INTROSPECTION AND ENGAGEMENT IN PROPERTIUS

Propertius repositions Latin love elegy in his third collection. Nearly a decade into the Augustan Principate, the early counter-cultural impulse of Propertius' first collections was losing its relevance. Challenged by the publication of Horace's *Odes*, and by the imminent arrival of Virgil's *Aeneid*, in 23 BCE Propertius produced a radical collection of elegies which critically interrogates elegy's own origins as a genre, and which directly faces off Horatian lyric and Virgilian epic, as part of an ambitious claim to Augustan pre-eminence. But this is no moment of cultural submission. In Book 3, elegy's key themes of love, fidelity and political independence are rebuilt from the beginning as part of a subtle critique of emerging Augustan *mores*. This book presents readings of fourteen individual elegies from Propertius Book 3, including nostalgic love poems, an elegiac hymn to Bacchus and a lament for Marcellus, the recently dead nephew of Augustus.

JONATHAN WALLIS is a Lecturer in Classics at the University of Tasmania. Jonathan's research focuses on Latin poetry, and on Roman culture and its reception. Jonathan also maintains a keen interest in Latin pedagogy. He is currently leading the development of an innovative suite of digital materials, with the aim of bringing Latin language and literature to new and wider audiences.

CAMBRIDGE CLASSICAL STUDIES

General editors
R. G. OSBORNE, W. M. BEARD, G. BETEGH,
J. P. T. CLACKSON, R. L. HUNTER, M. J. MILLETT,
S. P. OAKLEY, T. J. G. WHITMARSH

INTROSPECTION AND ENGAGEMENT IN PROPERTIUS

A Study of Book 3

JONATHAN WALLIS
University of Tasmania

CAMBRIDGE
UNIVERSITY PRESS

University Printing House, Cambridge CB2 8BS, United Kingdom

One Liberty Plaza, 20th Floor, New York, NY 10006, USA

477 Williamstown Road, Port Melbourne, VIC 3207, Australia

314–321, 3rd Floor, Plot 3, Splendor Forum, Jasola District Centre, New Delhi – 110025, India

79 Anson Road, #06-04/06, Singapore 079906

Cambridge University Press is part of the University of Cambridge.

It furthers the University's mission by disseminating knowledge in the pursuit of education, learning, and research at the highest international levels of excellence.

www.cambridge.org
Information on this title: www.cambridge.org/9781108417174
DOI: 10.1017/9781108265003

© Faculty of Classics, University of Cambridge 2018

This publication is in copyright. Subject to statutory exception and to the provisions of relevant collective licensing agreements, no reproduction of any part may take place without the written permission of Cambridge University Press.

First published 2018

Printed in the United Kingdom by Clays, St Ives plc

A catalogue record for this publication is available from the British Library.

Library of Congress Cataloging-in-Publication Data
Names: Wallis, Jonathan, author.
Title: Introspection and engagement in Propertius : a study of book 3 / Jonathan Wallis.
Other titles: Cambridge classical studies.
Description: Cambridge: Cambridge University Press, 2018. |
Series: Cambridge classical studies | Includes bibliographical references and index.
Identifiers: LCCN 2017057295 | ISBN 9781108417174 (hardback)
Subjects: LCSH: Propertius, Sextus. Elegiae. Liber 3. |
Elegiac poetry, Latin – History and criticism.
Classification: LCC PA6646.W355 2018 | DDC 874/.01–dc23
LC record available at https://lccn.loc.gov/2017057295

ISBN 978-1-108-41717-4 Hardback

Cambridge University Press has no responsibility for the persistence or accuracy of URLs for external or third-party internet websites referred to in this publication and does not guarantee that any content on such websites is, or will remain, accurate or appropriate.

CONTENTS

Preface		*page* ix
	Introduction	1
1	Turning Elegy Upside Down: Propertius 3.1–3	22
2	Seeking *Fides* in Poets and Poetry: Propertius 3.6	46
3	Thematic Experimentation: Propertius 3.9–11	63
4	Marriage and the Elegiac Woman: Propertius 3.12	93
5	Delays and Destinations: Propertius 3.16	118
6	A Hymn to Bacchus: Propertius 3.17	131
7	In Lament for Marcellus: Propertius 3.18	164
8	Renewing an Elegiac Contract: Propertius 3.20	187
9	Breaking up (with) *Cynthia*: Propertius 3.24	201
	Epilogue: The Apotheosis of *Amor*: Propertius 3.22	217
Bibliography		225
General Index		236
Index Locorum		239

PREFACE

This book about Propertius began as a doctoral thesis completed at the University of Cambridge nearly a decade ago. In the years since then it has been significantly revised, expanded in many areas, condensed in others. My thoughts on Propertius have inevitably evolved and matured in ongoing conversations with friends and colleagues (old and new), and in continuing to research and teach the Roman world at the University of Tasmania. But it strikes me, as I send in the final 'typescript' to Cambridge University Press, that the book has remained remarkably true to the inspiration of the original thesis, which I had titled 'Reading Backwards and Looking Forwards in Propertius Book 3'. The intervening years have allowed me to refine and bring new focus to my thinking (if you like, 'reading backwards' has become elegiac 'introspection', and 'looking forwards' has developed into Augustan 'engagement') but the two-pronged core of my argument about this fascinating collection of poems has remained throughout.

Many people have helped and encouraged me along the way, though I might name only a few here. John Henderson was my patient PhD supervisor, and has been a generous mentor since. His influence on this book is deep: I owe him the greatest thanks for his inspiration and ever-challenging perspective, and for the example he set in *really* reading a text as well as one could. Not least, I thank him deeply for the well-grounded sanity of his wisdom in that period of mania that comes with writing up a PhD. I could not have finished the book without the support and forgiveness of my partner, Susie, who has endured this project (and me) over many years and two hemispheres. The love, belief and generosity of my parents, Elizabeth and Peter, made the project possible in the first place; it is never possible to thanks one's parents enough, and this is just one

Preface

instance of many. The interest and insight of colleagues and friends have given me sustenance throughout. Very soon, I hope, I can cease testing the patience of those hardy few who have still not given up their enquiry about when this book of mine is finally coming out. Last of all I mention my daughter Winifred, who arrived in (and has done her level best to distract me from) the final stages of writing up. Freddie, I hope that you too might one day have a love for Latin poetry.

Hobart, August 2017

INTRODUCTION

Prologue

In the third-last poem of his third book, Propertius offers the following remarkable endorsement of Augustan Italy to his one-time patron Tullus:

> haec tibi, Tulle, parens, haec est pulcherrima sedes,
>   hic tibi pro digna gente petendus honos,
> hic tibi ad eloquium ciues, hic ampla nepotum
>   spes et uenturae coniugis aptus amor.
>
> 3.22.39–42

> This, Tullus, is your motherland, this your most beautiful home, here the public honour for you to seek as befits your distinguished family, here the citizens to move you to eloquence, here the ample hope of offspring and the suitable love of a wife to be.

As a product of the late 20s BCE, this elegant catalogue of Augustan virtues is hardly remarkable in itself – but hearing it issue from the mouth of an elegist surely is.[1] Tullus, the elegist's conservative foil in Book 1, has been living on the eastern fringe of the empire since leaving an indolent Propertius behind at Rome and pursuing a career move that, symbolically, placed *patria* above *puella* (1.6). In 3.22 Propertius seeks to entice Tullus back to Rome, but he does so with (of all things) an appeal to Tullus' sense of duty: Rome – now says the elegist – is the place to fulfil one's proper duty as a citizen, husband and father. Propertius' apparent change of heart is astounding. Here, in pair of couplets which evoke the controlled patriotism

---

[1] The paradox of Propertius' rhetoric is captured with typical vividness at Johnson (2009) 113–14.

1

Introduction

of Anchises commending Rome's future to Aeneas in Virgil's imminent *Aeneid*, Propertius appears to embrace precisely the kind of Roman and masculine orthodoxy which he had so vehemently rejected when last writing to Tullus (1.6, 1.14); in a vision of personal responsibility that evokes the balancing of individual and state in Horace's *Odes*, Propertius seemingly recants his generic objection to marriage and the expectation of producing Roman children (2.7). In short, if Propertius is to honour his triumphant rededication to amatory elegy in the poems that open Book 3, then the Augustan landscape of 3.22 seems an incredible place for Propertian elegy to find itself in. The following study – an exploration of fourteen poems in Propertius' crucial third book – is an investigation of how the elegist rebuilds his genre from the inside out in order to get there.

Starting Points

3.22 is one of several poems which give rise to a well-known pair of interpretive narratives concerning Propertius Book 3; these two stories are both significant and yet, taken on their own, inevitably superficial. On the one hand, we hear that Propertius' third book displays less sustained interest in erotic material than there had been in earlier books.[2] Whereas Cynthia had stood at the head of both Books 1 and 2, Book 3 opens symbolically with Callimachus instead – while Cynthia herself is not named until 3.21; this shapes up as an irreversible thematic withering that culminates in the climactic rejection of Cynthia as both muse and mistress in the collection's final poem. The second story notes that the scope of poetic subjects and elegiac voices in the book broadens noticeably.[3] The once tightly controlled elegiac landscape becomes increasingly populated with external characters that elicit a new expansiveness from Propertius himself: 3.7, for instance, is an unparalleled poem lamenting the death at sea of the drowned merchant Paetus, a symbolically transgressive figure only belatedly contrasted

---

[2] Esp. Cairns (2006) 348 and *passim*.
[3] Hubbard (1974) 75–115, Sullivan (1976) 70–1, Lyne (1980) 136–8.

Starting Points

with the private circumstances of the lover–poet; with the faithful Aelia Galla in 3.12, Propertius stages an unexpectedly enthusiastic celebration of married life right at the middle of the book, and so seemingly gestures towards a new respect in elegy for traditional Roman morality; and, perhaps most egregiously of all, 3.18 performs an elegiac lament for Marcellus, dead Augustan prince – a poem that aligns sympathetically with Augustan symbols in a way unthinkable in Book 1.

The interconnectedness of these narratives is immediately apparent. The new material that Book 3 displays – especially the new 'Augustanism' – does give credibility to the renunciation of Cynthia with which the book ends, just as the renunciation itself invites readings which emphasise a gradual Augustan conversion across the book. On this line of interpretation, Propertius' increasing thematic breadth looks designed to test what else elegiac verse is capable of accommodating and, in doing so, it pushes erotic elegy to the point of breakdown – with the closing *renuntiatio amoris* providing, it seems, the moment when it does break down. But the present study seeks to demonstrate that this inevitably partial portrait falls far short of telling the whole story. At the same time as he approaches new topics, Propertius deploys his 'new' material and any departure it might represent in a highly self-aware manner, as part of a book-wide self-commentary on the ongoing evolution of elegy itself. Paetus' poetically novel but ultimately disastrous journey in 3.7, for instance, invites a metapoetic reading which tropes the dangers – for the *poet* – of abandoning the restraint of an elegiac aesthetic;[4] thus 3.7 is not simply novel in itself, it also problematises at an early stage in the book the very drift towards a more public form of poetry that Propertius does indeed countenance widely in the collection. In chapter 4 we see that the marital fidelity of Aelia Galla – far from signalling a new elegiac morality – in fact realises on a central pedestal (and reclaims from Horace's lyric) the feminine ideal that elegy has sought of its *puella* since the beginning. In chapter 7, Propertius certainly mourns the

---

[4] Houghton (2007).

Introduction

death of Marcellus, but in a way that exposes the Augustan myth-making currently underway in Virgil's *Aeneid*, and in the veiled dynastic machinations of Augustus himself. Indeed, these last two elegies encapsulate particularly well the newly engaged role that Propertius envisions for elegy in Book 3, and we return to them below.

It becomes increasingly clear that Propertius Book 3 is a deeply multivocal collection, setting out a series of contrasting and even contradictory messages, often within the scope of a single poem. The aim of this study is certainly not to expose a hidden 'truth' within these twenty-four elegies, still less to argue that, contrary to appearances, Book 3 maintains an uncomplicated elegiac opposition to an Augustan programme (if, indeed, this was ever the case). Rather, it urges a full reading of these complex poems: the distinctive character of the collection lies in the friction it creates between elegy's proudly exclusive devotion to *amor* (and all this entails) and the seemingly inevitable need for elegy, along with the other Latin genres, to address the symbols of Augustus' new *Roma*.[5] If Book 3 ends by rejecting Cynthia, it turns out really to be the rejection of the tendentious portrait of Cynthia we (thought we) had known, the breaking up of the Cynthian caricature we fell for in Book 1. In her place the third book offers a rearticulation of 'Cynthia' and – as this study hopes to show – repositions Cynthian poetry in an emergent Augustan social and literary context.

Reception of Book 3

Heyworth & Morwood's excellent Oxford commentary from 2011 has brought long-overdue attention to the integrity and independence of Propertius Book 3 as a collection. Heyworth & Morwood rightly advertise the richness and diversity of a poetry book that accommodates the geography of Augustan imperial expansion, as well as the rising ambition of Augustan literature, especially through its interaction with Horace's

[5] On the latter point, see Ross (1975) 127–8.

just-published *Odes*, and with Virgil's imminent *Aeneid*. But the freshness of this commentary highlights the fact that it marks a notable departure from a very weary and for the most part cursory reception for Propertius' third collection in classical scholarship. In the past several decades, in fact, besides Heyworth & Morwood's commentary, Propertius Book 3 has largely escaped detailed reading on its own terms, or has been subject to readings which conspire against the capacity of the collection to speak with an original voice.[6]

We must look back some distance to find interpretative studies which seek to read Book 3 as a collection in its own right. The focus here is primarily structural. In the 1960s, a number of studies claimed to explain an elaborate symmetrical arrangement of the twenty-two poems of Propertius' first book.[7] Subsequently, several readers attempted to find similar concentric patterns in the third book,[8] encouraged by its similar size and by its many self-conscious allusions to Book 1. The usefulness of such schemes is questionable in any case;[9] and, certainly, these attempts to find coherence in the thematic diversity of Book 3 by making it work more like Book 1 (where Propertius is at his most thematically consistent) have largely been ineffective. But the spate of interest in the structure of Book 3 gave rise to a number of important readings which adopt a linear approach to short sequences of poems within the collection.[10] As outlined more fully below, the current study proposes a new way of reading the arrangement of poems in Book 3 – as a broad structure consisting of three series of eight poems – but a focus on linear reading remains fundamental, and sits at the foreground in chapters 1 and 3, discussing the sequences 3.1–3

---

[6] Greene & Welch (2012) – a collection which republishes a representative selection of scholarship on Propertius ranging from 1977 to 2007 – seemingly affirms a critical silence when it comes to Book 3: the focus of these pieces falls (almost) exclusively on poems from, or themes connected with, Books 1, 2 and 4.
[7] E.g. Otis (1965), Courtney (1968).
[8] E.g. Woolley (1967), Nethercut (1968), Marr (1978); for more linear approaches, cf. Courtney (1970), Jacobson (1976), Putnam (1980), Hutchinson (1984).
[9] Hutchinson (1984) 99.
[10] Nethercut (1970a) 385–407, Nethercut (1970b) 99–102, Jacobson (1976) 160–4, Courtney (1970) 48–53, Putnam (1980) 105–10 and *passim*.

Introduction

and 3.9–11, respectively. A consecutive reading of poems might be expected as an approach to an ancient poetry book;[11] but in the case of Book 3 it seems an approach that Propertius overtly encourages by employing a recurrent 'journey' metaphor across the collection as a whole,[12] and we will see it offer particular reward as metapoetic commentary on the process of reading through the evolution of a book and, indeed, a genre.

When we turn to more recent discussion, we find that a particular fate of Book 3 has been to serve the purposes of studies whose attention lies elsewhere. Excepting a recent cluster of more comprehensive studies (discussed below), most critical interest in Propertius since the mid-1980s has been concentrated on the two extremes of the Propertian corpus: on the beginning, where Propertius first establishes the *personae* of his elegiac poet–lover and the beloved *puella*, the poetic interaction between which, to various extents, governs his first three books;[13] and, more recently, on the end – on the final book in which, as *Romanus Callimachus*, Propertius blends his erotic poetics with a new aetiological investigation of stories associated with Roman myths and landscapes.[14] Caught between the different concerns of these two approaches, Book 3 is represented either as the final iteration of the first-person amatory paradigm established in Book 1,[15] or as bringing about the closing down of the subjective 'Cynthian' poetics of Books 1–3, a move necessary before the poet could progress to a more objective style of elegy in the fourth book.[16] As regards the

---

[11] Putnam (1980) 97, Hutchinson (1984) 100.
[12] There are over thirty specific references to pathways, streets and travel in Book 3, compared with a mere fifty or so in the other three books combined. On the metaphor of (sea-)travel in Latin love poetry, see Jacobson (1976) 165–6; for the metaphor's teleological drive especially in the second half of Propertius Book 3, see Clarke (2004). Yet Propertius' thematic interaction with 'journeying' frequently contradicts the sense of teleology that journey symbolism provides: see recently Phillips (2011) 125–6.
[13] On the identity and function of the elegiac *puella* in Books 1 and 2, see esp. Wyke (1987b), (1989a) and (1994), and Greene (1995) and (1998); on the persona of the poet–lover particularly in Book 2, see esp. Sharrock (2000) and Greene (2000) and (2005).
[14] See the full-length studies of Janan (2001), Debrohun (2003), Welch (2005).
[15] E.g. Ross (1975) 127–8: a 'half-hearted … attempt to retain the mask he had so proudly made his own'.
[16] E.g. Debrohun (2003) 131–4.

Reception of Book 3

focus of academic attention, that is to say, the position of the third book within the corpus has rendered it vulnerable to interpretation largely with reference to concerns outside itself, being read in terms of its similarity to, or difference from, the books that surround it.[17]

Given the paucity of interpretative studies whose focus is Book 3 itself, the most influential characterisations of the collection are to be found in studies which treat the breadth of the poet's work more fully. Though it has been left behind by developments in theoretical approaches to elegy,[18] Margaret Hubbard's 1974 monograph *Propertius* remains influential for her depiction of Propertius' third book as the elegist's attempt to find new subjects in order to reinvigorate a tired and restrictive genre. Discussing the novel poems in the book's centre, for instance, Hubbard writes:

> Mostly, they show an exhaustion of the genre, and give the impression that the poet is bored with love poetry and trying, though as yet unsuccessfully, to find new modes. ... In all this part of the book perhaps only the slight but amiable 3.16 and the hymn to Bacchus (3.17) avoid the tedium inescapable in the spectacle of a good poet in an impasse and looking for both a subject and a manner.[19]

The effect of an approach like this is to reinforce the perception of Propertian elegy as a static genre with a strictly limited range, based on a template established by the poet in Book 1; it precludes fuller study of creativity in the third collection by appealing to the notion of generic fatigue, where the presence of new material serves only to reinforce the perceived limitations of elegy in the first place. This has proved a persuasively pessimistic reading from which more recent discussions – though more sympathetic and sophisticated – have not managed fully to liberate Propertius' third book. Alison Keith, for instance, in her judicious overview of Propertius'

---

[17] E.g. Nethercut (1975) 74, Stahl (1985) 189–90. Miller (2004) 147 is more nuanced on this point.
[18] Gibson (2007) 173.
[19] Hubbard (1974) 89. For the clash of new and old in Book 3, see similarly Sullivan (1976) 70–1.

Introduction

poetry from 2008, quite rightly singles out Book 3 as the site of elegist's highly productive engagement with Horatian lyric (Propertius thus 'admits a new depth and generic complexity to his elegiac aesthetic'[20]). Yet, in the end, Keith nonetheless links Propertius' experimentalism with his 'disengagement' from love elegy, notwithstanding the extent to which Keith herself shows Propertius manipulating Horace to further the ends of an amatory elegiac programme.[21]

Two other recent discussions of Propertius' complete corpus adopt vastly differing approaches, and yet both further conspire to restrict the scope of Book 3 as an individual collection. Of these, Francis Cairns's massive 2006 study of Propertius is the more problematic.[22] Cairns regards the greater presence of historical and aetiological interests within Book 3 (and Book 4) as directly reflecting the poet's increasing political awareness and commitment to Augustan ideology – to the extent that it shows 'Propertius self-consciously speaking as a public mouthpiece of the regime'.[23] In these avowedly selective readings, the extent to which Cairns adopts Augustus as the central, sometimes sole, point of reference inevitably frustrates any broader significance that his very detailed analysis might offer. The obvious depth in Cairns's scholarship is frequently compelling (and useful, for instance, in providing a historical context for the composition and interpretation of 3.14 and 3.17).[24] But the uncomplicated certainty with which Cairns presents the thematic intricacy of Book 3 (combined with his frequent and blunt dismissal of alternative readings as

---

[20] Keith (2008) 63.
[21] Keith (2008) 56–65.
[22] Cairns's study revives a stream of historical and political approaches to Augustan elegy prevalent from the 1960s onwards: Cairns (2006) x cites Boucher (1965), Stahl (1985) and Newman (1997) as particular influences. It is a tendency of such political readings of elegy to establish the poet as uncomplicatedly pro- *or* anti-Augustan; this is a demonstrably problematic approach to a collection such as Propertius Book 3, which offers support for both viewpoints.
[23] Cairns (2006) 349.
[24] Cairns (2006) 362–403.

'misinterpretations')[25] results in a remarkably straightforward and univocal representation of what remains a complex collection of ideas and symbols. By contrast, W. R. Johnson depicts a recalcitrant Propertius who could hardly be more different from Cairns's (pro-) Augustan poet. Eschewing the kind of political transformation that Cairns sees, Johnson sketches instead an elegist who remains keenly at odds with Roman society as Augustus was seeking to reinvent it.[26] As will become clear, there is much sympathy in the present study for Johnson's instinctive portrait of a stubborn poet who never fully renounces the subversive voice that comes, in the Roman mindset, with being a lover. Here, Johnson's tracking of a resistant eroticism from Books 1–3 into Book 4 – and so, his reading of Propertius' claim to have moved on from Cynthia at the end of the third book as inevitably misguided and, in fact, generically inconceivable – provides refreshing insight into the overall coherence of an erotic poetry that shows greater loyalty to the central claim in Book 1 – that Cynthia will be the beginning and the end (*Cynthia prima fuit, Cynthia finis erit*, 1.12.20) – than many readers allow it to have. But, as will also become clear, we will not go as far as Johnson in refusing Propertius an increasingly constructive interaction with the Augustan subjects that loom ever larger in the period during which the third book was written. Seductive though it is, Johnson's portrait of a poet for whom Augustan integration was 'impossible' necessarily lends his characterisation of the public material in Book 3 a curiously ironic air, where sarcasm and satire must become the poetry's dominant modes. Like Johnson, we find a poet who resists official goading to turn his attention to properly 'Roman' verse, at least in the way that those who would pressure him might have hoped. But we also meet a poet whose

---

[25] E.g. Cairns (2006) 344–7, dismissing ironic readings of the Augustan content in Book 3 as found, for instance, in Stahl (1985) ch. 10.
[26] Heyworth (2010) similarly depicts Propertius' career as one which privileges stasis over evolution, even as it explores the friction between these competing aesthetic demands. See too Wilson (2009).

principles – for all the elegist's counter-cultural bluster – prove not *always* dissimilar to those traditional values which Augustus was seeking to reinvest in Roman culture.

Contextual Considerations

The Roman literary scene had progressed significantly by the time Propertius was completing his latest collection in 23 BCE.[27] The brutal politics of civil war, out of which grew the elegist's dissident manner in his first two books,[28] was now the best part of a decade distant. Augustus was busily bedding down a new Roman constitution, which, even if the extent of the Principate that would result was not yet fully apparent, nonetheless outlined ever more clearly the beginning of an Augustan dynasty, and provided Rome's artists with a wealth of new socio-political material to interrogate, as well as, very probably, the imperative to do so. The focus of Roman cultural attention was changing. The particular type of civil defiance which gave impetus to Propertius' early poetry was no longer relevant in the way it used to be.

For a start, in the late 20s BCE all eyes were turning towards Virgil's *Aeneid*. It was clear even at the time Propertius published his second book that Virgil's Augustan epic was destined to become a dominant cultural text (*cedite Romani scriptores, cedite Grai!|nescio quid maius nascitur Iliade*, 'Yield, Roman writers, yield Greeks too! Something greater than the *Iliad* is coming to birth', Prop. 2.34.65–6).[29] Just a few years later, the frequency of references to the *Aeneid* – including specific allusion – in Horace's subsequent *Odes* and in Propertius' third book affirm the extent to which the epic was commanding attention while it was still being written (as well as the extent

---

[27] For the dating of Book 3, see Fedeli (1985) 29, Goold (1990) 2; for the dating of all Propertius' collections, see Hubbard (1974) 43–4, and Lyne (1998a) 520–4 (with particular focus on Books 1 and 2).

[28] See esp. Breed (2010). Heyworth & Morwood (2011) 8–26 provide a useful overview of the political history preceding the Augustan Principate, and the significance of this in Propertius' first two books.

[29] On Propertius' representation of the *Aeneid* in 2.34, see O'Rourke (2011).

Contextual Considerations

to which significant parts of the poem were in circulation well before its 'publication'). The *Aeneid* – so it certainly seemed – was changing the way that poets and Roman society interacted. As a project designed to give Roman literature a gravitas equal to (ideally, surpassing) its Greek models, Virgil's incipient epic was shaping up as a peerless statement of Roman literary maturity and ambition. More particularly, in setting to Latin hexameters the story of the Trojan family whose legacy was Rome itself, and from whom Rome's first citizen Augustus claimed descent, the *Aeneid* would bring together individual and state, literature and politics, as well as narrative and national myth, at level not seen before in Rome.

The way that Virgil would achieve these fusions brings focus to one of the central aesthetic challenges of the period. The Augustan milieu brought with it both incentive and opportunity to create literature that celebrated Roman greatness – and, indeed, *imperium sine fine* ('empire without limit', *Aen.* 1.279) would be one of the *Aeneid*'s programmes – but how exactly this might be realised by a poet with a professed allegiance to an Alexandrian *deductum carmen* ('fine-spun song', *Ecl.* 6.5) was a point of some interest.[30] In this context, Virgil's extant proems in his second and third books of *Georgics* assume a heightened programmatic importance, particularly in hindsight. At the beginning of *Georgics* 2, Virgil had characterised his poem as a paradoxical hybrid in scope and style, asking his patron Maecenas metaphorically to join him in an epic voyage upon the open sea, and yet to keep modestly well within reach of land (*Geo.* 2.39–46). More significantly still, early in *Georgics* 3 Virgil promised soon to construct a metaphorical marble temple that would house Caesar himself (*templum de marmore ponam ... in medio mihi Caesar erit templumque tenebit*, *Geo.* 3.13, 16), offering an irresistible metaphor for a coming poem that would celebrate the military triumphs of Augustus. Yet Caesar's grand temple follows an allusion to Virgil's own poetic triumph, which, in 'leading down' the Muses from Mt Helicon, evokes the 'fine-spun song' from *Eclogue* 6

[30] On the dilemma, see Fowler (1995) 254.

Introduction

(*Aonio rediens deducam uertice Musas*, *Geo.* 3.11). The historical poem seemingly foreshadowed in the *Georgics* 3 proem sits at odds with the mythological epic which Virgil was currently completing,[31] but this matters less than the way that the two *Georgics* proems frame the new project as an Augustan fusion of a personal and disengaged Alexandrian literary aesthetic with a more public kind of poetry. The architectural metaphor in which Virgil appears to clothe his new project affirms a similar point: by promising to 'build a temple', Virgil foreshadows his capacity as a private poet to contribute to the Roman good by involving himself in a tradition of public building by the Roman elite,[32] of whom the most recent member to be doing so was, of course, Augustus himself.

If the *Aeneid* was still a tantalising work in progress, a powerfully concrete expression of Rome's new modernity and cultural confidence arrived in Horace's *Odes*, published as a three-book collection in 23 BCE.[33] In this momentous poetry, Horace too amplifies significantly the role of the personal poet at Rome. As the collection progresses, Horace's private lyric voice steadily gains scope and potency until, climactically, at the outset of the third book Horace addresses his audience as a priest of the Muses (*Musarum sacerdos*, 3.1.3).[34] Here, drawing no doubt on Augustus' current attempts to reinvigorate Roman religious life, Horace aligns the lyric poet with the most sacred of Rome's official symbols, claiming for himself the capacity to speak with sacral authority on matters of Roman ethics and morality. This marks the movement of Roman personal poetry out of (albeit thematised) sympotic space into civic terrain, a development that Horace emphasises metaphorically as he brings his collection to a close. In the final poem Horace claims that he has 'built a monument' (*exegi monumentum*,

---

[31] But cf. Schauer (2007) 48–56, Kirichenko (2013).
[32] Meban (2008) 167–9.
[33] For the unified publication of *Odes* 1–3, see Nisbet & Rudd (2004) xix; West (2002) ix. The suggestion by Hutchinson (2002) 528 that the third book of *Odes* was first published in a new edition that included republication of *Odes* 1–2 has not generally found favour.
[34] Lyne (1995) 23–4, 160.

Contextual Considerations

3.30.1) – just as Virgil promised to do – seeking to associate his literary achievement with the physical symbols of the political elite that shaped ancient cityscapes. But once again it seems the activities of Augustus himself are especially in mind. In claiming – hyperbolically – to have been 'the first' (*princeps*, 3.30.13) to have brought Greek song to Latin, Horace assumes in a literary context the political title Augustus had held since 27 BCE. The point seems less a sincere assertion of poetic originality than a claim to have shared with Augustus a leading role in (re)building Roman culture.

The positioning of the personal poet on the public stage raises the bar for other writers. The lyric poet's signature characterisation of himself gains a new social immediacy (and, seemingly, official sanction): as complement to his vatic role, the *Odes* allow Horace a mainstream platform from which he might explore and espouse Augustan values in his own person. Here Horace lays down a challenge to elegy in particular, and to the relevance of its recusant, fringe-dwelling protagonist. As does elegy, lyric verse takes love as a recurrent theme. But, for Horace, love forms part of a very different erotic morality. In the *Odes*, love is not a debilitating but an enabling theme, a motif that coheres broadly with his lyric philosophy of moderation in all things, and beyond that with Augustus' efforts to place personal (and especially sexual) virtue at the heart of Rome's transition away from a moral profligacy that attended the final decades of the old Republic. In this context, it is not that Horace adopts an abstemious or puritanical attitude to amatory matters (quite the reverse, of course); but, importantly, love becomes a theme through which Horace can affirm rather than compromise his masculine authority. In the *Odes*, erotic affairs are (mostly) harmless diversions, or past dangers which the wiser poet now avoids. More fundamentally, love and love poetry each reflect a broader moral resilience: in *Odes* 3.7 – a poem in which Horace pits his lyric values against those he perceives in elegy – the lovers Gyges and Asterie each espouse a very Augustan respect for amatory *fides* and, importantly, the strength to resist (elegiac) temptation; in *Odes* 1.22 the success of Horace's own love song for his mistress Lalage

Introduction

stems directly from the singer's moral 'wholeness' (*integer uitae*, 1.22.1). Overall, Horace's engagement with *amor* displays a control on a thematic level that coheres with the discipline for which his *Odes* are celebrated as poetry. Horace's amatory material plays its part in a collection which – with the notorious exception of his two odes to Bacchus, where Horace is dragged headlong by the god's overwhelming fervour towards direct poetic contact with Augustus himself – gradually consolidates Horace's poetic *auctoritas* over his lyric empire.[35]

Reading Propertius Book 3

Propertius Book 3 is the elegist's response to these substantial developments, and to Rome's shifting cultural priorities. In the study that follows we track Propertius as he explores two complementary thematic arcs. In the first of these, Propertius responds to the literary challenge apparent in Virgil's imminent *Aeneid* and in Horace's just-published *Odes* by looking ahead to elegy's potential as personal genre with newly overt interest in mainstream Roman topics. But this process necessarily involves the poet in a fundamental re-evaluation of existing elegy, too, and the second thematic concern within the collection involves looking backwards at elegy's foundational relationship with its mistress and with *amor* itself. Here, in an obsessive act of self-interrogation, Propertius exposes and (especially as the book closes) resolves several of elegy's early emblematic crises. In short, in Book 3 Propertius employs the writing especially of his Augustan contemporaries as an external catalyst in the development of elegy from within itself. The result is a genre whose self-declared thematic compass is significantly expanded – but also a genre which remains remarkably true to its own internal value system, even at the point Propertius purports to dismiss Cynthia as the book comes to a close (a threat, of course, the elegist has made before).[36]

---

[35] Oliensis (1998) 102–5.
[36] Wilson (2009) 186.

Reading Propertius Book 3

As a collection, Book 3 comprises three sequences of eight poems, each with a broadly distinct character. Reflecting the first of the book's thematic arcs, each sequence is headed by an overtly programmatic elegy in which engagement with Virgil and Horace is prominent. In 3.1–3 (chapter 1) Propertius asserts elegy's superior claim to public significance: 3.1 claims for elegy the symbolic role of Horace's *sacerdos* and Virgil's poetic triumph from *Georgics* 3, as well as the enviable legacy of Homeric epic; 3.2 coopts the language and imagery of Horace's *monumentum* to celebrate the public potency of elegy's eroticism, particularly among its female audience; 3.3 rounds off the triumphant tone of the opening set by staging Propertius' emphatic rededication to amatory verse in an Ennian initiation scene atop Mt Helicon. In 3.9 (chapter 3), an appeal to Maecenas – a figure with peerless connections to the Augustan administration – reunites Propertius with his two fellow client-poets,[37] and introduces a set of poems in which particularly Augustan themes are prominent. The precedent of Horace's own strategic addresses to Maecenas at 'middle' moments in his *Odes* affirms these poems as a 'central' sequence within Book 3, as well as Propertius' ambivalent attitude to official pressure to produce imperial poetry; at the same time, allusion to Virgil's two *Georgics* proems allows Propertius to signal that, in whatever expansion there might be to elegy's scope, Propertius will stay loyal to the Alexandrian principles for which 3.1–3 stands as the elegist's most powerful statement of allegiance. In 3.17 (chapter 6), a hymn to Bacchus looks ahead to the climactic rejection of Cynthia as mistress and elegiac muse in 3.24, the collection's final poem. Now, suddenly and ludicrously, Propertius threatens to forswear his Alexandrian loyalty: in 3.17 Propertius' rededication in the book's opening sequence both to amatory verse and to inspiration in Callimachean water is opposed by a closural sequence that begins with a desire to forget love (and so elegy), and which proposes a newly elevated form of poetry to be sealed with a sip of Bacchic wine. Yet here too Horace and Virgil are conspicuous,

---

[37] Cf. Heyworth (2007c) 101–8.

Introduction

emphasising that 3.17 in fact complements rather than contradicts the literary paths taken in both 3.1 and 3.9. Allusion to Virgil's Caesarian temple from *Georgics* 3 and to Horace's own Bacchic writing certainly signals that, with Propertius' proposed 'elevated' poetry, contact with the grandeur of Augustus himself is imminent (and it is, with a lament for Marcellus in 3.18). But here Propertius' cumulative engagement with these poets' own programmatic writing over the breadth of Book 3 comes to fruition: when Propertius finally does turn his elegiac couplets towards imperial material, then much like his fellow poets it will be on his terms that he does so.

When Book 3 reprises what has been elegy's 'customary' erotic material – the collection's second arc – it engages in overt re-evaluation of the genre's original and signature motifs. Particular moments in Book 1 are the subject of recurrent intratextual interrogation: Propertius' very first poem (1.1) in which he introduced himself as a lover inhabiting the margins of Roman society and enslaved to his mistress Cynthia, and where he first stated the amatory condition as degrading and yet inescapable; and the first book's central diptych (1.11–12), in which Propertius juxtaposed his fears about the fickleness of Cynthia's faith for him against the permanence of his own eroto-poetic fidelity to her. Of course, the early claim that Cynthia and elegy are indivisible bears particular significance in Book 3, which ends with the poet's claim to dismiss his mistress. In this context, it is unsurprising that the collection's final poem, 3.24 (chapter 9) offers the best-known retrospective moments: Propertius emphasises his climactic eviction of Cynthia by recalling and reversing the conditions in 1.1 which gave Cynthia her authority.[38] Yet the later poem ultimately fails to abandon Cynthia in the clear-cut manner for which Propertius evidently hopes. Especially in the light of Book 4, the undermining of elegy's early programme in 3.24 shows Propertius more casting aside the limitations of elegy's

---

[38] Barsby (1974) 135–7, Putnam (1980) 108–11.

autobiographical fiction than it shows him simplistically abandoning erotic verse, or even Cynthia herself, *tout court*.

Propertius' other 'erotic' poems in Book 3 similarly interrogate early material in the context of elegy's increasing openness and thematic scope. In some cases, elegiac motifs are juxtaposed starkly against Rome's own narratives: 3.11 (chapter 3) positions the Propertian lover's disgraced servility as an explanatory paradigm for the submission Rome nearly offered to the Egyptian queen Cleopatra, had it not been for the virile intervention of Octavian; here Propertius tests the relevance and the limits of elegy's early posturing when it comes to interpreting the stories of the early Augustan period. Commonly, the collection's amatory verse offers conspicuous metapoetic commentary on the genre's development. In 3.10 (chapter 3) and 3.16 (chapter 5) interaction with elegy's mistress invokes the book's pervasive travel motif, and so the sense of inevitable progress that comes with it. 3.10 figures Cynthia's birthday (and, it seems, Propertius' third anniversary as Cynthia's poet) as a ritual journey that pits thematic repetition against the relentless forward motion of time itself; 3.16 imagines a literal journey towards Cynthia that the poet wants not to end, but which he cannot postpone; in both cases, the sense is palpable that time is nearly up for Cynthia – as we knew her, at least.[39] Yet the book's erotic material is not always so pessimistic as to its future in Propertian verse. On several occasions Propertius' metapoetic focus falls on the poetics of reading elegy, and writing it: 3.6 and 3.20 (chapters 2 and 8) present a pair of contrasting studies that direct readers 'back to the beginning' in order to reconsider the pervasive theme of fidelity (*fides*) in elegy. In one sense, these poems might well seem to contribute to an impending sense of closure for erotic verse by affirming what readers will already suspect – that the lover's claim of faithfulness is a lie, that the story of 'Propertius' and 'Cynthia' is little more than a seductive fiction. In another sense, these

---

[39] When Cynthia returns as a ghost in 4.7, the mistress's own version of elegiac history conflicts sharply with what we have heard from Propertius himself: see esp. Janan (2001) 100–13.

Introduction

belated revelations invest what has been duplicitous Propertian poetry with a paradoxical sincerity, even as an ending for amatory verse looms. 3.20 in particular, through its invitation late in the piece to join Propertius in a new contract, holds out the opportunity to lover and beloved (and so to reader and writer) to begin all over again on new terms, just as elegy proceeds to a newly public discourse that was foreshadowed in the book's opening poems.

This brings us back to the two elegies – 3.12 and 3.18 – in which Propertius' new ambition is realised most effectively; here, the two thematic arcs of the third book come together to produce poetry in which a recognisably elegiac voice engages social and civic narratives of the kind espoused in the Augustan poetry of Horace and Virgil. Aelia Galla in 3.12 (chapter 4) sits prominently at the collection's centre. This poem is a remarkable celebration of marital fidelity; it is also a pointed response to the competitively centrist morality of Horace's Asterie poem (*Odes* 3.7), and of his lyric poetry more broadly. But while Propertius places at the heart of his new book a new and socially orthodox kind of *puella*, Galla is not so much a rejection of a fickle Cynthia as a realisation of the woman Propertius had always wanted Cynthia to be (and which, for the most part, she seemingly was).[40] In an Augustan context, Galla's married constancy in the middle of Book 3 celebrates the surprisingly conservative erotic ideal at the core of Propertian poetry, and foreshadows the faithfulness that Cynthia declares of herself in 4.7, and which the married Cornelia exemplifies in Propertius' very final poem, 4.11.

By contrast, 3.18 (chapter 7) is possibly the most 'Augustan' poem in Book 3,[41] but its public role is not necessarily the one that Maecenas (or Augustus) would have desired elegy to

---

[40] It is important to note that, at least in the limited 'history' Propertius gives us, Cynthia's reputation for fickleness stems almost entirely from the Propertian lover's paranoia (fears which usually prove unfounded) rather than from narrated acts of infidelity. Cf. James (2003b) *passim* for the 'professional' infidelity that characterises women like Cynthia in the world elegy evokes.
[41] Cairns (2006) 347.

adopt. In 3.18 Propertius joins with numerous other poets in lamenting the death of Marcellus in 23 BCE,[42] the young man seemingly marked out as a successor by a childless Augustus. At one level, Propertius' lament returns elegy to its supposed funerary origins. But he also uses the occasion of Marcellus' death to draw attention to an Augustan *Realpolitik* lying behind the Julian myth of Augustan pre-destiny which Augustus was carefully curating, and which is stated nowhere more powerfully than by Virgil in the parade of Roman heroes in *Aeneid* 6. Here, perhaps, we see most clearly the kind of mature elegy that would emerge eventually in Propertius' fourth book: a poetry that mounts an oblique and thoroughly independent interrogation of values, symbols and (Augustan) icons lodging at the heart of Roman identity.

Of course, there is a danger of overplaying the presence of thematic and structural schemes in any collection of poetry. Certainly, in Propertius Book 3 each individual poem has more at stake than just its place in the collection, or its role in advancing metapoetic commentary; similarly, the collection as a whole has more to say about literature and Roman culture than an interpretive reduction to two broad thematic arcs might suggest. The nine chapters that follow aim to achieve a balance between readings of individual elegies that make up the third book, and interpretation of the third book as a coherent collection with an artistic voice and distinct character of its own. The chapters are arranged by the order of the poems they discuss, rather than by theme – but the thematic significance of each poem in terms of the whole book is an important aspect of each reading. There is also conscious balance between individual readings and readings of sequences of poems.[43] Chapters 1 and 3 overtly treat two sequences within the collection (3.1–3 and 3.9–11), while the remaining chapters all analyse single poems. Even

---

[42] Falkner (1977) 11.
[43] On the interplay between single poems and the narrative movement of the third collection as a whole, see Phillips (2011) 125–8.

Introduction

here, though, sequence proves important – especially for the cumulative interpretation of 3.16, 3.17 and 3.18 (chapters 5, 6 and 7).

Textual Notes

The choice of a text is a significant issue for any analysis of Propertius' poetry.[44] The earliest drafts of this book were based on P. Fedeli's 1984 *Teubner* edition; the ideas in these readings were developed before the publication in 2007 of S. J. Heyworth's considerably more radical Oxford Classical Texts edition of Propertius. In almost every way Heyworth's edition (especially with its companion volume *Cynthia*) supersedes Fedeli as a textual resource. But Heyworth's text itself remains a controversial one, and it will take some time longer for the editorial decisions it makes to be assessed fully by Propertian readers.[45] In light of this I have decided to stick with the Teubner edition in which this study originated, but to do so mindful of the provocations provided by Heyworth's OCT. On some occasions, I have incorporated conjectures accepted or proposed by Heyworth (most conspiciously in 3.12 and at the end of 3.18). On other occasions, I have used footnotes to discuss pertinent differences from Fedeli in Heyworth's text, and suggested how they might alter the reading of the poems. The question of the unity or division of Propertius Book 2 (and so whether Book 3 is the third or fourth book of the corpus) is still current. Fedeli himself accepts the theory that what has been transmitted as 'Book 2' is the collation of an original two books,[46] as do the editions of Goold (1990) and Heyworth (2007a).[47] But the division of Book 2 is not

---

[44] Welch (2012), Tarrant (2016) 105–23.
[45] In particular it is worth nothing that Heyworth's text makes frequent emendation where readings of the editorial vulgate are not only defensible but arguably preferable in their poetic context: see e.g. Tarrant (2016) 115–23.
[46] Fedeli (2005) 21f.
[47] Goold (1990) 16–18; Heyworth (2007a) lxii–lxiv.

Textual Notes

universally accepted;[48] and even among those who agree that 'Book 2' comprises two individual books, there is disagreement about where the division lies.[49] The issue is not critical to the following discussion, although on occasion I do note where it would be attractive to read Book 3 as the third book (as for instance where Propertius' text interacts closely with Book 3 of Horace's *Odes*). Even in these instances the issue is raised only as additional support for a broader argument.

---

[48] E.g. Butrica (1996) esp. 89–98, Syndikus (2006) 273 n. 93.
[49] See Murgia (2000) 147–91, Lyne (1998b); see also Heyworth (2007b) x–xi.

CHAPTER I

TURNING ELEGY UPSIDE DOWN

Propertius 3.1–3

The opening of Propertius' third book marks an important elegiac restart during a crucial period for Augustan literature. Propertius Book 3 appears hot on the heels of Horace's *Odes* 1–3, and with Virgil's *Aeneid* looming on the literary horizon. This was a time of intense and self-conscious competition between genres to establish a pecking order of poetic authority – a rivalry no doubt fostered by Augustus' evident desire for a new imperial literature celebrating Roman (but particularly Augustan) achievement.[1] In this context, Propertius' new book opens with three overtly programmatic poems that offer sustained generic self-examination, and which engage challenges from both Horatian lyric and Virgil's imminent epic – significant parts of which were already in circulation[2] – in an effort to reposition elegy as a more open and socially engaged genre for the emergent Augustan Principate. These three elegies, in which Propertius will make the paradoxical claim that his third book offers new thematic scope while yet continuing in a familiar elegiac vein, are the focus of this opening chapter.

It is important to begin with a reminder of some elegiac commonplaces. Interrogation of generic identity and the rivalry between genres has long been a subject of elegiac discourse.

An earlier version of this chapter was published as Wallis, J. A. C. (2013) 'Turning Elegy Upside Down. Propertius 3.1–3', in M. Borg & G. Miles (eds.) *Approaches to Genre in the Ancient World*, 30–58. Newcastle. It is published here with the permission of Cambridge Scholars Publishing.

[1] Oliensis (1998) 102–5 argues that Horatian lyric poetry in particular displays a progression towards poetic potency in parallel with Augustus' movement towards imperial authority. For Horace's competitive engagement with Virgilian epic and Propertian elegy in his lyric poetry, see e.g. *Odes* 1.3 and 3.7, respectively; and Harrison (2006), Rutherford (2007) 250–3.

[2] Propertius' general foreknowledge of the *Aeneid* has been flagged since the publication of Book 2 (2.34.61–6; on which see esp. O'Rourke (2011) 464–73). In Book 3,

Turning Elegy Upside Down: Propertius 3.1–3

Elegy's self-proclaimed slightness as a genre (especially in a foundational binary it establishes with epic) is written onto the slender physique of the elegiac lover himself.[3] Elegy represents itself fundamentally as an inverted genre, becoming implicated in a series of symbolic oppositions so as to define itself as being everything that Rome and its imperial literature is not. Here, the lover–poet's effete body and leisured lifestyle correlate with an intensely personal literature that represents the antithesis (and rejection) of Rome's public value system and any poetry that celebrates it.[4] Yet elegy is also a paradoxical genre whose negative definitions bind it uncommonly closely to the ideals that it rejects. For all his declared preference for the isolation of his personal domain, the elegist repeatedly directs his attention back to the world from which he would cut himself off, 'tak[ing] advantage of his alternative, elegiac perspective to make himself a social commentator'.[5] Famously, elegy infuses its alternative world with those very Roman values of masculine militarism which Rome invests in both its (idealised) citizens and its sanctioned (epic) literature. Quite ironically, the thoroughly un-Roman lover–poet – elegy's enslaved, effeminate and peacenik protagonist – nonetheless coopts the symbols of military and mythic heroism in a paradoxically epicised characterisation of his inverted world and his role in it.[6]

All of this generic background matters because, in the following discussion, we will see that Book 3 presents as innovation what is essentially a re-inversion of elegy's already inverted oppositions. In particular, in 3.1–2 Propertius rebuilds elegy with an emphasis on the paradoxical heroism that has underpinned his role as reticent lover, and on the broader

---

sustained interaction with the *Aeneid*'s themes (esp. 3.1, 3.18, 3.22), as well as a number of specific allusions, suggest a more intimate knowledge.
[3] E.g. 2.22.21. Elegy's tendency to offer a literal embodiment of generic traits is famously taken to an extreme by Ovid's personification of Elegy and Tragedy as poetic characters in *Amores* 3.1: see Wyke (1989b).
[4] For an overview of the Romanly unorthodox elements of elegy, see Conte (1994b) 322–3, Farrell (2003) 397, Wilson (2009) 188.
[5] Farrell (2003) 397; see too Wilson (2009) 188. Here, 'love' becomes not merely a refuge from but also (even mostly) an allusive way of speaking about 'Rome'.
[6] On the paradoxes of elegiac characterisation, see esp. Sharrock (2000), Greene (2000), Greene (2005).

relevance that Propertius asserted from the beginning for the otherwise proudly private nature of elegiac poetry. Indeed, when the third book does stage a return to its erotic beginnings, what it casts as regression is in fact a reinvention of its amatory paradigm for a new social context, and a laying bare of elegy's foundational autobiographical fiction. Propertius' third book signals a reversal, too, of the way it approaches interaction with Augustan genres. Early elegy's strident self-declaration as a fiercely exclusive and differentiated genre had always concealed a practice of generic assimilation.[7] As Book 3 opens, we find a genre that is markedly inclusive of other generic modes and symbols, even as it seeks to define its superiority over other genres.[8]

Elegiac Expansion – 3.1

The opening poem of Book 3 presents elegiac Propertius in exultant mood, and as emancipated from the servility that marked the beginning of his first book as it is possible to imagine. Here Propertius – daunting, demanding – famously asserts his right as a Roman poet to tread the poetic landscape of Greek Callimachus and Philitas, and from their grove he lets loose a series of roaring couplets intended to dictate the nature of elegiac verse as Propertius envisages it. This indeed is elegy newly sung loud and clear:[9]

> Callimachi Manes et Coi sacra Philitae,
>   in uestrum, quaeso, me sinite ire nemus.
> primus ego ingredior puro de fonte sacerdos
>   Itala per Graios orgia ferre choros.
> dicite, quo pariter carmen tenuastis in antro?   5
>   quoue pede ingressi? quamue bibistis aquam?

---

[7] In fact, a mismatch between ancient genre theory and practice is widespread in antiquity: see esp. Hinds (2000), Farrell (2003).
[8] Elegy's transgression of genre boundaries is parodied by Ovid at *Am.* 1.1 (with e.g. Davis (2005) 177).
[9] See Hubbard (1974) 75 on the attention-seeking, hyperbolic nature of Propertius' imagery in 3.1. The swift shifts of imagery derive ultimately from Callimachus' own technique: see Heyworth & Morwood (2011) 30.

Elegiac Expansion – 3.1

a ualeat, Phoebum quicumque moratur in armis.
exactus tenui pumice uersus eat.
quo me Fama leuat terra sublimis, et a me
 nata coronatis Musa triumphat equis, 10
et mecum in curru parui uectantur Amores,
 scriptorumque meas turba secuta rotas.
quid frustra missis mecum certatis habenis?
 non datur ad Musas currere lata uia.
multi, Roma, tuas laudes annalibus addent, 15
 qui finem imperii Bactra futura canent;
sed, quod pace legas, opus hoc de monte Sororum
 detulit intacta pagina nostra uia.
               3.1.1–18

Spirit of Callimachus and sacred rites of Philitas, allow me, I pray, to go into your grove! I enter as the first priest from the pure spring to bring Italian mysteries by means of Greek music. Tell me, in what cave did you refine your song together? or with what foot did you enter? or what water did you drink? Ah farewell, whoever detains Phoebus under arms! Let the verse go, finished off by fine pumice – by such verse sublime Fame lifts me from the earth, and the Muse born of me triumphs with garlanded horses, and with me in the chariot ride tiny Cupids, and a crowd of writers pursue my wheels. Why in vain do you strive against me with loosened reins? A broad path is not given to run to the Muses. Many, Rome, shall add your praises to the annals, singing that Bactra will be the extent of empire; but, that you might read something in peacetime, my page has brought down this work from the mountain of the Sisters by an untrodden path.

Propertius' extravagant advertisement for elegy abounds paradoxically with the symbolic language of genres other than elegy.[10] Most dramatically of all, Propertius appropriates from Horace's recent lyric the guise of poetic priest (*sacerdos*, 3.1.3); the word even appears at the very same point in Propertius' third book as it had in Horace's.[11] Moments later, Propertius imports via Virgil's *Georgics* the heroic metaphor of a literary triumph (9–12), an allusive gesture that catches a number of writers besides Virgil in its sweep.[12] To be sure, Propertius' triumph will celebrate peace; the elegist disavows the martial themes customary to epic

---

[10] Miller (1983a) 290–1.
[11] For some readers, the closeness of Propertius' imitation of Horace begins to threaten elegy's identity: e.g. Nethercut (1970a) 386, Keith (2008) 56.
[12] Cf. Virg. *Geo.* 3.8–15. Virgil's passage already alludes to Ennius via the text of Lucretius (Hinds (1998) 52–5); while Propertius further builds an Ennian presence

literature (7, 17) just as he had at the outset of Book 2. Yet, as his Virgilian triumph blends into a Homeric chariot race (13),[13] Propertius inscribes his new book with an elevated and epicising ambition that sits now at the heart of the elegiac project, rather than belonging to the sort of writing Propertius would entertain should he turn away from elegy (cf. 2.10–13).

This is a bold moment. As a Roman priest and literary *triumphator*, Propertius provides his latest elegiac collection with a public platform from which he will soon address *Roma* directly (15) with an authority that provocatively displaces Augustus' own.[14] At the same time, the verse generates its excitement through an implication of broader novelty.[15] Taken as a whole, and without overlooking the Callimachean rhetoric aimed at distinguishing Propertian elegy from other writers and writing, the confidence and flamboyantly allusive character of these opening lines rests on a generic openness, and sets up a sense of thematic adventure for the new collection.[16] Just as Callimachus has displaced Cynthia for the first time from the book's opening lines (cf. 1.1.1, 2.1.1–4) – heralding, we might presume, a tightened focus on the literary over the personal – so Propertius' vatic and triumphant persona seems to signal the promotion of public engagement over the private verse that had been the elegist's hallmark.[17]

The poem's interrogation of generic identity is flagged for its readers at an early stage. As a link between the poet's Callimachean (and Horatian) initiation scene and his Virgilian triumph, Propertius places a series of questions which occupy

---

at the beginning of Book 3 through *annalibus* at 3.1.15 (see generally Miller (1983b)).
[13] Fowler (2002) 154.
[14] In 3.1 Propertius develops his previous engagement with the triumph motif (for instance, at 2.1, 2.7, 2.15) which – like the metaphor of *militia amoris* in which it is grounded – works to distinguish between and yet also to associate the private realm of elegy and the public world of epic/Augustus. On the triumph metaphor in Propertius generally, see Galinsky (1969) 80–91; on the triumph motif in 3.1 particularly, cf. Fowler (2002) 154–5.
[15] E.g. Putnam (1980) 97. Propertius' novel tone here matches Horace's explicit statement of poetic innovation at *Odes* 3.1.2–4, on which see Lyne (1995) 160.
[16] Miller (1983a) 290–1.
[17] Wyke (2002) 225; see too Nethercut (1970a) 387–8.

Elegiac Expansion – 3.1

wholly the third couplet of the poem, and which foreshadow the exploratory tone of the poem that follows:

> dicite, quo pariter carmen tenuastis in antro? 5
> quoue pede ingressi? quamue bibistis aquam?
>
> 3.1.5–6

These three questions foreground programmatic aspects of literary inspiration and generic composition at the outset of the new collection. In the first instance, as questions to the ghostly guardians of the sacred grove, these lines look backwards, seeking to understand the nature of the writing that granted Callimachus and Philetas their posthumous renown. At the same time, as questions posed by a poet just beginning his new project, they imply a willingness to take guidance as to the direction and shape of the coming poetry.[18] At this level, these questions about literary identity stand programmatically open-ended at the head of a poem (and a book) that goes on to explore new scope and tone for Propertian elegy. The shifting imagery of lines 9–14 then further reinforces the lack of fixity that arises from an approach that prioritises questions over answers. Here Propertius presents an elusively metamorphic persona which seems to resist reduction at each point into any one stable identity: Propertius is first borne aloft by Fame, before transforming into *triumphator*, then, finally, into race-leading chariot driver. As the first half of the poem comes to a close, Propertius in fact eschews all interest in poetic constraint, assigning this instead to the un-Callimachean multitude that will seek, ironically, to impose limitation on Roman imperial expansion (*multi ... qui finem imperii Bactra futura canent*, 15–16).[19]

In the concluding section of 3.1 Propertius further manipulates the presence of Horace's *Odes* to recast elegy's long-standing opposition with the values of epic poetry in a way that reflects the greater prestige Propertius grants elegy as his

---

[18] Cf. Baker (1968b) 37, Nethercut (1975) 74–5, where readerly anxiety about change is palpable.

[19] On the seeming incompatibility of Callimachean poetry and Roman imperial expansion, see Fowler (1995) 254.

third book commences. To begin with, Propertius combines Callimachean distrust that a poet will ever receive the respect he is due while alive with a bold embrace of the increasing fame won by Homer's poetry since his death:[20]

> at mihi quod uiuo detraxerit inuida turba,
>   post obitum duplici faenore reddet honos.
> omnia post obitum fingit maiora uetustas;
>   maius ab exsequiis nomen in ora uenit.
> nam quis equo pulsas abiegno nosceret arces ...
>   3.1.21–5

> But as for what the jealous throng detracts from me while I live, after death glory will restore it with doubled interest. After death, antiquity fashions everything greater: after his burial, a man's name comes greater onto the lips of men. For who would know that the citadel was struck by a wooden horse ...

In the second half of 3.1 Propertius' greatness as already figured especially through his role as literary *imperator* now finds a parallel in the type of poetry which is suited to the celebration of just such heroic success in warfare. Propertius' transition to discussion of epic writing also facilitates the poem's continued emphasis on development and expansion. The elegist predicts that his reputation will receive a 'two-fold increase' (*duplici faenore*, 22); and, in the mannered repetition of *maiora* and *maius* (23–4), we must surely hear suggestive echoes of Virgil's 'second proem' at the beginning of *Aeneid* 7,[21] providing particularly Roman authorisation for a poet setting himself for (or claiming for himself) 'bigger' and 'greater' things. Such Propertian engagement with epic is not new in itself. At the beginning of Book 2, in a poem that otherwise recuses the elegist from writing Augustan epic on the familiar ground of incapacity, Propertius nonetheless elevates the ostensibly intimate status of his sex life with Cynthia (and so the elegiac poetry that narrates it) by association with the composition of

---

[20] For 'Envy' denying a poet his due renown, cf. Callimachus' *Hymn to Apollo* 105–13; for the theme of the Trojan War(riors) becoming famous only through their presence in (Homeric) poetry, cf. Theocritus 16.48–50.

[21] *maior rerum mihi nascitur ordo, | maius opus moueo* ('A greater array of material opens up before me, I undertake a greater task', Virg. *Aen.* 7.44–5).

lengthy *Iliad*s;[22] later, in 2.10, Propertius contrives an apparent intent to write an epic poem in part so that he might comment upon his heightened literary reputation, now that his amatory project 'has been completed'.[23] Yet, in these previous instances (and for all the constant slippage between 'elegiac' and 'epic' symbolism), the value of epic as a comparison for elegy lies in the frisson of its otherness to elegiac writing. In 3.1, by contrast, Propertius sets out to communicate the literary renown he has attained through his elegy, and here he does little to distinguish between the successful precedents of Homer and Callimachus himself. Rather, in this latest programmatic elegy, Propertius moves to assimilate his new elegiac project with the scale and legacy of Homeric epic without apology (cf. 2.1.17–18, 41–2; 2.10.25–6).

From *Amor* to *Roma*

Such undeniable novelty in Propertius' self-characterisation in 3.1 provides an important glance ahead. In particular, the vatic role that Propertius adopts at the poem's outset provides a glimpse of the manner of 'public' Roman elegy that Propertius will present subsequently, and more fully developed, in his fourth book. Nonetheless, it is equally important to recognise that the abrupt confidence of Book 3's opening, and elegy's 'novel' interest in Roman themes and literatures, effectively present a further inversion of an always-inverted genre which ever oscillates between *Roma* and *amor*. Here Propertius' incarnation as (Horatian) priest and (Virgilian) *triumphator* reworks the intensely competitive, ritualistic and heroic heart of the alternative world the elegist has already created for himself. It also flags the way in which elegy will engage two contemporary icons of Roman poetry – Virgil and Horace – to bring about renewed focus on elegy's social engagement.

---

[22] 2.1.13–14. On the paradoxically heroic characterisation of elegiac Propertius in 2.1, see Greene (2000).
[23] 2.10.8: *bella canam, quando scripta puella mea est*. On generic and geographical interaction in 2.10, see Tatum (2000). For the performative nature of Propertius' regular threats to abandon elegy for epic, see Wilson (2009).

Turning Elegy Upside Down: Propertius 3.1–3

Virgil deserves first glance, given that Propertius employs epic poetry as a generic reference point for Book 3's opening poem.[24] Propertius' choice to personify the epic genre via Homer is obvious enough, even if the Greek poet is described misleadingly as the commemorator of Troy's fall (*tui casus memorator Homerus*, 3.1.33). In programmatic terms, the unusual word *memorator* ('narrator', but also 'rememberer')[25] recalls *moratur* from line 7 ('Ah farewell, whoever *detains* Phoebus under arms') and so links epic's cultural longevity with Propertius' own intent for elegy.[26] But this striking phrase surely also contrives the presence of Virgil,[27] the *Roman* Homer, to whom responsibility for memorialising the fall of Troy might be attributed far more meaningfully. Here the word *memorator* assumes sudden contemporary relevance, particularly given apparent pressure in the 20s BCE to produce Roman celebration for the new *princeps* (e.g. 2.1.17–18, 3.9.1–4). Propertius' announcement of the *Aeneid* at 2.34.61–6 makes it clear that the elegist knew of Virgil's complicity in rendering Troy's legacy inseparable from Augustus' personal narrative. Yet the prompt to memory might remind us that elegy also commemorates loss in warfare. This is especially pertinent at 1.21–2, a two-poem *sphragis* for Book 1 which positions elegiac erotics retrospectively on the wrong side of Roman civil conflict:[28] recollection of warfare in elegy likewise engages Augustus' personal narrative but perhaps not in the way he would have welcomed.[29]

It is Horace's new lyric poetry, however, which most enables Propertius to re-address elegy's relationship with epic

---

[24] Galinsky (1969) 88, Miller (1983a) 292.
[25] *memoratur* is attested in classical Latin only here at Prop. 3.1.33.
[26] This is also a familiar act of differentiation in which the elegist once again sets his 'peaceful' material (e.g. 3.1.17) against the military subjects typical of epic.
[27] Thus establishing an allusive Virgilian frame for the Trojan sequence in 3.1 as a whole: see n. 21. In addition to the sack of Troy (32–3), Propertius' Trojan *exempla* in 3.1 include the wooden horse (25) – neither episode is treated in the *Iliad* (and feature only indirectly in the *Odyssey*), but both appear at length in the *Aeneid*; on this 'anomaly' see Heyworth & Morwood (2011) 103.
[28] See esp. Breed (2010).
[29] In the same vein, at 2.1.25–36 the epic that Propertius promises Maecenas he would write (had he the capacity) recalls the recent battles of Octavian that *Augustus* might have preferred forgotten.

From *Amor* to *Roma*

verse and the national significance epic claims.[30] Horatian lyric shares with elegy a primarily personal voice and a regular focus on the poet's own, often ephemeral experience. But, building explicitly on the precedent of Greek lyric poetry, in his *Odes* Horace increasingly endows his private voice with overt public capacity; indeed, as the three-book collection unfolds, Horace maps a trajectory towards complete authority over his poetic domain in a way that seeks association with Augustus' own ascent to imperial control over the Roman Principate.[31] Horace makes this explicit in the collection's final poem by embedding his poetry within the physical environment shaped by the ancient world's rulers:

> exegi monumentum aere perennius
> regalique situ pyramidum altius,
> quod non imber edax, non Aquilo impotens
> possit diruere aut innumerabilis
> annorum series et fuga temporum.
>
> Hor. *Od.* 3.30.1–5

I have completed a monument more lasting than bronze and higher than the royal tomb of the pyramids, which neither gnawing rain nor the north wind in its impotence are able to destroy, nor the innumerable series of years and the flight of time.

Horace's reference to himself as a builder of monuments and, later, as *princeps* (*Od.* 3.30.13), invites direct comparison with Augustus, the political *princeps* to whom Suetonius attributes a boast that he 'found Rome built of brick and left it in marble'.[32] The significance of Horace's bold claim to civic capacity plays out especially in the context of Propertius 3.2, but for the moment significance lies in the way that Horace's ending for the *Odes* becomes Propertius' starting point in Book 3. In the middle of his lyric *sphragis,* Horace predicts that his own fame will increase among succeeding generations (*ego postera crescam laude recens,* 'I shall grow renewed in the praise of

---

[30] Putnam (1980) 98.
[31] Lyne (1995) 23–4, 160; Oliensis (1998) 102–5.
[32] Suet. *Div. Aug.* 28.

31

posterity', *Od.* 3.30.7–8). Propertius uses this Horatian sentiment as a bridge between Homeric precedent and the future fame that Propertius prophesies for himself in 3.1:

> necnon ille tui casus memorator Homerus
> *posteritate* suum *crescere* sensit opus;
> meque inter seros *laudabit* Roma nepotes:
> illum post cineres auguror ipse diem.
> 3.1.33–6

> Even Homer, the commemorator of your fall, has felt his work increase through the passage of time. And me too Rome shall praise among its belated generations: I myself predict that day after my cremation.

In one basic sense, at 33–4 Propertius caps his expansive poem with the boldly hyperbolic image of an epic poem that grows even longer over time.[33] More significantly, Propertius adapts Horace's lyric language so as to convey the incomparable esteem in which Homer and Homeric epic are held by posterity, and to claim this legacy for elegy – and so he finally closes the gap between the elevated status he grants elegiac poetry as 3.1 begins and the epic idiom it evokes.[34] Finally, in the use of *auguror* ('I prophesy', 36) the poem comes full circle. Propertius concludes an elegy which aspires to Homeric heights by characterising it as a priestly utterance which recalls his opening entrance as Horatian *sacerdos*. In this way, as the introductory poem ends Propertius addresses posterity as an elegist whose capacity embraces lyric and epic discourse as well.

---

[33] Propertius possibly undermines the apparent epicisation of his new programme with a lewdly erotic double entendre based on the capacity of *opus* to mean both 'work' and 'penis': Adams (1982) 156–7. This might be seen more clearly through the rear-vision mirror of Ovidian elegy which also glosses the thematic expansiveness of hexametric writing in suggestively sexualised terms: *sex mihi surgat opus, in quinque residat*, 'My work(/penis) rises in six feet, and sinks back in five' (*Am.* 1.1.27: on which see Kennedy (1993) 59–60).

[34] How things have changed: at 1.7.1–6 it was Ponticus whose Theban poetry 'rivals that of peerless Homer' (*primo contendis Homero*, 1.7.3), a point Propertius makes in order to distinguish his own amatory material from the martial themes of epic (*nos, ut consuemus, nostros agitamus amores*, 1.7.5). In 3.1 Propertius still rejects war as subject, but not the competitive comparison with Homer.

Erotic Regression – 3.2

Notwithstanding the ways in which 3.1 foreshadows a re-inversion of existing elegiac traits, the extent to which the triumphant programme that Propertius announces there represents, simultaneously, a different mode of writing from what had come before is marked very clearly by the opening of 3.2:

> carminis interea nostri redeamus in orbem:
> gaudeat in solito tacta puella sono.
>
> 3.2.1–2
>
> Meanwhile let us return to the round of our song: let the girl rejoice, touched by the familiar sound.

In the first poem we followed Propertius rising aloft from the ground (*me Fama leuat terra sublimis*, 3.1.9); but now 3.2 promises our collective safe passage back to earth (as it were: *redeamus in orbem*, 3.2.1) with the claim to resume the poet's usual 'sphere' of writing.[35] Moreover, by flagging a return to a familiar kind of poetry (*redeamus*, 1; *solito sono*, 2), the collection's second poem not only situates the opening poem exactly as a transgressive novelty but, as a programme poem in its own right, also establishes through its connection to 3.1 a dialogue between innovation and thematic recapitulation that will prove crucial to the poetry that follows.[36] At this level, the poet's initial swing from *amor* back to *Roma* is represented as creating a crisis of identity for elegy between its past and future directions – a tension only resolved (perhaps) by the climactic renunciation of Cynthia with which the collection ends.

---

[35] Cf. Richardson (1977) 322, seeking to reduce the tension between 3.1 and 3.2 by assigning *interea* (3.2.1) the unusual sense of 'occasionally'.

[36] The collection as a whole is marked by an oscillation between poems which outwardly seek to extend elegiac compass and those which appear to recall the manner of Propertius' earlier writing. The sequence 3.7–10 is one example: in 3.7 Propertius presents an unparalleled lament for an external figure, Paetus, followed in 3.8 by an erotic narrative similar to those found especially in Book 2; in 3.9 Propertius all but promises Maecenas an Augustan epic – but the poem we get in 3.10 is a birthday hymn for Cynthia that recalls very closely the opening poems of Book 1.

Turning Elegy Upside Down: Propertius 3.1–3

Nonetheless, 3.2 itself proceeds to play with its readers' understanding of exactly what is 'familiar' to elegiac writing; in this sense, the collection's second poem in fact continues the programmatic interrogation of elegiac identity that began in the first poem (esp. 3.1.5–6). The grand ambition of 3.1 sought confrontation with epic literature; now the (re)turn towards more personal and, especially, erotic material invites further, more sustained interaction with Horace's lyric. But rather than engage Horace as a fellow private poet, as might have been suspected, Propertius concludes his revival of 'erotic' elegy by plundering further from *Odes* 3.30 (quoted above),[37] so continuing to engage Horace at the moment Horace himself confirms his place in Rome's socio-political landscape:

> fortunata, meo si qua es celebrata libello:
>   carmina erunt formae tot *monumenta* tuae.
> nam neque *pyramidum* sumptus ad sidera ducti,
>   nec Iouis Elei caelum imitata domus,
> nec Mausolei diues fortuna sepulcri
>   mortis ab extrema condicione uacant.
> aut illis flamma aut *imber* subducet honores,
>   *annorum* aut ictu, pondere uicta, ruent.
> at non ingenio quaesitum nomen ab aeuo
>   excidet: ingenio stat sine morte decus.
>   Prop. 3.2.17–26

Happy are you, whoever you are that is celebrated in my book. My songs will be so many monuments to your beauty. For neither the extravagance of the pyramids raised to the stars, nor the house of Jove at Elis that imitates heaven, nor the rich fortune of Mausolus' tomb are exempt from the final condition of death. Either flame or rain will take away their glories, or they will fall to ruin at the impact of the years, overcome by the weight. But the name earned by a poet's talent will not fall in all eternity: due to such talent, splendour stands deathless.

The broad significance of such symbolism deserves more emphasis. While Horace establishes competition between

---

[37] The sheer extent of Horatian material in 3.2 already complicates the claim that this poem offers a return to familiar elegiac territory: Miller (1983a) 292, Richardson (1977) 322. Keith (2008) 63 – more constructive – sees increasing diversity itself as Propertius' elegiac statement, notwithstanding his claim to be reverting to earlier elegiac modes.

Erotic Regression – 3.2

poetry and politics, Propertius is typically seen to compete simply with Horace alone, redirecting Horatian sentiment in support of a differentiated elegiac project.[38] This is not inaccurate, so far as it goes: the elegist caps the lyric poet by extending the comparison of poetry with cityscape to include other wonders of the ancient world (3.2.19–22); in a similar spirit Propertius multiplies and yet diminishes the scale of Horace's Augustan *monumentum*, transforming it into so many *monumenta* for the elegiac *puella*, whose unconventional relationship with the poet has lent Propertian elegy its proudly private character.[39]

But 3.2 also continues Propertius' use of Horace's *Odes* as a generic catalyst to reposition elegy as a genre more overt in its public capacity – and so precisely less concerned to maintain its pretence as personal confession and lament. Over and above its differentiation from Horace's lyric values, elegiac identity is newly articulated in a way that signals elegy's prior claim to the kind of literary authority that Horace espouses. Yet the foundations from which Propertius' 'new' modality develops are drawn from earlier elegiac modes – precisely from the 'accustomed song' to which the poem's opening lines claim to return us (furthermore, inasmuch as these lines usher in a new, seemingly 'Horatian' form of elegy, then Horace's lyricism is positioned paradoxically as already 'familiar' to elegy). In line with the inversion of elegiac norms in 3.1, now Propertius uses Horace's closural detachment to further expose a very literary nature of elegy that had previously been overshadowed by the passionate narrative of what now must seem an increasingly fictional love affair.[40]

3.2 stages the first appearance of an elegiac *puella* in Book 3, but when it does so the effect is oddly distancing. The reference to a *tacta puella* in the poem's second line might be expected to serve as a prompt for renewed erotic reminiscence but instead

---

[38] Mader (1993) 330–1, Keith (2008) 59–60, Heyworth & Morwood (2011) 111–12; also Nethercut (1970a) 387–8 for a reading that has Propertius having fun in these lines at Horace's expense.
[39] For this reading of 3.2, see Miller (1983a) 295, 298–9 and esp. Keith (2008) 57–60.
[40] Wyke (1987b) is groundbreaking for unpacking the tension between elegy's realism and its literariness, especially in the context of Books 1 and 2.

Turning Elegy Upside Down: Propertius 3.1–3

acts as a springboard for further meditation on the potency granted a poet by his poetry:

> Orphea detinuisse feras et concita dicunt
> flumina Threicia sustinuisse lyra;
> saxa Cithaeronis Thebas agitata per artem   5
> sponte sua in muri membra coisse ferunt;
> quin etiam, Polypheme, fera Galatea sub Aetna
> ad tua rorantis carmina flexit equos.
>
> 3.2.3–8

> They say that Orpheus restrained the wild beasts and held back the rushing rivers with his Thracian lyre; they tell that Cithaeron's rocks, driven to Thebes by the singer's skill, of their own accord came together to form parts of a wall; what is more, Polyphemus, even Galatea below wild Aetna turned her dewy horses at your songs.

In this mythic triptych, 3.2 focuses not on erotic subjects but on erotic writing itself. Just as at the beginning of 3.1, the poem's attention falls on the successful artist and the influence of his art: Orpheus (3–4) and Amphion (5–6) serve as stock *exempla* for the ability of song to exert an almost magical control over things both animate and inanimate; while Polyphemus, who appears as the climax of the tricolon (7–8), exemplifies poetry's erotic authority through (what Propertius presents here as) his successful wooing of the nymph Galatea.[41] All three myths direct the poem's erotic regression towards another triumphant ending – a celebration of Propertius' talent as an erotic artist, and the everlasting name it has won for him. In this context, the poem's heavy allusion to *Odes* 3.30 serves a similar end to that it served in 3.1: to 'authorise' the poet's closing declaration through reference to another writer making the same declaration (cf. 3.1.37–8).

When Propertius brings the lesson of these myths to bear on his own writing, the poetry he describes is not written for the seduction of one beloved but has instead a wider female audience:

---

[41] These myths – that of Orpheus in particular – might also serve as warning about 'the overmastering power of music', and so further the implicit suggestion at the beginning of the poem that the poetic ambition of 3.1 represents dangerous extravagance for an elegist: Heyworth & Morwood (2011) 111.

Erotic Regression – 3.2

> miremur, nobis et Baccho et Apolline dextro,
> turba puellarum si mea uerba colit?
>
> 3.2.9–10
>
> Why be amazed, with both Bacchus and Apollo at my right, that a crowd of girls cherishes my words?

In Books 1 and 2 Propertius identifies both as poet and lover with the totemic figure of one girl – Cynthia. Right at the heart of Book 1, Propertius had asserted that Cynthia was the first and would be the last (1.12.20); and he opens Book 2 with the bold claim that his poetic impulse comes not from Calliope or Apollo, but from his girl alone (2.1.3–4; see too the primacy of Cynthia at 2.34.93, just two poems earlier).[42] But here Propertius introduces us to a bevy of girls who are all represented as readers of his verse, and each as a potential subject for celebration in it.[43] The change in emphasis is highly significant for Propertian elegy, especially at the head of a collection which will withhold Cynthia's name until its twenty-first poem. The reference to *turba puellarum* (10) – conspicuously balancing *scriptorum turba* at 3.1.12 – further suggests the way that 3.2 works programmatically in support of 3.1; indeed, 3.2 tracks thematic expansion in Propertius' amatory sphere, too, moving from one girl at 3.2.2 to a crowd of girls at 3.2.10. Introducing a number of girls to elegy is also a markedly Horatian touch, right at the moment that the poem initiates a series of close lexical borrowings from Horace (3.2.11–26); in contrast to elegy's obsessive fidelity to one *puella*, Horace's notably lighter lyric persona flirts with a variety of girls across the three books of the *Odes* (and here, too, perhaps Propertius' crowd of girls seeks to outnumber Horace's mere several *puellae*).

Most significantly, Propertius flags a broadening in the way elegy seeks to identify itself. In particular, the *turba puellarum* continues the trend at the start of Book 3 of placing elegy in a civic setting with a public readership, and, consequently, of

---

[42] It is significant in this context that Propertius will receive literary counsel from both Apollo and Calliope in the following poem, 3.3. For the centrality of the poet's mistress as both subject and reader of his poetry, see too 1.7.11, 2.13.11–14.

[43] For *turba puellarum* as in fact a departure from a 'familiar' position, see Heyworth & Morwood (2011) 109.

moving the genre further away from the conceit that it represents a largely private correspondence primarily addressed to one beloved girl (or to the poet's individual male friends about one beloved girl).[44] In 3.2 Propertius presents his poetry as though it were a social artefact in the hands of 'actual' readers, and he foregrounds his own erotic role as 'an observer rather than a participant',[45] a small novelty which brings about further subtle but significant transformations. The single elegiac *puella* becomes a crowd of girls that worships (*colit*, 3.2.10) the poet's words – developing the poet's sacerdotal imagery from 3.1, especially in the connection with Bacchus and Apollo (3.2.9). Yet Propertius' general audience now replicates, as individuals, the role of the single female reader which formerly it had been Cynthia's privilege to perform. Now it seems that any of these readers may choose to enter into the fiction that Propertius' poetry is about her, effectively conjuring the possibility of an indefinite number of individual 'beloveds'. Here we might revisit the poem's pivotal engagement with Horace, where once again all these threads come together:

> miremur, nobis et Baccho et Apolline dextro,
> turba puellarum si mea uerba colit?
> ...
>
> at Musae comites, et carmina cara legenti,
> nec defessa choris Calliopea meis.
> fortunata meo si qua es celebrata libello:
> carmina erunt formae tot monumenta tuae.
>   3.2.9–10, 15–18

Why be amazed, with both Bacchus and Apollo at my right, that a crowd of girls cherishes my words? ... but Muses are my companions and my songs are dear to the one reading them, nor is Calliope wearied

---

[44] Such a move towards exposing an external 'reality' usually has closural force in fictional writing. For instance, Propertius allows himself the 'realistic' image of his reigning among a *number* of girls at the literary conuiuium in the closing poem of Book 2 (*ut regnem mixtas inter conuiua puellas*, 2.34.57) – nothwithstanding that the poem's final couplet reasserts Cynthia's primacy. So too, at the end of Book 3, one of Propertius' closural moves will be to suggest that Cynthia's literary persona has in fact been composed from the figures of various girls (*mixtam te uaria laudaui saepe figura*, 3.24.5).
[45] Mader (1993) 326.

by my music. Happy are you, whoever you are that is celebrated in my book: my songs will be so many monuments to your beauty.

Here Propertius' crowd of female admirers becomes so many single readers (*carmina cara legenti*, 3.2.15). In this context, the pointed indeterminacy (*si qua es*, 3.2.17) of the girl's identity whose beauty the poetry celebrates invites a radical reappraisal of our response to earlier elegy, which encourages us to identify the poetry's female addressee with Cynthia herself. Propertius' allusion to Horace's *monumentum* at this point offers further significance. While Propertius' many monuments to female beauty surely do seek to trump Horace's single structure, they also symbolise very effectively the sudden multiplicity of potential 'lyric-style' mistresses as Propertius addresses his *turba puellarum* with words that each girl wishes were hers alone.

In contrast with the generalising identity and comparatively timeless quality of Horace's new personal verse, elegy's signature restriction to a specific amatory scenario centred on the poet and his mistress locks the elegist into a particular (and particularly limited) way of connecting with the external readers whose concerns the poet seldom acknowledges.[46] Book 3 clearly seeks to reset elegy's bearings by focusing on its place in a social environment.[47] Yet it is important to realise that this transition once again represents an inversion of aesthetic priorities which elegy has always held. As with 3.1 in the context of heroic literature, in 3.2 the innovation for amatory elegy lies in developing the poetry's veiled interest in poetics which has underpinned its more immediate focus on erotic realism. We might recall, for instance, that from the beginning 'Cynthia' – as first word of Book 1 – both establishes eroticism as the poet's theme (writing about loving a girl) and yet gives a name to a collection of poetry (writing and reading *Cynthia*); and that, as the corpus progresses, 'Cynthia' slips increasingly from easy identification with a 'flesh-and-blood' woman and more towards representation of a literary discourse (a symbol for

---

[46] Conte (1994b).
[47] Putnam (1980) 98.

Turning Elegy Upside Down: Propertius 3.1–3

elegy itself).[48] Against this background, when Book 3 explicitly claims literature itself as its primary focus by addressing Callimachus and Philetas in its first line,[49] it represents as much the continuation of an elegiac trend as it does genuine generic innovation.

Moreover, the 'shift' represented in 3.2 by focusing on erotic writing and an indefinite (even multiple) identity for elegy's beloved *puella* simultaneously opens elegy up in response to the broader amatory mode of Horatian lyric and exposes a 'truth' that Cynthia – ever a literary metaphor clothed in Coan silk – was never really one girl in the first place but is, rather, the name Propertius has given the 'endlessly adaptable'[50] female fantasy which sits at the heart of his poetry. Even the climactic statement in 3.2 that Propertius' talent in erotic writing has granted him everlasting public renown (3.2.25–6, itself a refinement of the similar claim at the end of the previous poem at 3.1.35–8) is essentially the rearticulation of a social role Propertius has long claimed for elegy.[51] The concluding lines from 1.7 foreshadow very closely the kind of sublime authority that Propertius claims as Book 3 opens:

> tum me non humilem mirabere saepe poetam,
>   tunc ego Romanis praeferar ingeniis;
> nec poterunt iuuenes nostro reticere sepulcro
>   'ardoris nostri magne poeta, iaces.'
>   1.7.21–4

Then you will marvel that I am no humble poet; then I shall be ranked above other Roman talents; nor will young men be able to stay silent at my tomb: 'Here you lie, great poet of our passion.'

At this point not yet halfway through Book 1, Propertius already envisions an elegiac greatness that lets him rival epic poets

---

[48] See esp. Wyke (1987b), Greene (1998). For an overview of the reflexivity of life and literature in elegiac discourse, see Kennedy (1993) 1–15; for a significant reading which recuperates realistic circumstances underpinning the lives of (fictional) elegiac women, see James (2003b).

[49] E.g. Ross (1975) 121, Putnam (1980) 98, Nethercut (1970a) 387–8, Wyke (1987a) 154 and (1989a) 30, Debrohun (2003) 130, Clarke (2004) 127–8.

[50] Gold (1993) 88.

[51] Nethercut (1970a) 388.

(*non humilem poetam*, 1.7.21) and lead other poets in triumph (*Romanis praeferar ingeniis*, 1.7.22). More pertinently for 3.2, Propertius articulates at an early stage the essential relevance of his personal narrative to a wider audience. Crucially, in 1.7 an audience of young men (*iuuenes*, 1.7.23; in 3.2 the audience comprises young women) recognises Propertius' personal relationship with Cynthia as offering a paradigmatic exploration of love as a general condition that affects them, too (*ardoris nostri poeta*, 1.7.24). It is this implicit social connection which Propertius promotes loudly in 3.1–2 as he reconstructs elegy in inverted fashion for an increasingly crowded public stage that it shares with Horatian lyric already, and soon will share with Virgilian epic as well.

Recapitulation and Coda – 3.3

Propertius Book 3 might commence by repositioning elegy as a more public genre, and do so by giving renewed attention to an underlying Romanness already present in elegy, but this does not mean the collection opens with any sudden clarification of the thematic confusions and oppositions that elegiac verse has displayed in earlier books. By inverting anew the relationship in his opening poem between *amor* and *Roma* (for, while *Roma* is now represented inclusively in 3.1, *amor* is still present – though it has been relegated to the back seat of the poet's triumphal car: *et mecum in curru parui uectantur Amores*, 3.1.11) Propertius essentially maintains the thematic tension between these two symbols but now probes it from a different direction. By way of closing we look briefly at the third poem of Book 3, not least because Propertius positions it as providing answers to the generic questions posed at the beginning of 3.1.[52] Yet the poem also represents a telling summation both of the disparate programmatic strategies of the collection's first two poems and of the tensions between these poems that do (and, in an elegiac sense, must) remain unresolved.

---

[52] Nethercut (1970a) 385.

Book 3 opened with Propertius seeking literary instruction from the spirits of Callimachus and Philitas: metaphorically, Propertius asked which water they had drunk to inspire the writing that brought them fame. Now, in 3.3, Propertius dreams that he is reclining at leisure on Mt Helicon (*uisus eram molli recubans Heliconis in umbra*, 3.3.1), about to drink from the stream which had inspired Ennius in the composition of his *Annales*.[53] But Propertius' inceptive epic on Roman history is brought up short by the intervention of Apollo, who directs the elegiac poet to a secluded grove where Calliope points out the more appropriate inspirational font containing the water Philitas had drunk (*ora Philitea nostra rigauit aqua*, 3.3.52). The final couplet of 3.3 thus offers neat ring-reference to the opening couplet of 3.1, and so affirms the first three poems of Book 3 as a programmatic unit which explores and (seemingly) resolves the issue of Propertian generic identity.

But, in doing so, 3.3 essentially restages the dynamic of transgression and retraction that has been at work across the first two poems of the new collection. 3.1 expressed a newfound confidence and excitement expressed in swelling verse which, for all that it disavowed martial themes, revealed deep interest in the success of epic writing; 3.2 then flagged the opening poem as an aesthetic transgression by promising a return to the confines of familiar erotic material (even if the promised familiarity proved rather 'Horatian'). 3.3 marks such generic oscillation as intrinsic to elegy itself – and particularly to the programme of Book 3 – through repetition of the opening poems' swing between aesthetic poles: the dreaming poet placing his small lips against Ennius' great font (*parvaque iam magnis admoram fontibus ora*, 3.3.5) paraphrases Propertius' flirtation with epic's grand scale of values in 3.1 (and in earlier poetry); while Apollo's interruption and Propertius' subsequent initiation with Philitan water tropes the interventionist force and erotic regression of 3.2 (the poet

---

[53] The Ennian episode is foreshadowed with *annalibus* at 3.1.15. For the use of Ennius in elegy as a symbol for epic poetry, see generally Miller (1983b).

Recapitulation and Coda – 3.3

always comes back to elegy). Apollo himself – as the voice that mediates between the extremes of epic and elegiac writing – is even characterised in 3.3 as leaning on a lyre (*sic ait aurata nixus ad antra lyra*, 3.3.14), recalling the intermediary role performed by Horace's lyric poetry especially in 3.1. Further suggesting elegy's status as neither one nor the other, but instead as a (nearly) balanced negotiation of both literary opposites, each of Apollo's and Calliope's speeches to the dreaming Propertius is divided (almost) evenly between reference to 'epic' and 'elegiac' material.[54] Even the conventional gendered imagery of elegy as 'soft' and epic as 'hard' seems interdependent in this dreamlike poem: Calliope's verb as she wet Propertius' lips with Philetan water – *rigauit* – evokes uncannily the verb *riguit* ('hardened'), while the Heliconian shade from which Propertius had originally contemplated Ennian epic is 'soft' (*molli in umbra*).

More importantly, 3.3 further confirms the inverted stance which Book 3 adopts with respect to earlier programmatic statements, where the lover's lifestyle serves as metaphor for elegiac poetics. Ostensibly, like the poems before it, 3.3 claims to confirm that in Book 3 Propertius will continue in the manner which has defined his earlier books; this is the message that Calliope delivers. Yet, exactly in making this claim, the current poem up-ends the relationship established in earlier Propertian poetry between life and literature, and so continues the elegy's third-book focus on Propertius as poet rather than lover. At the start of Book 1, Cynthia had received instruction from both Apollo and Calliope (1.2.25–8), while in Book 2 Propertius had claimed that he received inspiration from Cynthia alone and not from Calliope or Apollo (2.1.3–4); in other words, previously it was the poet's mistress who served as metaphor for his engagement with elegiac poetics, within a poetry which more persistently maintained its

---

[54] Both speeches define elegy precisely as a dialogue between the opposed extremes of epic and elegiac stereotypes. Apollo's speech (3.3.15–24) switches between lines evoking the unsuitability of epic and lines promoting the appropriateness of elegy, while Calliope's speech (3.3.39–50) lists 'epic' themes at 40–6 before closing – a little more briefly – with reference to 'elegiac' material at 47–50.

43

autobiographical conceit.[55] Now, as Book 3 begins, Propertius himself takes counsel directly from both Apollo and Calliope, while Cynthia is as yet nowhere to be seen. Poetics are prioritised above mistress; Cynthia has given way to Cynthius.

3.3 also reinforces subtly the new kind of 'objective' love elegy that appears in 3.2, even as it claims to affirm the manner of subjective elegy with which Propertius began his career. After cataloguing the sort of warlike material that Propertius should not attempt (3.3.41–6), Calliope sets out proper subjects for an elegist:

> quippe coronatos alienum ad limen amantis
> nocturnaeque canes ebria signa fugae,
> ut per te clausas sciat excantare puellas,
> qui uolet austeros arte ferire uiros.
>
> 3.3.47–50

Indeed you will sing of garlanded lovers before another's threshold, and of drunken tokens of nocturnal flight, so that he who would like to cheat strict husbands by his skill might learn to charm out locked-up girls.

Calliope's edict remembers elegy's emblematic motif of the locked-out lover who sings drunkenly on his mistress's doorstep in the hope of gaining entrance to the girl's house or enticing his *puella* out. She also unavoidably recalls the erotic elegy particularly of Propertius' first book where the erotic narrative most 'realistically' depicts the interaction of lover and mistress, and which even contains an elegy almost entirely voiced in grumpy couplets by the locked door itself (1.16). But the effect of recalling Book 1 at this point is to highlight the extent to which, in Book 3, Calliope now decrees a less personal style of elegy. Calliope continues the trend in 3.2 of downplaying the elegist's role in chronicling his own erotic adventures in favour of writing about love affairs in more general terms (and Calliope plays up Propertius' role as an erotic instructor of other lovers,[56] which has a further distancing effect: the focus

---

[55] On the strategies of realism in Propertius' early books, see esp. Wyke (1987b); cf. Greene (1998) *passim*.
[56] Cf. e.g. 1.7.13–14.

Recapitulation and Coda – 3.3

falls not on Propertius' own seduction of Cynthia but on the seductions Propertius should teach others to perform).

It has been remarked that Propertius' description of Ennian epic at the beginning of the poem (3.3.7–12) seems 'somehow wrong'.[57] But it is not observed that Calliope's tightly focused and symbolic representation of what Propertius should be writing bears only partial resemblance to the varied kind of elegy that Propertius has indeed produced – a poetry which has underscored the triumphant tone of 3.1 as much as the erotic potency of 3.2. One effect of coming across such a definition of elegy now in a third book (and especially after reading through the provocatively expansive and Cynthia-free material in both opening poems) might well be a sudden awareness of how long it has been since elegy has looked as Calliope describes it. In this case, 3.3's dream on Mt Helicon becomes a nostalgically selective fantasy about elegy's early period – the value of which lies not in defining what elegy ought to be but rather in pointing out what it is no longer. This point seems affirmed in the very next poem when Propertius wakes from his elegiac dream only to utter the un-elegiac sentiments *arma deus Caesar* (3.4.1). And the fact that the book continues after 3.3 in a spirit of modal exploration intermixed with further backward glances suggests that, as elegy continues to reinvent itself, the programmatic function of the collection's opening questions of generic method lies as much in their asking as in their answer.

---

[57] Miller (1983b) 281.

CHAPTER 2

SEEKING *FIDES* IN POETS AND POETRY

Propertius 3.6

This chapter is the first of three contrasting studies of *fides* within Book 3 – this series continues in chapter 4 (3.12), and in chapter 8 (3.20). The focus of the opening study falls on 3.6, Book 3's first 'love' elegy. This poem is an obsessive exploration of one's desire for faithfulness in love, and in the act of telling stories about love: the poem presents a dramatic monologue in which the poet seeks *honest* assurance from an intermediary (Cynthia's hapless slave Lygdamus) about the *sincerity* of his mistress's affections for him during a period of separation. This chapter examines in particular the way that Propertius conflates these different senses of 'fidelity'. Here the poet desires *fides* of both mistress and messenger in an elegy which dramatises ironically the vulnerability of truth to manipulation in narrative (a point that should not be lost on the elegy's gullible reader).

The Metapoetry of Propertian Love

The narrative of 3.6 pivots on vagaries of trust and interpretation. As the poem begins, Propertius interrogates Cynthia's slave Lygdamus for information about the behaviour of their common mistress, from which the poet hopes to glean the 'truth' about Cynthia's feelings; here, the poet's obsessive questioning in the first half of the poem creates the impression that he fears Cynthia no longer loves him. Then, in the second half of the poem, a report of Cynthia's own words (or the poet's fantasy about what she might have said) suggests that she suspects in turn that Propertius now loves someone else. In its focus on erotic tension, 3.6 provides a sustained example of the way in which Propertius' poetry employs amatory dynamics

The Metapoetry of Propertian Love

to interrogate the acts of writing and reading – and it is precisely this duality which gives the poem's thematic obsession with 'fidelity' its potency. At narrative level, 3.6 performs the lover's desire to suspend disbelief, and so to trust that his mistress's affection for him is 'real'. At a subtextual level, the poem explores an affinity between a lover's willingness to suspend disbelief and a reader's desire to embrace the realism of erotic narrative, and so to believe that the story they are reading is 'true'. In effect, 3.6 employs the mutual suspicions held by the poet and mistress of each other to offer commentary upon the fraught relationship of trust between reader and writer, and the ways in which this relationship affects the reader's attempts to extract 'meaning' from the poetry.

A vital prompt to read 3.6 for its concern with (meta)literary as well as erotic dynamics comes in a non-scanning pun in the poem's final line. Propertius ends his poem by promising Lygdamus 'you will be *free*' (*liber eris*, 3.6.42), should only the poet and mistress be reunited. Here, the long first syllable in the adjective *līber* confirms the narrative sense of the slave's potential 'liberation' – but Propertius quips that Lygdamus 'will be a *book*' at the same time, by suggesting the noun *lĭber*, a word with the same spelling but an unmetrical short initial syllable. In a general sense, Propertius' 'book' joke caps his poem with a closing gesture to an underlying textuality in the poem's lineage: notwithstanding the apparent return to the realism of poet's personal world, the poem's quasi-dialogic structure is notably informed by Greek epigram and Roman satire;[1] the poem as a whole has close affinity with mime,[2] and its thematic focus on appearances and mistrust derives from Roman comedy, especially Terence's *Heauton Timorumenos*.[3] More specifically, the joke affirms the metapoetic significance assigned to Lygdamus himself – that elusive slave with a poet's name.[4] As 3.6 ends, we are invited to reflect upon the transformation of message-bearing

---

[1] Heyworth & Morwood (2011) 146.
[2] Camps (1966) 78–9, Richardson (1977) 337, Fedeli (1985) 205–6.
[3] Butler & Barber (1933) 273, Yardley (1972) 135, and esp. Butrica (1983) 33–7.
[4] The elegiac poet Lygdamus, whose work is transmitted as Book 3.1–6 of the *Corpus Tibullianum*. On the paradoxes of Lygdamus' position within the Propertian corpus, see Richardson (1977) 337.

Seeking *Fides* in Poets and Poetry: Propertius 3.6

slave into an allegory for the poetic text itself. Already, though, Propertius has positioned Lygdamus as his own authorial surrogate: by embedding representation of his mistress within a report brought to him by the slave, in 3.6 Propertius dramatically cedes to Lygdamus responsibility for narrating *Cynthia*.

The poem's comedic background is instrumental not only in setting up such a reading of Lygdamus, but also in colouring it. The role of a slave as go-between is a narrative commonplace in Roman comedy; and Propertius' requests for information about Cynthia in 3.6 echo specifically the interrogation of the slave Syrus by the young Clinias concerning his beloved Antiphila at *Heauton Timorumenos* 264–307. But comedy's own metapoetic game at such moments already plays on the identification of its cunning slaves as 'poets' who are responsible for shaping the play's plot.[5] Comedy's slave–poet synergy is addressed explicitly with Plautus' eponymous Pseudolus. Needing to find a way to extort money, the Plautine slave appeals to the literary world for inspiration:

> sed quasi poeta, tabulas cum cepit sibi,
> quaerit quod nusquamst gentium, reperit tamen,
> facit illud ueri simile, quod mendacium est,
> nunc ego poeta fiam: uiginti minas,
> quae nusquam nunc sunt gentium, inueniam tamen.
> Plaut. *Pseud.* 401–5

> But just as the poet, when he has taken up his tablets, seeks what exists nowhere in the world, finds it nonetheless, and makes what is a fiction have the appearance of truth; now *I* shall become a poet; twenty *minae*, which currently exist nowhere in the world, nonetheless I will find.

The dynamics of this metapoetic relationship work in two directions simultaneously. Pseudolus' confidence in his cleverness to 'plot' his way out a predicament justifies his self-identification *as* a poet. At the same time, Pseudolus' poet simile neatly figures his own creative ingenuity in the first place – *like* the poet, the comedic slave is able to contrive a plausible truth out of what is really a lie. Both these generic associations from comedy inform the representation of

---

[5] Sharrock (1996) 164–5, Fitzgerald (2000) 44.

Lygdamus in 3.6. By building his poem on a comedic model, Propertius invites recognition of his decision to grant control of the poem's plot to a slave. Yet the same frame should lead us to suspect that any 'story' told by Lygdamus will be less than straight.

In sum, the first love poem of Book 3 reintroduces erotic narrative to Propertian verse in a way that juxtaposes the celebrated realism of his early books with an ostentatious staginess. By entrusting a (fellow) slave with responsibility for conveying messages to his mistress in a poem with a marked theatrical lineage, Propertius embarks on an elaborate masquerade of his own. The elegist purports to lay aside the role of creative poet for a moment, and to give that role to another figure who, just like Propertius, is enslaved to Cynthia. The poem's narrative conceit invites us to view Lygdamus as encapsulating a deceptive quality in the Propertian text itself, and it bestows metapoetic value on Propertius' own role as well. In 3.6 the erstwhile poet puts to Lygdamus the kind of questions elegy's suspicious reader might have for Propertius himself.

Elegiac Narration and the Fictional Contract

Forsaking for the moment his customary control over the representation of Cynthia, Propertius opens the poem by asking the slave Lygdamus to tell *him* about the behaviour of his mistress:

> Dic mihi de nostra quae sentis uera puella:
>   sic tibi sint dominae, Lygdame, dempta iuga.
> num me laetitia tumefactum fallis inani,
>   haec referens, quae me credere uelle putas?
> omnis enim debet sine uano nuntius esse,   5
>   maioremque timens seruus habere fidem.
> nunc mihi, si qua tenes, ab origine dicere prima
>   incipe: suspensis auribus ista bibam.
>   3.6.1–8[6]

---

[6] Heyworth (2007a) transposes 5–6 to after 1–2, and 3–4 into what he argues is a

Seeking *Fides* in Poets and Poetry: Propertius 3.6

> Tell me the truth that you have perceived about our girl: thus may the yoke of your mistress be removed from you, Lygdamus. Surely you don't deceive me and make me swell up with empty joy, telling me these things which you think I want to believe? For every messenger ought to be without deceit, and slave to have greater reliability because of his fear. Now, if you know anything, begin to speak from the very beginning: I shall drink in your words with pricked ears.

Here Lygdamus effectively gains the poet's responsibility for narrative, while Propertius himself takes up a position analogous to that of elegy's reader – or, perhaps, to that of an audience member 'listening' at a *recitatio* (*suspensis auribus ista bibam*, 8). This elaborate charade of role-switching draws attention to the performance of poetic narration and, especially, to the way that poems and poets convey 'meaning'. Through the interrogation of the messenger Lygdamus by the eager poet, the poem rehearses for its actual reader one of the ways in which elegy itself might be read.

Subject now to Lygdamus' representations, Propertius asks to be told the truth – *dic mihi uera* (1). Yet the poem's opening establishes 'truth' as a matter of performance in which two closely related traits act in concert. On the one hand, Propertius admits a suspicion that his narrator (the book-like Lygdamus, for the poetic text itself) has the capacity to deceive (*fallis*, 3) – and this is very much in keeping with the slavish duplicity in comedy from which Lygdamus' role derives. On the other hand, Propertius acknowledges a certain credulity on his own part, and so on the part of elegy's reader, whom he resembles: this is an awareness that he receives pleasure (*laetitia*, 3) from being told 'things he likes to believe' (4). Propertius may well begin the poem claiming a desire for truth, but in the end – as Propertius shows here by moving swiftly to a revealing series of credulous questions (9–18) which betray very much the sort of things he would like to hear – Propertius (and his reader surrogate) is shown to be content with being duped,[7] as long as

---

lacuna after 11–12; see Heyworth (2007b) 304–5. Heyworth suggests (304) that in 3–4 the narrator must react to news already received, and so places that couplet after the first pair of questions in which (in one possible reading; see below, n. 15) the poet repeats the slave's report.

[7] Insofar as Propertius thus adopts the persona of a reader, cf. Sharrock (1996) 152.

the deception is not so apparent as to prevent the suspension of his disbelief – that is, to render his desired pleasure effectively 'empty' (*inanis*, 3).

Constructing *Fides*

To regain their *laetitia* and propel them towards a desired *concordia* (41), when asking Lygdamus to tell them the truth both the poet and the *puella* place weight on the messenger's *fides*. To begin with, Propertius admonishes Lygdamus:

> omnis enim debet sine uano nuntius esse,
> maioremque timens seruus habere fidem.
>
> 3.6.5–6

For every messenger ought to be without deceit, and slave to have greater reliability because of his fear.

The phrase *habere fidem* (literally, 'to have trust') is a crucial but elusive one in the present context.[8] The phrase is usually employed actively to describe the placing of faith in someone or something.[9] Here, though, the use is quasi-passive, and conveys figuratively the sense of 'to be truthful'. Behind this must lie a more fundamental sense of 'to have credence' – that is, to be believable;[10] what matters above all in the generation of 'truthfulness' is that the story, or the storyteller, be convincing.

This point is reinforced when the phrase *habere fidem* recurs in 3.23. Once again the phrase applies to the role of 'messenger' – in this case, the messenger is a pair of wax tablets which convey written messages between the poet and his mistress:

> has quondam nostris manibus detriuerat usus,
> qui non signatas iussit habere fidem.

---

[8] Camps (1966) 79, 162 (in relation to 3.6.6 and 3.23.4, respectively).
[9] E.g. Cat. 30.6: *quid faciant, dic, homines, cuiue habeant fidem?* ('Tell me, what are men to do, in whom are they to put their trust?'); Lucan, *B.C.* 7.139: *nec gladiis habuere fidem* ('They put no trust in their swords').
[10] E.g. Cic. *Epist. ad Fam.* 6.6.7: *debebit habere fidem nostra praedictio* ('My skill at prediction will be bound to be believed'); Hor. *A.P.* 52: *noua fictaque nuper habebunt uerba fidem* ('New words, ones coined recently, will gain acceptance').

> illae iam sine me norant placare puellas
> et quaedam sine me uerba diserta loqui.
>
> 3.23.3–6

> These tablets had been worn down by long use at my hands, which bid them believable (as mine), even without a seal. They knew how to please girls in my absence and, in my absence, to speak certain clever words.

Propertius' recollection of the good *fides* of his tablets gains poignancy from its position just before the poet's final realisation of Cynthia's lack of faith in 3.24.[11] But the two cases of 'fidelity' are not entirely dissimilar; both depend on fashioning a successful impression. In 3.23 the phrase *habere fidem* highlights the value of having an appearance that gives rise to trust: the worn tablets prove convincing in affirming Propertius' authorship, and so in effecting the poet's seduction. Propertius' description of his poetic vocabulary as *diserta* – 'carefully arranged', 'clever' – points similarly to the importance of artfulness in persuading the girl to believe what the poet says. This is, in fact, an erotic truism that Ovid would later observe very bluntly. Looking back critically at amatory elegy in his *Ars Amatoria*, Ovid asserts that (elegiac) *fides* is more closely linked with *ars* than with *uera*:

> est tibi agendus amans, imitandaque uulnera uerbis;
> haec tibi quaeratur *qualibet arte* fides.
>
> *Ars Am.* 1.611–12

> You must perform the role of lover, and imitate his suffering with words; belief in this must be acquired by any artful means.

These poems teach that 'truth' is the product of 'belief' – even that being believed is more important than telling the truth. Here lies an ironic link back to Propertius' desire for facts and a faithful messenger in 3.6. The poet has claimed that a slave ought to have '*greater* fidelity because of his fear' (*maioremque timens seruus habere fidem*, 6): and well he might, for a slave who will be

---

[11] See in particular Pelling (2002) for a double reading of 3.23, one which examines the poem optimistically on its own terms, and one which then places the poem in a pessimistic closural context at the end of Book 3.

punished for dishonesty, or who is interrogated under torture, has all the more reason to be convincing in selling his words as 'truth'.[12]

It is revealing that in this poem both parties place emphasis on the fidelity of the messenger, when in the end they are both suspicious of the fidelity of each other: Propertius seeks evidence that the *puella* has not been dressing up to attract other men's attention (11–14) but has instead been cloistered chastely in female company (15–18); whereas the *puella* herself imagines that another deceitful girl (*illa improba*, 25) has succeeded in winning over Propertius through use of magic (25–30). In part, this reflects the projection of interpersonal insecurities onto the bearer of potentially unwelcome news, and so reveals that the honesty of the messenger acts as a metaphor for the fidelity of the lovers.[13] In this context, the implied movement back and forth of the 'faithful' messenger Lygdamus reinforces the fact that this relationship is inherently reported, making what each party believes of the other all the more important. When Propertius demands in 3.6 that Lygdamus *debet habere fidem*, there is strong implication that he desires that the narration of fidelity be convincing perhaps more than that the amatory parties should themselves be faithful in fact.[14]

This brings us to an interdependent – in fact, almost circular – relationship between the two interests which shape

---

[12] The use of fear or torture as a means of discovering truth is therefore a risky strategy: in order to escape punishment, the person under interrogation is all the more likely to say exactly what (he thinks) his torturer wants to hear: see e.g. Bradley (1987) 39, who uses Plautus to demonstrate the unreliability of a servile *fides* constructed from a desire to avoid punishment. This point is acknowledged by the Romans themselves: at *Pro Sulla* 78, for instance, Cicero argues specifically that 'fear invalidates' (*infirmat metus*) evidence given by slaves under torture; see Bradley (1994) 167 generally for a short discussion of Roman ambivalence about the evidential value of torturing slaves.

[13] And vice versa. There is a close correlation between the 'faithfulness' of the characters in this poem and the 'faithfulness' of the medium through which their activities are narrated.

[14] This abstraction has not always been the norm in Propertius' poetry: see Lilja (1965) 172–86 and Lyne (1980) 65–7 for the ideal of actual (and especially male) amatory fidelity in elegy. The desire for faithfulness in elegiac erotic relationships is discussed in detail in chapter 4 (in the context of 3.12) and chapter 8 (in the context of 3.20).

the poem's narrative. The listening lover (for the poem's reader) desires the narrator to be believable, yet the narrator will be most believable when telling the lover what he wants to hear. This point is reinforced by the series of questions Propertius puts to Lygdamus regarding the behaviour of his mistress:

>   sicin eam incomptis uidisti flere capillis?
>   illius ex oculis multa cadebat aqua?   10
>   nec speculum strato uidisti, Lygdame, lecto   11
>   scriniaque ad lecti clausa iacere pedes   14
>   ac maestam teneris uestem pendere lacertis?   13
>   ornabat niueas nullane gemma manus?   12
>   tristis erat domus, et tristes sua pensa ministrae   15
>   carpebant, medio nebat et ipsa loco,
>   umidaque impressa siccabat lumina lana,
>   rettulit et querulo iurgia nostra sono?
>   3.6.9–18

> Did you see her like this, weeping, with her hair unkempt? Much water was falling from her eyes? Did you not see a mirror, and was her bed made? And her make-up chest was lying closed at the foot of her bed? Did her dress hang mournful from her delicate arms? No jewel adorned her snowy hands? Was the house sad, were her maids sad as they plucked their measures of wool, and she herself was spinning in their midst, drying her damp eyes by pressing wool against them, and did she relate our argument in plaintive tone?

Rather than allowing Lygdamus to report the 'truth' as the poet has requested in the poem's opening lines, instead Propertius continues in his own voice, listing the types of information that he would like the slave to report.[15] This is not unusual in itself. Since early in Book 1, Cynthia's contrived absence has allowed

---

[15] There is no consensus as to whether lines 9–18 represent an actual report from Lygdamus as repeated 'word for word' by Propertius, or whether the questions in these lines represent the anxious imagination of the poet, revealing what the poet would like to hear. For the former position, see Camps (1966) 79, Hubbard (1974) 137, 139, Richardson (1977) 337 (but cf. 338), Fedeli (1985) 205–7; for the latter position, see Butler & Barber (1933) 273, Warden (1980) 100, Newman (1997) 305–6. The merits of the two contrasting readings are discussed by Butrica (1983), 23–9, who finally rejects the latter position, albeit through an overly strict interpretation of 3.6.35–57 (see esp. Butrica (1983) 24). Heyworth (2007a) follows Butrica, but goes further in positing a lacuna after 12 (see above, n. 6) in which he argues for a lost couplet explicitly marking Lygdamus as beginning to speak: on this see Heyworth (2007b) 305.

Constructing *Fides*

the poet to indulge in make-believe, providing 'a *tabula rasa* on which [the poet] can project his fantasies and desires'.[16] Significantly, the very reason that the details at 3.6.9–18 represent an attractive fantasy for Propertius is that they make up a convincing narrative that the *puella* does indeed love the poet. In effect, Propertius' anxious series of questions offers the slave a script through which he can best demonstrate his *fides*. And here, within 3.6's self-reflexive scheme, Lygdamus' own *fides* will stand or fall on the persuasiveness of the tale he can tell about the *fides* of the *puella*.

Two aspects of the story that Propertius desires to hear are obvious enough in their evidence of the *puella*'s apparent chastity.[17] One is that she has refrained from doing her hair, and from using make-up and jewellery, means through which she might otherwise seek to attract other men (11–12);[18] the other is that by spinning wool in female company (15–16) she has adopted the persona of a chaste Penelope, that most famously constant female figure,[19] or of a virtuous Lucretia.[20] But the most dominant aspect of Propertius' desired narrative is that his mistress weep, and that her household be sorrowful: *flere* (9), *ex oculis multa cadebat aqua* (10), *maestam uestem* (13), *tristis domus, tristes ministrae* (15), *umida lana* (17). At one level this may be because the lover gains a form of pleasure from imagining his mistress crying;[21] but above all the poet–lover desires to see his mistress in tears because female sorrow is the most faithful indication of erotic devotion.[22] This is emphasised just two poems later, when Propertius declares

---

[16] Greene (1995) 313, commenting in relation to Prop. 1.3 (the mistress is absent through sleep) and 1.11 (the mistress is physically absent from Rome).
[17] Both elements are present at Terence *Heauton Timorumenus* 285–310 where a young man also seeks evidence of a girl's *fides*, a passage which Propertius may well be adapting here. On broader similarities between Terence's play and Prop. 3.6, see also Yardley (1972) 135 and Butrica (1983) 34–6.
[18] For the *puella*'s use of an elaborate hairstyle, make-up and jewellery to win male attention, see Propertius 1.15.5–8. On cosmetic artifice in 1.15 see Bennett (1972) 37f.; and on the connection between 1.15 and 3.6 see Butrica (1983) 29 n. 24.
[19] Fedeli (1985) 210.
[20] Livy *Ab Urbe Condita* 1.57.4–10. See Richardson (1977) 339.
[21] James (2003a) 99; also Lilja (1965) 125, Butrica (1983) 28. Similar examples are found at Propertius 1.19.23, 2.17.18.
[22] James (2003a) 100, 109.

himself the 'sure interpreter' (*uerus haruspex,* 3.8.18) of the indications of true passion (*certo in amore notas,* 3.8.18):

> aut in amore dolere uolo aut audire dolentem,
>   siue meas lacrimas siue uidere tuas.
> 3.8.23–4
>
> I want either to feel pain in love or to hear another in pain, to see either my own tears or yours.

If crying is seen as an intrinsic part of love, then a lack of tears would suggest the absence of love. As such, in the narrative context of 3.6 there is nothing Lygdamus could tell Propertius that the poet would rather hear – nothing he would rather believe – than that his *puella* has been weeping. Such convincingly 'faithful' behaviour generates a correspondingly convincing narrative for the 'faithful' slave to report. Yet tears are not always to be trusted, and we return to them below.

Deconstructing *Fides*

While the convincing performance of fidelity proves programmatic in the poem's first half, the second half of the poem is governed by progressive unravelling of fidelity as it applies to both lovers and readers at the same time. First we learn, to our surprise,[23] that the cause of the quarrel between poet and mistress was the *puella*'s suspicion of a lack of faith on Propertius' part:

> Haec te teste mihi promissa est, Lygdame, merces?
>   est poena et seruo rumpere teste fidem.   20
> ille potest nullo miseram me linquere facto
>   et qualem nolo dicere habere domi!
> gaudet me uacuo solam tabescere lecto:
>   si placet, insultet, Lygdame, morte mea!
> non me moribus illa, sed herbis improba uicit: 25
>   staminea rhombi ducitur ille rota;
> illum turgentis ranae portenta rubetae
>   et lecta exsuctis anguibus ossa trahunt

---

[23] On the use of narrative deceit, paradox and surprise in 3.6 see Butrica (1983) 29–31, Richardson (1977) 337–8. Lilja (1965) 175–6 observes a decreasing reliance on the ideal of *fides* across the books of Propertius.

Deconstructing *Fides*

et strigis inuentae per busta iacentia plumae
cinctaque funesto lanea uitta rogo. 30
3.6.19–30

Is this the reward he promised me, Lygdamus, with you as witness? There is a penalty for breaking faith, even when a slave is witness. He is able to abandon me to my misery, though I've done nothing, and to have in his house such a woman as I don't want to say! He rejoices that I'm wasting away alone on an empty bed: if it pleases him, let him mock me even in death! That woman has beaten me not with her character but – the witch – with herbs. He is drawn by the threaded wheel of the rhombus; the powers of the toad swollen with gore and the bones picked from sucked-out snakes drag him in, and the feathers of owls found among the broken tombs, and the woollen fillets bound around the funeral pyre.

This reported (or imagined) speech from the *puella* to Lygdamus balances the earlier questions put to Lygdamus by the poet, but focus now switches from the artful means by which fidelity might be believed (glossed by the crucial phrase *habere fidem*, 6) to the mystical skills which might induce good faith to be broken (now glossed in the phrase *rumpere fidem*, 20). This thematic reversal amplifies the message in the poem's metapoetic link between life and literature. At a literal level, the *puella* dwells at length on the magical implements which she believes have caused her to lose in love to a rival (*me improba uicit*, 25). Figuratively, magic and poetry have a long-standing affinity (often flagged in the ambiguity of the word *carmen* – both 'poem' and 'spell', e.g. Prop. 1.1.24, 3.2.8) in their common ability to manipulate behaviour and perception. Propertius' own anxious questioning of Lygdamus has already come framed by suspicion that erotic narrative might compel belief in things that are not 'true'; now, the *puella*'s speech positions such artificial quality as outright trickery and deception. It is not surprising that the threat of punishment at the climax of her speech comes loaded with typical elegiac slippage between literal and literary:

si non uana canunt mea somnia, Lygdame, testor,
   poena erit ante meos sera sed ampla pedes,
putris et in uacuo texetur aranea lecto:
   noctibus illorum dormiet ipsa Venus.
3.6.31–4

Seeking *Fides* in Poets and Poetry: Propertius 3.6

I call upon you as witness, Lygdamus: if my dreams do not sing in vain, there shall be punishment, late but ample, as he lies before my feet; a rotten spiderweb shall be woven on his empty bed; Venus herself shall sleep on their nights together.'

As commonly, *pedes* (32) links the mistress's physical feet with the metrical feet of elegy, while *texetur* (33) activates the metaphor of weaving for the writing of verse; here the *puella*'s threat is doubled, cursing the lover with a loveless night, and the poet with a loveless text. Both these terms are prepared by the prophetic power the *puella* attributes to her dreams, where the verb *canunt* (31) appeals to the figure of the seer and so also to the poet, and is the expression *par excellence* for poetic utterance. Yet, in ironic affirmation of her focus on the breaking of trust, the *puella* admits the possibility that such discourse might be illusory: that her dreams might bear hollow prophecy (*uana*, 31) balances the poet's own fear that Lygdamus' narrative might inspire empty joy (*laetitia inani*, 3).

The prospect of love's absence, in combination with the poem's closing focus on infidelity and especially its examination throughout of erotic pretence and deceit, creates a closural effect for a body of erotic poetry even at so early a stage in the collection. This is true for the love poet himself, though it is not yet apparent to the Propertian narrator who ends the poem still thinking of a reunion with his mistress, despite his suspicions at the poem's beginning:

> quod mihi si e tanto felix concordia bello
> exstiterit, per me, Lygdame, liber eris.
> 3.6.41–2

If a happy peace arises for me out of so great a war, as far as concerns me, Lygdamus, you will be free.

Yet these final lines have ironic force for the poet–lover in terms of the collection as a whole. The desired *concordia* (41) never takes place within the scope of Book 3, which famously ends in erotic *discidium*; instead, the relevance of the poem's final lines for the book's ending lies in the promise of freedom given to Lygdamus (42). Propertius and Lygdamus bear an uncanny and ultimately programmatic

Deconstructing *Fides*

similarity: in 3.6 Lydgamus assumes Propertius' authorative role; Lygdamus is the name of a slave but also of an elegiac poet, while Propertius is a poet but also (and as such) a slave – and as slaves both figures have the same mistress. The poem's climactic assertion *liber eris* ('you will be free') has already associated the slave with the poet's text; now Lygdamus' prospective freedom anticipates Propertius' liberation from love's thrall as the book concludes.[24] From this perspective, it is telling that in the book's final poem Propertius signals his own release from love (and, it would seem, from love poetry) by his awareness that his *puella*'s tears – which in 3.6 had been the most desired indicator of her good faith – have in fact been strategic artifice:[25]

>nil moueor lacrimis: ista sum captus ab arte;
>semper ab insidiis, Cynthia, flere soles.
>
>3.24.25–6

I am not moved at all by tears: I have been caught by that artifice; you are always accustomed, Cynthia, to weep on account of trickery.

Propertius' belated epiphany offers erotic closure in its own right, while also realising the closural effect of the poet's wary interrogation of Lygdamus in 3.6. If Lygdamus did report to Propertius that the girl and her household were in tears (3.6.9–18),[26] the ironic result in hindsight – if not at the time – is not to prove the girl's *fides* but to intensify the poet's opening suspicion that erotic narrative itself is tailored carefully to create the appearance but not the substance of truth.

The suspicion and especially the exposure of artifice in realistic narrative means that 3.6 is a closural poem for elegy's reader as well, since it compromises exactly that reader's ability to believe that its fiction is true.[27] The point here is not that readers of elegy (ancient or modern) have previously misunderstood the elegy's inherent fictionality, since Propertian poetry has always expected its readers to appreciate its realism

---

[24] Butrica (1983) 37.
[25] On strategic tears in elegy, see James (2003a) 104.
[26] See n. 17.
[27] For the exposure of fiction as a closural device, see Fowler (2000) 8–10.

as an artistic construct.[28] But the continuation of such a text depends on maintaining a precarious balance between illusion and self-awareness.[29] While one may have always understood, implicitly, the reader's role in a mimetic game with the poet, in 3.6 the poetry invites our direct gaze upon its central conceit, and so makes it more difficult to suspend disbelief. Symbolically, this is apparent even at the narrative level where Propertian elegy represents the poet's 'love songs' for his mistress: the lesson of hindsight for the poet has been not to trust a girl's tears, but the result for the reader is an increasingly cynical attitude to Propertius himself. Just as the poem ends, for instance, Propertius prepares for his closing appeal to an eventual *concordia* by instructing Lygdamus to set in motion a reconciliation with the *puella* by declaring to her the poet's own *fides*:

> quae tibi si ueris animis est questa puella,   35
>   hac eadem rursus, Lygdame, curre uia,
> et mea cum multis lacrimis mandata reporta,
>   iram, non fraudes esse in amore meo.
>   3.6.35–8

If the girl issued these complaints to you with a sincere heart, Lygdamus, run back again by this same route, and carry back my instructions given with many tears: that there is anger but no deceit in my love.

By denying the presence of deception, Propertius' return message to his mistress intends to assert the truth of the poet's love; and the indication that Propertius too has been crying is included, we must presume, to make his claim of sincerity more convincing. But an irony is immediately apparent in the telling juxtaposition of tears and deceit, even if the deceit is

---

[28] The argument that Roman elegy should in fact only be read (and only was read by its contemporaries) as 'a fantasy that makes fun of itself' (94) is central to Veyne (1988). Veyne's approach has not found favour in subsequent criticism: see in particular Kennedy (1993) 91–100, and Conte (1994a) 158–60.

[29] Fowler (2000) 25.

Deconstructing *Fides*

denied (*multis lacrimis*, 37; *(non) fraudes*, 38).[30] Perhaps the reader suspected Propertius' honesty at the time;[31] certainly, after reading Propertius' closural revelation about the calculated art in elegiac tears, it is difficult not to harbour similarly closural suspicion about the poet's claim to lack pretence in the declaring of his love. In 3.6 we have seen poet and *puella* voice their mutual mistrust by questioning the honesty of their messenger; but, in the end, it is precisely the dubious reliability of the go-between Lygdamus which serves as symbol for the illusory relationship between two characters intent on deceiving each other, and us.

A final irony lies in the poem's opening appeal for honesty, and in the link made in the opening couplet between telling the truth and escaping from slavery:

> Dic mihi de nostra quae sentis uera puella:
> sic tibi sint dominae, Lygdame, dempta iuga.
> 3.6.1–2

Tell me the truth that you have perceived about our girl: thus may the yoke of your mistress be removed from you, Lygdamus.

In the discussion above, 'truth' has been the object of frustrated desire – an unattainable goal or negotiated construct. Yet by the end of the poem (perhaps, by the end of the book) there is a real sense in which 3.6 does indeed 'tell the truth' precisely by exploring the complicity of lovers (and readers) in upholding the layered deceptions present in erotic–elegiac narration. Such mimetic analysis especially of the process of reading love poetry does indeed set in train a closural turn towards 'freedom' for both the erotic poet and his audience. In one sense 3.6 thus creates thematic space for an investigation of new poetic modes beginning immediately with the lament

---

[30] On the combination of 'deception' and 'infidelity' in the word *fraus*, see Camps (1966) 83, Richardson (1977) 340, Butrica (1983) 32 n. 31. See also Prop. 2.20.3–4 for the opposition of *fraus* to *fides*.

[31] Although not Butrica (1983) 32: 'It is not likely that [Propertius] has taken a new mistress but swears falsely; his eagerness to be reconciled is too apparent.'

for Paetus at 3.7, and in the next chapter we explore an experimental sequence of elegies starting at 3.9. In another sense, the focus in 3.6 on the self-delusion necessary in love and love poetry paradoxically equips us to renew a relationship with elegiac *fides* in 3.20. As we will see in chapter 8, there remains time still in Book 3 for Propertian love elegy to reinvent itself.

CHAPTER 3

THEMATIC EXPERIMENTATION

Propertius 3.9–11

The central sequence of Book 3 throws critical light on the genre's sense of identity by parading characters and themes external (or presented as external) to elegy's typically introspective world view.[1] At 3.9 an address to Maecenas once more acknowledges the demands of a 'real world' that should lie safely beyond the remit of a private love poet (in a way that the novel but fictitious Paetus at 3.7 does not); at 3.11 Propertius denounces Cleopatra, and so engages the political threat of Mark Antony; 3.12 celebrates the idealised Augustan chastity of the married Aelia Galla; 3.15 admits a mistress who existed before Cynthia (!) – and here Propertius toys not only with elegy's chronology and celebrated amatory exclusivity but also with its claim of generic independence: in 3.15 Propertius conflates elegy with tragedy, using his accustomed erotic scenario to frame the inset tragic narrative of Dirce.

Such overt experimentation with the thematic scope of elegiac verse is an aspect of the collection most noted in commentary.[2] Yet, through a discussion of the sequence 3.9–11, this chapter argues that Propertius pre-empts his critics by annotating for us the novelty of these thematic intrusions, as well as the disruptive potential they possess for erotic elegy as we have known it. It is significant that an address to Maecenas in 3.9 and the poet's vehement attack on Cleopatra in 3.11 are separated

---

[1] For the novelty of Book 3's middle poems, see e.g. Gold (1982) 103. For a fluent discussion of elegy's embedded instability – arising, as here, from a manufactured conflict between 'reality' and the partial elegiac representation of reality – see Conte (1994a) 36–42.
[2] Typically this is seen simply in the introduction of novel subjects, and in new roles assigned to elegy's *puella*: for a positive response, see Wyke (1987a) 154; for a negative view, Hubbard (1974) 71. Others argue that, in doing so, Propertian elegy increasingly abandons its youthfully dissident voice for a more mature Augustanism: e.g. Fantham (2000) 198, and esp. Cairns (2006) 343, 438.

by a nostalgic birthday poem for Cynthia at 3.10; thus two elegies with potent connections to an Augustan 'reality'[3] make a poignant frame for a poem which recalls the escapist beginning of Propertius' amatory poetry, and expresses a desire to return there. As Book 3 approaches its centre, the increasing presence of more varied material – as noted widely by Propertius' readers – is underpinned by an aspect that has largely passed unremarked: a sustained metapoetic reflection on tensions inherent in the very process of generic development.

3.9 – Addressing Maecenas

The following discussion focuses on Maecenas' symbolic role within 3.9 both as an intervening outsider and yet as an internalised 'elegiac' figure whose aesthetics resemble Propertius' own. 3.9 is the second of only two poems which Propertius addresses to Maecenas – the first is the opening elegy of Book 2. As does the earlier poem, 3.9 begins as a *recusatio*: Propertius reprises arguments that he has employed in 2.1 (and 1.6) that different people are naturally suited to different tasks.[4] In 3.9 Propertius extends this train of thought to include and to spring from Maecenas himself. Propertius praises his patron for his own moderation, and states that he follows Maecenas' own modest principles in his approach to poetry (esp. 21–2).[5]

The highly conventional terms of a *recusatio* provide an important frame for reading the thematic role of the poet's patron within the elegy.[6] A *recusatio* sets out a poet's polite

---

[3] For engagement with the 'real world' in Propertian elegy, see Williams (1968) 557–9. Typically, this offers a point of departure for Propertius, who invokes mainstream values so as to assert his elegiac difference: 2.7 and 2.15 are useful examples. Ironically, elegy also threatens continually to embrace those very values from which it cuts itself off: Greene (1995) 316–17, Conte (1994a) 42.

[4] See in particular 1.6.29–30, 2.1.39–45.

[5] Butler & Barber (1933) 281, Camps (1966) 93, Richardson (1977) 351, Gold (1982) 104–5, Zetzel (1982) 97. See Nisbet & Hubbard (1970) 81–3 on the history of the *recusatio* as a literary motif.

[6] Zetzel (1982) demonstrates that Maecenas' several appearances in Augustan poetry show the patron being called upon not as a historical individual but as an artistic symbol; also Santirocco (1984) 241, Barchiesi (2007) 156–8, White (2007) 202–4.

3.9 – Addressing Maecenas

deflection of an apparent request to write on public themes; a poet will usually plead incapacity, as Propertius does in 3.9 by appealing to the metaphor of an ocean voyage:

> Maecenas, eques Etrusco de sanguine regum,
>   intra fortunam qui cupis esse tuam,
> quid me scribendi tam uastum mittis in aequor?
>   non sunt apta meae grandia uela rati.
>
>   3.9.1–4

Maecenas, knight from the blood of Etruscan kings, you who desire to remain within the scope of your good fortune, why do you send me into so vast an ocean of writing? Great sails are not fitting for my boat.

Notwithstanding any general desire within the Augustan regime for Rome's artists to produce celebratory material, the specific request presented here from Maecenas is likely fictive; it serves as elsewhere as an effective starting point for a monologue in which the poet asserts his own independent programme.[7] But the effect in this case proves ironic. Within the compass of Propertius' third book, the (staged) interference with Propertius' poetic programme from an Augustan official prefigures the external – and notably Augustan – thematic incursions into the private world of Propertian elegy which occur in the collection's central sequence. In one sense, Propertius' rejection of 'great sails' (4) sets a resistant frame for these imminent generic experiments by reminding us in advance that certain modes are acceptable to the poet while others are not. In another sense, Propertius actually coopts Maecenas' apparent interest in the direction of the poet's career to figure the poet's active examination of genre itself.

Maecenas' symbolic function in 3.9 is prompted by comparison with Horace's *Odes*. First of all, Horace's addresses to his patron reinforce the way that Propertius' Maecenas poem initiates a middle sequence within Book 3, as well as 3.9's central position (as the second of the collection's three programmatic

---

[7] See esp. Williams (1968) 558, Ross (1975) 124. For 3.9 as a 'programme' poem, cf. Hubbard (1974) 114–15, Richardson (1977) 348, Ross (1975) 126–7, Heyworth (2007c) 103–8.

Thematic Experimentation: Propertius 3.9–11

set pieces) between 3.1 and 3.17;[8] Horace had already made prominent use of the centre of poems and books for significant statements,[9] while the 'middles' of Horace's three collections are marked by poems addressed to Maecenas.[10] But Horace also makes strategic use of the central 'Maecenas odes' in charting his poetic development across the breadth of the collection.[11] Against a backdrop of Horatian programmatic writing, Propertius similarly conjures Maecenas as a conspicuous and stable point of reference outside the text – either a semiotic bulwark against which Propertius, like Horace, might gain leverage while attempting to change the direction of his poetic project, or, more actively, an independent catalyst which, on its own authority, can itself influence the direction of the work.

The patron's authority is conspicuous in Maecenas' reappearance towards the end of 3.9. After invoking Maecenas himself (*cogor et exemplis te superare tuis*, 'I am compelled to surpass you by your own example', 22) as precedent for not attempting historical epic, Propertius places at the heart of his poem a conventional list of epic *topoi* that he, as a Callimachean, will not attempt (23–42). But the poem's final section reintroduces Maecenas and sees Propertius abruptly changing direction.[12] In this climactic passage, Propertius claims that, should Maecenas inspire him, he will indeed write in the grand manner that he rejected as the poem begins, and now on the very themes he had rejected in 2.1 – on the Titans, on early Roman history and on the triumphs of Augustus:[13]

    te duce uel Iouis arma canam caeloque minantem
        Coeum et Phlegraeis Eurymedonta iugis;
    celsaque Romanis decerpta Palatia tauris
        ordiar et caeso moenia firma Remo,   50

---

[8] For 'central' programmatic statements, see generally Conte (1992); also Gold (1982) 103.
[9] See generally Moritz (1968); more recently, Harrison (2004).
[10] *Odes* 1.20, 2.12, 3.16, with Santirocco (1984) 242–3; see also Moritz (1968) 118.
[11] Santirocco (1980a) 52 and (1984) 252–3.
[12] Heyworth (2007b) 326–7 finds problematic the suddenness of this change combined with the 'abrupt' return to the addressee Maecenas; he therefore posits a lacuna before 47, into which he places the penultimate couplet 57–8, lines which themselves contain an address to Maecenas.
[13] Cf. 3.9.47–56 with 2.1.19–38: Cairns (2006) 268; also Gold (1982) 108–9.

3.9 – Addressing Maecenas

eductosque pares siluestri ex ubere reges,
crescet et ingenium sub tua iussa meum.
3.9.47–52

With you as my leader, I will sing of the arms of Jove and of Coeus threatening heaven and Eurymedon on Phlegraean mountains; I will begin to write of the lofty Palatine grazed by Roman bulls, and the walls made firm by the killing of Remus, and the paired kings raised from the wild beast's teat, and my talent will increase to meet your orders.

A poem which began as a *recusatio* reminiscent of the poet's first Maecenas elegy now ends paradoxically with Propertius seeking his patron's support for a grander (if elusive)[14] literary endeavour. But, in doing so, the shape of the poem reflects that of the book, so far:[15] after an initial recommitment to Callimachean ideals (3.1–3) Propertius employs his second Maecenas elegy as an introduction to a sequence of more experimental poems; similarly, within 3.9 itself, a direct appeal to Maecenas (*te duce*, 47) suddenly threatens to send the poet's programme in a new direction. The figure of Maecenas features symbolically in each case – precisely at the point of the poet's equivocation within the poem and within the book.

A Lucretian echo in Propertius' phrase *te duce* emphasises the numinous power and external perspective with which Propertius colours Maecenas at this point. Pausing before beginning the concluding section of *De Rerum Natura*, the didactic poet addresses his muse Calliope:

tu mihi supremae praescripta ad candida callis
currenti spatium praemonstra, callida musa
Calliope, requies hominum diuomque uoluptas,
te duce ut insigni capiam cum laude coronam.
Lucretius, *De Rerum Natura* 6.92–5

You go ahead of me and show me the course, as I run to the gleaming finishing line of my final path, Calliope artful Muse, repose of men and

---

[14] On the deliberate ambiguity of the closing passage of 3.9 see Hubbard (1974) 109–10; cf. Shackleton Bailey (1956) 165 and Bennett (1968) 322, arguing that the closing lines refer exclusively to the proposed task of writing about Rome and Augustus.
[15] Fantham (2000) 198.

the gods' delight, so that with you as my leader I might take the crown with distinguished praise.

Here Lucretius asks for guidance and inspiration at a crucial point in his poem; to the extent that we hear an echo of Lucretius' *te duce* at the similarly critical juncture in Propertius 3.9, Maecenas can be seen as literary *dux* to Propertius in the same way that Calliope was to Lucretius.[16] This is significant, for the elevation of Maecenas to muse-like status displaces a role formerly given to the poet's *puella* – as made clear in the poet's first elegy for Maecenas:

> Quaeritis unde mihi totiens scribantur amores,
>   unde meus ueniat mollis in ore liber.
> non haec Calliope, non haec mihi cantat Apollo:
>   ingenium nobis ipsa puella facit.
>   2.1.1–4

> You ask from what source love affairs come to be written by me so often, from what source my book comes softly on people's lips. It is not Calliope, it is not Apollo who sings these things for me: a girl herself makes my poetic talent.

Propertius claims a fundamental creative connection between his inspirational *puella* and his poetic *ingenium* (4), explicitly rejecting inspiration external to his amatory paradigm (3). As Book 2 begins, the poet's muse is static and internalised: she grants the poet by her very presence in his text a seemingly inexhaustible number of amatory subjects to write about (2.1.5–16). By contrast, in 3.9 Propertius links his *ingenium* with an inspirational Maecenas, and the effect now suggests intervention and development: *crescet et ingenium sub tua iussa meum* ('my talent will increase to meet your orders', 52). In the midst of Book 3 (and unlike the *puella* in 2.1), Maecenas' value lies symbolically outside the existing text, as Calliope's value had done for Lucretius: it is through Maecenas' imperial contact, and through his own independent authority, that he can pull the poet in new

---

[16] So Maecenas is inscribed with the divinely inspirational power of a Muse: Bennett (1968) 324; cf. Cairns (2006) 267–8.

3.9 – Addressing Maecenas

directions;[17] and the inspirational shift across Propertius' two Maecenas poems from *puella* to patron annotates the thematic transition from private to public sphere which the elegist had rejected as the poem began.

But this is only half the story. As much as Maecenas, especially as envoy of the *princeps*, offers an external Augustan waypoint against which a poet might measure (or effect, or deny) the development of his literary programme, as a patron of fellow poets Maecenas also represents an internal marker of a dialogue between poets about literary development itself. In this context Propertius 3.9 and its address to Maecenas revisits elegiac engagement with programmatic passages from Virgil's *Georgics* where Virgil had proposed his own thematic switch towards patriotic poetry.[18]

When Propertius employs a nautical metaphor to clothe an implied request from Maecenas to write in an epic mode (3.9.1–4), he draws pointedly upon imagery used by Virgil in his own address to Maecenas at the outset of *Georgics* 2. Here Virgil had already evoked the composition of grander or slighter poetry in terms of either voyaging on the ocean's depths or keeping close to shore:[19]

> tuque ades inceptumque una decurre laborem,
> o decus, o famae merito pars maxima nostrae,   40
> Maecenas, pelagoque uolans da uela patenti.
> non ego cuncta meis amplecti uersibus opto,
> non, mihi si linguae centum sint oraque centum,
> ferrea uox. ades et primi lege litoris oram;
> in manibus terrae. non hic te carmine ficto   45
> atque per ambages et longa exorsa tenebo.
>   Virgil, *Georgics* 2.39–46

---

[17] Propertius' promise to follow Maecenas' lead is usually regarded as self-defeating, since Propertius might safely assume his patron will not change his modest ways: Butler & Barber (1933) 281, 285 and Camps (1966) 99, Gold (1982) 110, Cairns (2006) 267–8. For a history of the interpretation of *te duce* within the context of the poem's argument, see Fedeli (1985) 326–8.
[18] See generally Bennett (1968); also Fantham (2000) 196.
[19] For discussion of this Virgilian passage in the context of Propertius 3.9, see Bennett (1968) 327. For the metaphor of sea voyaging in this passage, see Thomas (1999) 111.

Thematic Experimentation: Propertius 3.9–11

> You be present and, together with me, run over the laborious course I have undertaken – O you my pride, O you rightfully the greatest part of my renown, Maecenas – and spread your sails as you fly over the open sea. I have no desire to embrace every subject within my verse – no, though I should have a hundred tongues and a hundred mouths, and a voice of iron. You be present and pass by the edge of the nearby coastline, within reach of land. Not here will I detain you with contrived song, and through digressions and long preambles.

This famous passage will prove crucial for Propertius' renewed ambition to discover new material in 3.17, and the stylistic equivocation that Virgil expresses here is examined fully in that context (chapter 6). The striking point for present purposes is precisely that the Virgilian metaphor which Propertius imports brings with it the suggestion of generic ascent: Virgil notoriously precedes his closing affirmation of Callimachean restraint in shallow coastal waters with an ambitious plea for Maecenas to join him on a voyage 'over the open sea' at the same time (*pelagoque uolans da uela patenti*, 41).[20] As such, even as Propertius rejects the demands of epic composition as beyond the capacity of his humble raft in 3.9's opening *recusatio*, his nautical metaphor annotates the coming 'surprise' of a programmatic shift towards elevated Roman poetry in the poem's final section. More than this, Propertius flags the embrace of generic ascent as a move he shares with Virgil himself.

The sense in which generic slippage is presented as an inherited Augustan *topos* is reinforced in the concluding section of 3.9, just as Propertius appeals to Maecenas for guidance in a future composition on Roman history. As he promises Maecenas a new epic project 'under your leadership' and 'in accordance with your instructions' – *te duce* (47), *sub tua iussa* (52) – Propertius gestures now towards the proem to *Georgics* 3: Propertius rephrases in positive form what Virgil had put negatively when himself addressing Maecenas:[21]

> interea Dryadum siluas saltusque sequamur
> intactos, *tua*, Maecenas, haud mollia *iussa*.
> *te sine* nil altum mens incohat.
>
> Virgil, *Georgics* 3.40–2

[20] Thomas (1999) 111–12.
[21] Cairns (2006) 268.

3.9 – Addressing Maecenas

> In the meantime let us pursue the Dryads' woods and untouched glades, Maecenas – no gentle decree of yours. Without you, my mind undertakes nothing lofty.

As with Propertius' borrowed metaphor at the beginning of the poem, the value of this allusion lies in catching Virgil at a prolonged moment of modal ambiguity. To begin with, the lines that represent the immediate target of Propertius' reference show Virgil resuming just past its midpoint a current project which resists grand themes and modes – yet Virgil characterises Maecenas' decrees as 'not gentle' (*haud mollia*) and the project itself as 'lofty' (*altum*). More pertinently, these lines lie between a pair of passages in which Virgil makes provocative reference to a later epic project that would appear eventually as the *Aeneid*. At *Geo.* 3.13–15 Virgil refers to constructing a metaphorical temple that will house Caesar himself;[22] and only four lines after the target of Propertius' allusion Virgil promises a future celebration of Caesar's military successes:[23]

> mox tamen ardentis accingar dicere pugnas
> Caesaris et nomen fama tot ferre per annos,
> Tithoni prima quot abest ab origine Caesar.
> Virgil, *Georgics* 3.46–8

> Soon, though, I will ready myself to speak of Caesar's blazing battles and to bear his name in story through as many years as Caesar is distant from the birth of Tithonus long ago.

The *Georgics* represent an 'exquisitely intermediate stage'[24] of Virgil's teleological generic progression from the *Eclogues* to the *Aeneid*. This seems precisely the aspect of Virgil's poetry targeted allusively by Propertius in a poem which begins as a celebration of Callimachean restraint but which ends with a teasing promise of historical and mythic grandeur. The presence of 'Maecenas' at pivotal points in 3.9 draws attention to Propertius' participation in a dialogue with Virgil about generic expansion for which, in Augustan terms, Virgil himself

---

[22] Kirichenko (2013) 2 and *passim*.
[23] Esp. Schauer (2007) 48–56; see further discussion in chapter 6.
[24] Thomas (1999) 111; see generally 101–13.

has provided the blueprint. This is a conversation to which Propertius returns in 3.17.

If an address to Maecenas seems to import divergent and even contradictory symbolism into Propertius 3.9, one final glance at Horace's poetic engagement with his patron offers an opportunity to draw several threads together. Like 3.9, *Odes* 2.12 is a *recusatio*.[25] In general terms a *recusatio* – inasmuch as it deflects unwelcome pressure to write on a particular theme or subject – seeks to establish a poet's independence from the social clout and literary taste of his addressee.[26] But, in *Odes* 2.12, Horace presents a significant innovation by essentially aligning the personae of the poet and addressee, rather than emphasising the difference between them. In its first three stanzas, this poem rehearses episodes from Roman history and myth with a governing rhetorical strategy that the poem's addressee – revealed to be Maecenas at line 11[27] – would not wish (*nolis*, 2.12.1) such themes to be treated in lyric verse. In this way, instead of proving typically divergent, the values represented by the writer and the reader here coalesce on a matter of literary taste; Maecenas (who would otherwise symbolise the subjects on which Horace does not wish to write: see 2.12.9–12) is 'coopted' as a programmatic representation of the poet's own point of view, and as an official embodiment of the poetry's aesthetic system.[28]

In the same way Propertius adopts Maecenas as a definitional *exemplum* within the context of his own *recusatio*.[29] Propertius already cites Maecenas' real-life example as a guiding principle in his own rejection of Maecenas' request to write in a grand style (3.9.21–2), and the pivotal *te duce* (47) similarly implies an assimilation of the values associated with the poet's persona with those represented by Maecenas. The potential

---

[25] For similarities between Horace *Od.* 2.12 and Propertius 3.9, see esp. Santirocco (1980b) 233–6.
[26] Santirocco (1980b) 223; cf. Davis (1975) 81.
[27] For relevance of the delayed introduction of Maecenas, and thus the conflation of the poem's general reader with the perspective of Maecenas, see Henderson (1998) 155.
[28] Henderson (1998) 156.
[29] Cf. Comber (1998) 47, who implies that this move is a Propertian innovation.

3.9 – Addressing Maecenas

integration of poet and patron is in fact the subject of the poem's final couplet:

> hoc mihi, Maecenas, laudis concedis, et a te est
> quod ferar in partis ipse fuisse tuas.
>
> 3.9.59–60
>
> This glory you grant to me, Maecenas, and it is due to you that I myself am said to have been a member of your party.

Just as Horace had done in the middle of the *Odes*, Propertius positions his patron in 3.9 not only as the addressee of a *recusatio* but ultimately as an authoritative rationale that explains and justifies the poet's aesthetic choices.

Yet this is a complex manoeuvre, for Maecenas' symbolic value is employed within the poem in a contradictory manner. Inasmuch as 3.9 operates as a *recusatio*, the addressee Maecenas is positioned as an interventionist external figure (troping the poet's own generic investigations in Book 3); he is associated, too, with the various thematic grandeurs of state, the 'external' material to which he would seek to divert Propertius at the poem's beginning and to which Propertius, under Maecenas' inspiration and leadership, latterly promises to turn. But Maecenas is also employed as an internalised literary symbol, marking the current poet's dialogue with earlier poets who have previously engaged with the challenges and limitations of generic poetry. By providing the poem with the overriding programmatic rationale that Maecenas offers a peerless model for the poetry dedicated to him, Propertius attempts to signal the accommodation within his poetry of all the divergent aspects that Maecenas represents (or Maecenas' own contradictions are mobilised to reflect the discursive conflicts of elegy itself). In the end, *Maecenas eques* (3.9.1) is represented as being 'just like' the equestrian Propertius.[30] As a poetic metaphor, Maecenas offers the parallel image of an insider: a literary politician, an aesthetically appropriate figure who rises high while remaining modest, who performs official duty with unostentatious grace. In programmatic terms,

---

[30] Cf. Comber (1998) 47.

Thematic Experimentation: Propertius 3.9–11

Maecenas thus demonstrates how a Callimachean poet might interact with an increasing array of thematic material: through the exercise of aesthetic restraint in the treatment of any subject, no matter how elevated. This is the manner of leadership under which Propertius feels confident of contemplating his own version of *reges et proelia* at 3.9.47–56.

3.10 and the Recovery of Theme

In the first elegy after proposing a radical departure from erotic material, Propertius offers his readers a love poem that purports to celebrate Cynthia's birthday.[31] In fact, this passionately wistful elegy delivers a full-scale erotic fantasy: as it explores a romanticised sequence of events, 3.10 charts the progress (in the poet's imagination) of his mistress's birthday from beginning till bedtime. The poem's position immediately after 3.9 adds depth to what is already a poignant narrative moment.[32] In an important sense Propertius reverts to type in 3.10; rather than following through on his grand promise of patriotic verse in 3.9, the poet sets out obsessively a step-by-step plan for the celebration of an idealised erotic occasion. Thus 3.10 indicates how the love elegist might get back on track – but it also reveals that Propertian love elegy is no longer the same as it used to be.

A 'Birthday' Poem

3.10 flaunts its literariness right upfront. The poem does not start directly with Cynthia's birthday but rather with the poet's own confusion at an unexpected visit from his Muses; it is they

---

[31] E.g. Fedeli (1985) 336. For the literary *topoi* of conventional birthday poems, see generally Cairns (1971); also Bramble (1973) 155–7.

[32] Here Richardson (1977) 348 misses the bigger picture when he comments simply that 3.10 'blatantly contradict[s]' the poem before it. Other critics emphasise not the poem's place in a sequence after 3.9 but its position in a book which narrates the eventual ending of Propertius' affair with Cynthia: e.g. Lyne & Morwood (1973), Bramble (1973). Valeri-Tomaszuk (1976) treats 3.10 as an 'ironical escape poem' (827) in which the poet briefly abandons the otherwise erotically pessimistic tone of Book 3.

A 'Birthday' Poem

who then announce the theme of the poem to Propertius, and so to us:

> Mirabar, quidnam uisissent mane Camenae,
> ante meum stantes sole rubente torum.
> natalis nostrae signum misere puellae
> et manibus faustos ter crepuere sonos.
> 3.10.1–4

> I was marvelling at why the Muses had visited me in the morning, standing before my bed as the sun was reddening. They sent me the sign that it was my girl's birthday and three times they clapped their hands propitiously.

The presence of the Muses in the opening line foregrounds artistic concerns ahead of any erotic ones – ahead even of the theme of the mistress's birthday itself.[33] The symbolism in these opening four lines also plays provocatively with the promise of new poetry that closed out the previous poem. The initial couplet emphasises the sense of a 'beginning' through the motif of dawn (*sole rubente*, 2), while the propitious clapping of the Muses' hands (3–4) similarly suggests the signal that marks the beginning of a race.[34] Indeed, here the new poem's beginning offers the kind of 'sign' which Propertius – as the ambitious driver of his poetic racing-chariot – had desired of Maecenas in the penultimate couplet of 3.9 (*da mihi signa*, 3.9.58;[35] *signum misere*, 3.10.4). Almost as if 3.9's Roman ending were a programmatic vision (as it was in Propertius' Ennian dream in 3.3), the confused poet now wakes amid the symbolism of a new dawn to find the Muses duly come to inspire him to new poetry.

Yet the Muses provide the poet not with stuff of patriotic verse but with a timely remembrance of his *puella* instead (perhaps Propertius has forgotten that it is her birthday). For

---

[33] Bramble (1973) 158. The immediately ensuing sequence that imagines the beginning of Cynthia's birthday (3.10.5–10) reworks Callimachus' *Hymn* 2.17–24 (to Apollo): Heyworth & Morwood (2011) 199.
[34] Camps (1966) 102, Lyne & Morwood (1973) 46, Heyworth & Morwood (2011) 198.
[35] Cf. the transposition of this couplet by Heyworth (2007a), above n. 12. Both these instances of racing imagery in turn pick up the programmatic metaphor of the literary racing-chariot at 3.1.10–12.

the reader, of course, there is a basic sense in which this news comes simply as a surprise after the mooted nationalism of 3.9; the poet's opening astonishment stands in for our own (*mirabar*, 3.10.1).[36] But the Muses have signalled a theme remarkably apposite for the broader context of the poem. The sense of a fresh start that we might have expected in 3.10 comes prefigured (via 3.9's *recusatio*) explicitly in terms of difference from the past. Now, the announcement of a 'birthday' provides an ideal opportunity to reflect on the past while yet looking to the future. In this sense, and prompted by the mannered literariness of its opening, 3.10 becomes a poem that remembers the birth of Cynthian verse as much as that of Cynthia herself. Mostly, Cynthia's birthday becomes a device through which Propertius can reflect upon his own third anniversary as poet.[37]

The Birth of *Cynthia*

3.10 proceeds within the timeless framework of a daydream in which the poet seeks to elide the difference between past and future. Cynthia as beloved, as object of the poet's writing, is presented as held in a kind of stasis wherein her future is composed from elements of her past, and (such is the nature of a birthday) where the past is presented as a pattern to be repeated into the future. Yet such a representation of static timelessness creates tension with the poem's otherwise relentlessly onward motion, as it tracks the progression of the day with teleological certainty from auspicious beginning to inevitable conclusion.[38]

The manner in which the imagined birthday rituals in 3.10 recall Cynthia's entrance into Propertius' poetry is explicit and

---

[36] Within the central sequence of Book 3, 'astonishment' is itself a prominent theme: *mirabar* at 3.10.1 anticipates *quid mirare* ...? at 3.11.1, and *miramur* at 3.14.1. See Bramble (1973) 158, Heyworth & Morwood (2011) 198.
[37] Bramble (1973) 158. Several critics have further noted the paradoxical absence of Cynthia's voice from a poem that would plan her birthday: Lyne & Morwood (1973), Bramble (1973) 159, Richardson (1977) 357.
[38] Putnam (1980) 101.

The Birth of *Cynthia*

has been well documented.[39] Four central lines of 3.10 (where Propertius alludes overtly to the start of the affair) share significant imagery and programmatic vocabulary with the opening four lines of 1.1:[40]

> dein, qua primum oculos cepisti ueste Properti,
>   indue, nec uacuum flore relinque caput;
> et pete, qua polles, ut sit tibi forma perennis,
>   inque meum semper stent tua regna caput.
>   3.10.15–18

Then put on the dress with which you first captured Propertius' eyes, and do not leave your head free of flowers; and seek that your beauty (which grants you your power) be everlasting, and that your reign over my life stand for ever.

> Cynthia prima suis miserum me cepit ocellis,
>   contactum nullis ante Cupidinibus.
> tum mihi constantis deiecit lumina fastus
>   et caput impositis pressit Amor pedibus.
>   1.1.1–4

Cynthia was the first to capture me with her eyes, making me wretched – I who had not before been infected with desire. Then Love threw down my gaze of stubborn pride, placed his feet on my head and pressed it down.

Here, the 'real' beginning and the literary beginning of the affair are conflated and asserted as a permanent model.[41] Besides the verbal reminiscences which serve to recall the first poem of the collection, Propertius seeks explicitly to dress Cynthia now in the way she was clothed when he first saw her (3.10.15); and Propertius' prayer that Cynthia's domination of his life (*in meum caput*, 3.10.18) may always continue seeks to extend his programmatic submission to Amor at the very beginning (*caput pressit Amor*, 1.1.4). In essence, here Propertius aspires to an aesthetic ideal of continuity and

---
[39] E.g. Lyne & Morwood (1973) 39–40, Bramble (1973) 160, Richardson (1977) 358.
[40] Fedeli (1985) 345.
[41] Bramble (1973) 159 notes that 3.10 furthers its connection with the poetics of Book 1 by using the desolate imagery of 1.17 as a basis for the initial prayers at 3.10.5–10. Significantly, the tone in 3.10 reverses that of its model, and the contradiction perhaps injects some latent pessimism within its idealistic evocation of a perfect day. Cf. Valeri-Tomaszuk (1976) 828–9.

consistency as symbolised precisely by his desire for Cynthia's inspiring beauty to be everlasting – *sit tibi forma perennis* (17). May Cynthia never change, just as the poet's love for her (he has said) will never end. Many happy returns, in other words.

At the same time, in a broader sense the poem parades an awareness of the power of movement and progression. This is true at a thematic level, in the sense that a birthday itself provides an annual reminder that time is passing.[42] But the passage of time itself also sustains the narrative thrust of the poem. 3.10 employs sequence as a structural device (*primum*, 13; *dein*, 15; *inde*, 19); and, in contrast to its idealised and seemingly static representation of Cynthia, the poem's narrative – through which the poet sets out the events of the day in their proper order – is one in which time should not stand still (*transeat dies*, 5)[43] but rather move on relentlessly and speedily (*nox currat*, 21).[44] In this context, the poem concludes significantly by casting the events of the day and the poem itself as a 'journey':

> cum fuerit multis exacta trientibus hora,
>   noctis et instituet sacra ministra Venus,
> annua soluamus thalamo sollemnia nostro,
>   natalisque tui sic peragamus iter.
>
> 3.10.29–32

When the hours have passed with many cups, and attendant Venus sets up the sacred rites of the night, let us perform our annual observances solemnly in our bedchamber, and so complete the journey of your birthday.

---

[42] Lyne & Morwood (1973) 43.

[43] 3.10.5 marks the beginning of the poet's imagined celebration of the birthday, and it establishes immediately a contrast between progression and immobility, by desiring both the movement of the day (*transeat dies*) and the winds' lack of motion (*stent aere uenti*).

[44] Heyworth (2007a) emends *currat* at 3.10.21 to *surgat* on subjective grounds: 'the jump to night-time is sudden; and in a poem concerned with sequence ... the desire for night to pass quickly is inappropriate' ((2007b) 329). Given that Propertius' fantasy ends in bed with Cynthia, it might equally be argued that the poet is demonstrably eager to get there. Moreover, *currat* extends the racing metaphor which concludes 3.9 and which is picked up by the clapping of the Muses' hands at 3.10.4 (see too n. 35 above). On the issue of time in 3.10, see also Lyne & Morwood (1973) 44–5, Bramble (1973) 160–1.

The Birth of *Cynthia*

With *iter* as its final emphatic word (in combination with the verb *peragamus*), 3.10 reinforces the representation of Cynthia's birthday as a progressive narrative with a beginning and an end, a story in which one proceeds from morning to night, and one in which the final erotic climax[45] is intensified by the developments which have preceded it. When cast in metapoetic terms, the narrative drive of 3.10 at this milestone point urges a dynamic rather than static appraisal of Propertian elegy, with the text suggesting the interpretive reward that stems from developing an appreciation of the poetry's continuing reinvention (this point returns at the close of the discussion).

Propertius' evocation of a timeless Cynthia, dressed now as she was when the poet first saw her, already directs the poem's reader back to the start of the Propertian corpus. Paradoxically, the poem's contrasting emphasis on steady progression across 3.10 also reveals a marked circularity. The climactic *iter* of the poem's final verse is presented in tandem with the 'annual rites' in the preceding line (*annua sollemnia*, 31): this is a journey that is and has been repeated year after year. Similarly, the narrative journey of the poem itself brings us ultimately back to where we began – in bed with Propertius. But it becomes apparent that when revisiting the beginning a second or third time, both lover and reader will find that some things have changed. Superficially, Propertius advances from beginning the day in bed alone to ending it in bed with Cynthia (in his imagination at least). More significantly, Cynthia herself and the poetics she represents gain new sophistication and flexibility – a development made all the clearer by her poet's outward attempts to hold her still.

While the depiction of Cynthia in 3.10 seems certainly intended to – and does – recall Cynthia from the start of Book 1, aspects of the mistress's portrait in the current poem remain disconcertingly unfamiliar. The vivid connection of 'capture' and 'eyes' at 3.10.15 (*oculos cepisti*) clearly alludes to the famous first line of Book 1 (*cepit ocellis*), but the closeness of the reference serves also to remind the reader that

---

[45] For the erotic pun in *iter*, see Camps (1967) 104, Richardson (1977) 359.

Thematic Experimentation: Propertius 3.9–11

the later recollection is importantly different: whereas in 1.1 Propertius had been caught by Cynthia's eyes, now the poet places emphasis on his own eyes being captured. Indeed, the powerful agency of Cynthia herself in 1.1 is absent in 3.10; it is not even she that has captured Propertius' eyes, but rather her dress. The focus on Cynthia's clothing at 3.10.15 further suggests an area of erotic aesthetics where the latest representation of Cynthia can be seen to have developed significantly, a phenomenon that can be brought out clearly through a comparison of 3.10 with 1.2.[46] In 1.2 Propertius establishes very early on a particular perspective on the desirable aesthetics of Amor, as realised by a critique of Cynthia's appearance:

> Quid iuuat ornato procedere, uita, capillo
>   et tenuis Coa ueste mouere sinus,
> aut quid Orontea crines perfundere murra,
>   teque peregrinis uendere muneribus,
> naturaeque decus mercato perdere cultu,   5
>   nec sinere in propriis membra nitere bonis?
> crede mihi, non ulla tuae est medicina figurae:
>   nudus Amor formae non amat artificem.
>   1.2.1–8

What is the point, my life, of setting out with an elaborate hairstyle, or moving the fine curves of a Coan garment? – or of drenching your hair with Orontean myrrh, and selling yourself with foreign accessories, destroying your natural beauty with purchased fashion, and preventing your body from showing off its innate qualities? Believe me, there is no treatment that should improve your figure: Love is naked, and is no lover of one who contrives beauty.

This aesthetically programmatic passage anticipates several aspects of Cynthia's appearance that are prominent in 3.10, in particular adopting an elaborate hairstyle (*ornato capillo*, 1) and donning a fine dress (*Coa ueste*, 2), as well as the use of myrrh as a perfume (*murra*, 3; cf. *et crocino nares murreus ungat onyx*, 3.10.22).

---

[46] Given that both 1.2 and 3.10 dwell at length on female 'toilette', it is surprising that Propertian commentary avoids pressing any interaction between the poems. Lyne & Morwood (1973) 42 link the poems in a footnote, remarking only that 'To re-read 1.2 is illuminating'.

The Birth of *Cynthia*

It is clear immediately that Propertius differs between the two poems in his appreciation of these details, dismissing them in 1.2 and desiring them in 3.10.[47] But more significant are the changing priorities of the literary-aesthetic scheme to which these attributes cohere. When in 1.2 Propertius prefers a naked Cynthia, and chides her for dressing herself in fancy or exotic garb, he is promoting a poetic which, in Book 1, would see amatory realism hold sway over overt literary artifice;[48] the Propertian narrator states explicitly that, as god of love and love poetry, 'Amor is no lover of contrived beauty' (*Amor formae non amat artificem*, 1.2.8). In contrast, the depiction of Cynthia in 3.10 emphasises precisely her artificiality at the expense of her natural qualities. In the middle of the poem Propertius imagines Cynthia rising from bed and dressing for the day to come:

> tuque, o cara mihi, felicibus edita pennis,
>   surge et poscentis iusta precare deos.
> ac primum pura somnum tibi discute lympha
>   et nitidas presso pollice finge comas;
> dein, qua primum oculos cepisti ueste Properti,   15
>   indue, nec uacuum flore relinque caput;
> et pete, qua polles, ut sit tibi forma perennis,
>   inque meum semper stent tua regna caput.
>   3.10.11–18

And you, my dear girl, born under fortunate auspices, rise and pray justly to the gods as they demand. First shake off sleep from yourself with pure water and tidy your shining hair with the press of your thumb; then put on the dress with which you first captured Propertius' eyes, and do not leave your head free of flowers; and seek that your beauty (which grants you your power) be everlasting, and that your reign over my life stand for ever.

Here Propertius prioritises only the decorative elements that might augment or conceal Cynthia in her natural state: there is a flower for her hair (16), and a dress for her body (15). That Cynthia should do her hair (*nitidas presso pollice finge comas*, 14) reverses his preference for untamed locks at 1.2.1;

---

[47] On the 'oddity' of Propertius' perspective in 1.2, see Gibson (2006) 135–6.
[48] See esp. Wyke (1987b), Greene (1995).

Thematic Experimentation: Propertius 3.9–11

in addition, here the verb *fingere* emphasises Cynthia's constructed existence within the poem by treating her appearance as vividly statuesque, as if she were clay to be shaped at the will of a sculptor's hands.[49] Even at the moment Propertius introduces Cynthia to the poem (*tuque, o cara mihi, felicibus edita pennis*, 11), he suggests immediately the textuality underpinning his mistress's existence: *edita* implies equally that Cynthia was 'born' and 'published' under happy auspices. In sum, the mannered prompts in 3.10 to compare the representation of Cynthia now with her appearance at the start of Book 1 ironically reveal a figure that has developed significantly over time. The Cynthia who began life as a (comparatively) realistic figure with fearful authority over Propertius has become in 3.10 a more outwardly literary creature, overtly subject to her poet's artistic whim. Besides the poet's new interest in the poetic arrangement of Cynthia's superficial garb, even the switch at 3.10.15 from her eyes to his has the effect of acknowledging Cynthia now as the focus of the poet's gaze rather than suggesting, as at 1.1.1, his submission to hers.[50]

After Propertius' promise to Maecenas at the end of 3.9 to embark on more patriotic poetry, the poet's methodical progress through the hours of his mistress's birthday in 3.10 resembles instead a set of instructions for the recuperation of amatory elegy. Yet it is equally possible to read the new poem in a way that builds on its predecessor, where the progressive dressing of Cynthia in 3.10 demonstrates her essential adaptability to Propertius' developing aesthetic and literary programme. When she reappears on her birthday, Cynthia resides

---

[49] Propertius frequently associates the verb *fingere* with artistic contrivance. Of the twelve occurrences of *fingere* in the Propertian corpus (not including adjectival/ participial variants of *fictus*), seven are found in Book 3, and of these the two most recent occur in relation to sculptors (Prometheus at 3.5.7, and Lysippus at 3.9.9).

[50] The connections that Propertius suggests here between vision and authority do not sit neatly either with ancient theories of looking or with more modern conceptions of an objectifying gaze. Ancient theory emphasises the vulnerability of a lover's eyes to erotic looking, yet in 1.1 Cynthia is made powerful by her gaze; while in 3.10, where we have seen Propertius seek to objectify Cynthia in his mind's eye, her constructed appearance is said to have rendered his eyes captured. On ancient optics, see Bartsch (2006) esp. 58–83; on the erotic gaze in Propertius, see Greene (1995), O'Neill (2005).

completely in her poet's imagination; physically she resembles an elegiac mannequin, ready to be fashioned in accordance with her author's needs.[51] In contrast especially with the emphasis on her nakedness and its relatively straightforward identification with erotic elegy in 1.1 and 1.2, the focus on clothing and styling in 3.10 adds now increased sophistication to the relationship between the *puella* and poetry – and at least grants the possibility that the poet might choose to clothe her differently. The reflection on past and future that forms part of the annual ritual of a birthday has revealed a Cynthia who has grown up to the point where she might even be capable of assuming the mantle of new poetry – as mooted more explicitly at the end of the previous poem.

Propertius 3.11

The private amatory world of 3.10 and the move towards public Roman poetry mooted at the end of 3.9 come crashing together in 3.11, a deeply riven poem in which Propertius offers a paradoxical celebration both of his submission to his mistress and of Octavian's victory at Actium over Antony and the Egyptian queen Cleopatra. In one sense, Propertius attempts to bridge the gap that he has long maintained between his own literary-erotic business and the broader pursuit of Rome's imperial ambition (a programmatic distinction asserted early on, in the diptych 1.6–7), by offering his own amatory predicament as an explanatory paradigm for recent Roman politics. In another sense, the collision of these disparate worlds in 3.11 serves precisely to reassert their incompatibility: Propertius' closing praise for Augustus' virility in subduing a transgressive Cleopatra remains fundamentally at odds with the lover–poet's implicit empathy for Antony's unspoken submission to the very same woman.[52]

---

[51] On the *topos* of fine dressing in birthday poems, see Cairns (1971) 152–5.
[52] Griffin (1977) is influential for recognising in the character of the Propertian narrator 'more resemblance to the life ascribed to Antony than to that of a good

Thematic Experimentation: Propertius 3.9–11

Once again, the poem's opening emphasises ironic association with its predecessors in order to further a sequential exploration of elegiac identity which calls into question the poet's superficial claims of generic allegiance. Just as 3.10 springs teasingly – and, in the end, misleadingly – from the new beginning promised in 3.9, so the initial couplets of 3.11 present an inverted relationship with 3.10:

> *Quid mirare*, meam si uersat femina uitam
>   et trahit addictum sub sua iura uirum,
> criminaque ignaui capitis mihi turpia fingis,
>   quod nequeam fracto rumpere uincla iugo?
>   3.11.1–4

Why be amazed that a woman rules my life and drags a man enslaved to her rule? Why do you contrive shameful charges of cowardice against me, on the grounds that I am unable to shatter the yoke and break my bonds?

Here Propertius signals that the new poem will offer a public recontextualisation of the lover's *seruitium* that had been reprised intimately at the heart of the preceding elegy. The poet's personal astonishment at the appearance of the Muses (*mirabar*, 3.10.1) becomes the abrupt criticism of an unspecified third party (*quid mirare?*, 3.11.1); private commemoration transforms into a matter of public censure.

3.11 also revives explicitly the focus on exemplarity in 3.9, and in their parallel engagement with Augustan symbols the two poems form an expansive public frame for the contained nature of erotic reminiscence in 3.10. But here too the new poem inverts the approach of the earlier poem. In 3.9, Maecenas had served as the climax of a series of *exempla* in which different people are shown to have different talents; in 3.11, Propertius himself becomes an *exemplum* at the beginning of a sequence exploring cases of female authority and male submission. The parallels between the two moments are striking:

Augustan citizen' (23) – but, in terms of 3.11, he glosses over the tension thereby established with the poem's strongly 'Augustan' closing tone; cf. Wyke (2002) 200, Gibson (2007) 60. By contrast, for a reading that overlooks the poem's dissident beginning in favour of its later 'overt Augustan material', see Cairns (2006) 350–1.

> at *tua*, Maecenas, uitae praecepta recepi,
> *cogor* et <u>exemplis</u> te superare <u>tuis</u>.
>> 3.9.21–2

But I have received your intructions for life, Maecenas, and I am compelled to outdo you by following your own example.

> ista *ego* praeterita iactaui uerba iuuenta:
> *tu* nunc <u>exemplo</u> disce timere <u>meo</u>.
>> 3.11.7–8

I hurled such words as those long ago when I was young: now do you learn to fear from my example.

In the repeated appeal to exemplarity and highly mannered inversion of first- and second-person gestures, Propertius draws attention to a general switch between external and internal paradigms: in 3.9 Propertius looks outside elegy to find (in Maecenas) a definitional model for elegy's paradoxical synthesis of contradictory values; now in 3.11 he looks inwards to reclaim elegy's earliest archetype – his own initial submission to Cynthia – and then attempts precisely to impose this personal paradigm on the outside world at large.[53]

Yet the real counterpart to Maecenas in 3.11 turns out not to be Propertius but rather Cleopatra herself. As he had done with Maecenas in 3.9, Propertius places Cleopatra at a point of sudden transition, where she provides the point of contact for 3.11's starkly opposed representations of female power and male authority.[54] The poem's initial section purports to explain the power held over Propertius by his mistress by citing a list of similarly dominant female figures from myth and legend whose names outshine even the heroes with whom they are associated: Medea (9–12), Penthesilea (13–16), Omphale

---

[53] The sense of reversal is enhanced by an inverted echo in the opening couplet of 3.11 of a crucial moment in 3.9: where Propertius had promised Maecanas that his talent would increase 'under your command' (*crescet et ingenium <u>sub tua iussa</u> meum*, 3.9.52), now he declares that his very masculinity is indentured 'to his mistress's authority' (*et trahit addictum <u>sub sua iura</u> uirum*, 3.11.2).
[54] On 3.11 as a thematic 'disunity', see e.g. Camps (1966) 104 and Richardson (1977) 359; cf. Weinlich (2003) 111 and (2005).

Thematic Experimentation: Propertius 3.9–11

(17–20) and the Babylonian Semiramis (21–6).[55] At this point Propertius switches abruptly from mythic past to recent history by introducing the defeated Egyptian queen:

> nam quid ego heroas, quid raptem in crimina diuos?
> Iuppiter infamat seque suamque domum.
> quid, modo quae nostris opprobria nexerit armis,
>   et (famulos inter femina trita suos!)   30
> coniugis obsceni pretium Romana poposcit
>   moenia et addictos in sua regna Patres.
>   3.11.27–32[56]

Why should I drag heroes under accusation, why the gods? Jupiter brings disgrace upon himself and his house. What of her who recently devised disgrace for our arms, and (a woman used among her own slaves!) demanded Roman walls as the price of her obscene marriage, and Senators enslaved to her rule.

As the climax of a list of sexually dominant women with more than a passing resemblance to elegy's *domina*,[57] Propertius' Cleopatra undermines the neat distinction between the Roman 'real world' occupied by elegy's readers and the literary escapism of the poet's amatory enslavement. Cleopatra's eroto-political seduction of Roman statesmen provides a striking 'historical'[58] model which, precisely in its resemblance to Cynthia's conquest of Propertius, brings the elegiac paradigm right to the Roman doorstep.

Yet in 3.11 Cleopatra also serves as introduction to the poem's reassertion of masculine authority through its concluding celebration of Roman historical success. Just as Horace had done in *Odes* 1.37, Propertius represses Cleopatra's name in 3.11. In Augustan literature, the Egyptian queen is

---

[55] On these *exempla* and their relationship to the ensuing 'political' second section of the poem, see esp. Nethercut (1971) 422–6. On the poetics of obscuring male names in this sequence, see Gurval (1995) 195.

[56] Heyworth (2007a) accepts Baehrens's *qui* for the transmitted *quae* in line 29, so that the hexameter of this pivotal couplet refers first to Antony, with Cleopatra being introduced in the pentameter at line 30.

[57] Nethercut (1971) 321–2, Wyke (2002) 196.

[58] Notwithstanding that the dramatic narrative of Cleopatra's life and death has been held up as a notorious fiction: Gurval (1995) 29–30, Tronson (1998) and (1999). The Egyptian queen is virtually a creature of the texts that speak about her: esp. Hor. *Od.* 1.37, Prop. 3.11, Virg. *Aen.* 8, with Wyke (2002) 196–223.

portrayed persistently as a transgressive female outrageously wielding male authority; to name her would grant her the masculine dignity of her title 'glory of the father'.[59] In Propertius' poem, Cleopatra's lack of a name also provides a symbolic turning point. Cleopatra enters the poem as culmination of a sequence of powerful female figures, but she is conspicuously the first of these women not to be named. In the opening section of the poem, the names of these women (and the simultaneous occlusion of male names) emphasises a narrative of female dominance; in the poem's middle, Cleopatra's lack of name triggers a sudden proliferation of male titles – Pompey, Marius, Scipio, Camillus, Decius, Cocles and Caesar Augustus himself (3.11.35–66). Together these symbolise the poem's paradigm shift in its second section towards a celebration of male success and, especially, signal the return in gender terms of social and political orthodoxy. The explosion of historically significant titles also shows the extent to which Propertius' elegiac lens widens dramatically over the course of the poem and the corpus as a whole. 3.11 begins by revisiting the personal scenario of the lover's submission to his mistress (in lines that parade shared imagery with the first programmatic statement of Propertian *seruitium amoris* in 1.1).[60] But the poem ends with a public embrace of the three biggest names of all: the mighty triumvirate of the Roman state – Caesar, Jove and Rome itself (*uix timeat saluo Caesare Roma Iouem*, 'Rome should scarcely fear Jove, while Caesar is safe', 3.11.66).[61] The magnitude of this expansion vehemently 'corrects' the inverted authority paradigm with which Propertius opens the poem, and so invites radical reappraisal not only of the gendered identity of the elegiac poet, but also of the nature of elegy as a 'private' genre.

---

[59] Esp. Wyke (2002) 207. Yet the queen's name is not entirely absent in Propertius' poem. At 3.11.28, in the couplet immediately before introducing Cleopatra, Propertius foreshadows her appearance with an oblique Latin translation of the queen's Greek title: *Iup-piter in-fama-t*.

[60] Cf. Weinlich (2003) 111 and (2005), esp. 140–6.

[61] On the emphatic juxtaposition of proper names, see Fedeli (1985) 393–4; cf. Richardson (1977) 368 (a 'curious near blasphemy').

In this broader context, Cleopatra's pivotal role in 3.11 underpins her position alongside Maecenas as a central character in a metapoetic drama about a poet losing control of his genre – a narrative that has been underway since Propertius' abrupt promise of patriotic verse at the end of 3.9. In thematic terms, Cleopatra crucially resists the elegist's attempt to bring her into the service of his own regressive elegiac agenda.[62] In fact, the poet's appeal to the Egyptian queen immediately sends the poem careering in what seems an unintended direction: what begins as a defence of erotic abjection becomes suddenly a vehement condemnation of submission as shameful. Similarly, the attempt to deploy Cleopatra within an erotic paradigm as the prototypical elegiac mistress brings the poet into contact – inevitably and at length – with other very public narratives in which Cleopatra is also implicated, and from which she cannot be isolated. Here the private poet is drawn from the literary abstraction of myth to the bloody reality of civil war in Rome's recent past: the threat ascribed to Cleopatra's Egyptian base occasions a Propertian apostrophe to the murder of Pompey (3.11.33–8); while the gravitational pull of the Cleopatra narrative promoted by Octavian, in which Roman liberty fights a foreign war against Egyptian tyranny, seemingly compels Propertius into retelling an Actian legend where Tiber faces up to the menaces of the Nile (3.11.39–56). The narratives which Propertius ends up acknowledging because of his choice to invoke Cleopatra actually undermine the fundamental elegiac logic which Cleopatra had been invoked to demonstrate in the first place.

Exemplarity and Elegy's Ideological Tensions

For these reasons 3.11 remains a poem that defies stable interpretation, since the opposing models of authority that collide in Propertius' characterisation of Cleopatra are never fully

---

[62] Similarly, the legend of Cleopatra as an eastern female ruler already exists as part of a far wider cultural narrative which ultimately eludes the grasp of the Augustan poets and their sponsors: Wyke (2002) 209.

Exemplarity and Elegy's Ideological Tensions

reconciled. In elegiac terms, for instance, the poem ultimately invites its readers to consider two lessons, each stemming from the poet's appeal to exemplarity. Is it that Cleopatra's fearsome qualities offer a contemporary public paradigm to help the reader better understand elegiac amatory enslavement? Or does Cleopatra's final submission to a virile Octavian expose a myth at the heart of elegy, and map out a recuperation of the genre towards an acceptable orthodoxy?[63] The external voice of Roman masculinity might have the final say, yet the narrating lover never rescinds his initial position of unmanned subservience.[64] Any resolution is left to the judgement of the poem's audience.

Similarly, the poem's unprecedented engagement with Roman public narrative abandons elegy's aversion to playing a role in Augustan myth-making (most famously in 2.7), yet it stops short of uncomplicated endorsement of an Augustan ethos. 3.11 certainly offers vocal support for Rome's official line on foreign affairs, and for Augustus in particular (esp. 3.11.49–50, 65–6, 71–2).[65] But the poem also dwells at length on the aspects of Cleopatra's legend – her gender, the 'nobility' of her suicide – which caused her to drop swiftly from the official storybook soon after Actium.[66] From a cultural perspective this poem keeps an ultimately troublesome image of a tragic Cleopatra before the eyes of a Roman audience and, in doing so, both champions Octavian's victory and exposes it to the possibility of belittlement.

Yet one final return to the metapoetics of sequence offers an opportunity not only to bring together the clashing ideologies in 3.11 but the disparate concerns of the two previous elegies as well. We have seen that at the start of 3.11 Propertius grants his reproving interlocutor the conventional line that the

---

[63] For this programme as an elegiac strategy of closure, see Fear (2005).
[64] On this paradox, Gibson (2007) 60; cf. Weinlich (2003) 111 for the assimilation of erotic poetry and Augustan propaganda. Weinlich (2005) regards 3.11 as emblematic of the blending of the two 'souls' of the Propertian narrator – 'den Liebenden wie den Patriotik' (143).
[65] Richardson (1977) 359.
[66] See esp. Wyke (2002) 242–50; cf. Gurval (1995) 204.

poet's submissive amatory lifestyle is a thing of cowardice and shame (an accusation rejected vehemently by the Propertian narrator). Here again is the lover's self-defence, with attention drawn now to particular details of vocabulary and syntax underpinning the slavish imagery:

> criminaque ignaui *capitis* mihi *turpia* fingis,
> quod nequeam fracto rumpere uincla iugo?
> 3.11.3–4

> Why do you contrive shameful charges of cowardice against me, on the grounds that I am unable to shatter the yoke and break my bonds?

Propertius' language recalls very closely the metaphoric opening of 3.9, when Propertius had similarly appealed to the imagery of (suggestively servile)[67] submission, in order to justify to Maecenas why he should remain a love elegist rather than become overburdened by the weighty task of serious poetry:

> *turpe* est, quod nequeas, *capite* committere pondus
> et pressum inflexo mox dare terga genu.
> 3.9.5–6

> It is shameful to commit your head to a burden which you cannot bear, and then, weighed down, bend your knee and give way.

In a straightforward sense, here 3.11 furthers a sense of linear variation and reinvention as the collection advances: the literary metaphor addressed to Maecenas by a humble poet becomes a social slur hurled at the poet by a judgemental reader.[68] But, while both these couplets affirm the Roman dictum that a lack of agency is a shameful thing (*turpe est*, 3.9.5; *crimina ... turpia*, 3.11.4), taking up the invitation to read the two against each other establishes a suggestive paradox. In 3.9, Propertius decries the shame that would stem, if he were

---

[67] See Heyworth & Morwood (2011) 198 on reading *dare terga* at 3.9.6 as signifying, in context, submission rather than retreat.
[68] The redeployment of imagery is neatly suggested at a linguistic level by a variation of syntax governing the same vocabulary: the relative clause *quod nequeas* becomes an adverbial clause in *quod nequeam*.

Exemplarity and Elegy's Ideological Tensions

to attempt epic, from his limp 'incapacity' to bear a burden (*quod nequeas* ... *committere pondus*), and so he remains a love poet – while 3.11 employs the accusation of 'incapacity' to break one's bonds (*quod nequeam* ... *rumpere uincla*) as a description of the already shameful slavery of the love poet in the first place. In other words, when we approach these poems as a sequence, Propertius himself enters 3.11 already embodying the opposed paradigms of servility and dominance that the poem itself will bring crashing together. By wishing to remain an elegist in 3.9, Propertius already resists as a poet the kind of unmanned abjection that he exhibits as a lover in 3.11.

Hearing the (un)subtle echo of 3.9's *recusatio* in 3.11's opening depiction of *seruitium* considerably escalates a reading of Propertius' engagement with Augustan literary politics. Reading backwards, suddenly Maecenas' request to extol Roman achievement in epic verse looms as an attempt (which Propertius resists, at least initially) to impose a shameful form of literary slavery on a par with the erotic slavery that the Roman mainstream so disparages. But the consequence is especially significant if one has read 3.9 as a *recusatio* that fails. In this case, 3.11 might well seem to end up where 3.9 left off, offering 'sincere' praise for Augustus in accordance with the upbeat Roman programme that 3.9 ends by promising.[69] But, if so, 3.11 must seem also to realise the kind of crushing literary burden that Propertius had begun the earlier poem wishing to avoid. In writing these (outrageously) Augustan lines,[70] does Propertius 'submit' shamefully to Maecenas' imperial authority, after all? Or, perhaps, does he perform by exaggeration the kind of submission he perceives in other writers? Here the extended justifications of debased servitude assume a new relevance for the poet's remarkable change in tone halfway through the poem. By opening with a reminiscence of his earlier address to Maecenas, 3.11 threatens to link an emasculated servility with the delivery of Augustan praise as a satire

---

[69] Cairns (2006) 350–1.
[70] For the patriotism of 3.11 as hyperbolic irony, see Nethercut (1971) 439–43.

of literary patronage under the Principate. The poem's celebratory words seem the sort uttered under compulsion by a poet who even introduces himself as not his own master – as unable, indeed, to escape the shameful condition of his (literary) bondage.

CHAPTER 4

MARRIAGE AND THE ELEGIAC WOMAN

Propertius 3.12

3.12 leads us right to the middle of Book 3, and should have attracted more attention than it has.[1] Sitting as the twelfth of Book 3's twenty-four poems, it negotiates the reader's passage into the second half of the book – and it does so by introducing what must seem at first glance a new kind of elegiac *puella* and, indeed, by foreshadowing a new kind of Propertian elegy: in this poem we meet the chaste wife Aelia Galla, upon whose marriage Propertius reflects with uncharacteristic favour. In one sense, Galla is another of the 'external' characters which Propertius gathers in the central sequence of his third book. We have already explored the potential disruption of Propertius' elegiac programme represented by Maecenas and Cleopatra in the previous chapter; now, at the very heart of the book, the beloved Aelia Galla seems to challenge the most basic assumptions that we hold of elegy's female protagonist. Significantly, Galla is both married and chaste – characteristics which should, at first glance, mark her as a misfit in the elegiac world.[2] After all, Propertius had declared his 'hatred' for chaste girls (*castas odisse puellas*, 1.1.5) in his very

---

An earlier version of this chapter was published as Wallis, J. A. C. (2011) 'Marriage and the Elegiac Woman in Propertius 3.12', *Ramus* 40, 106–29.

[1] For rare treatments of 3.12 on its own terms, see Nethercut (1970b), Cairns (1972) 197–201, Jacobson (1976), Lieberg (1999), Brouwers (2006). Otherwise, scholarly interest in 3.12 comes largely from the external perspective of other poems or broader themes. Galla herself has attracted comment as the novel and sympathetic portrait of a married woman which Propertius would later develop through Arethusa in 4.3 and Cornelia in 4.11: see here Becker (1971) 469–71, Fantham (2006) 196–7; and, briefly, Günther (2006). Others have been concerned with the historical identity of the addressee Postumus, and with whether he is the same figure to whom Horace *Odes* 2.14 is addressed: see here White (1995), Keith (2008) 5–7 (White argues no; Keith, yes).

[2] For such a view of Galla, see Fantham (2006) 195–6. Maltby (1981) discusses the critical unease that has attended Arethusa's open declaration of her married status even early in Book 4.

first elegy, the poem in which he presents Cynthia, instead; and in 2.7 Propertius had positioned marriage (specifically Augustus' proposed legislation which would have compelled elite Romans to marry)[3] as antithetical to elegiac continuation. And so in 3.12, by bestowing his approval both on Galla and on the institution of marriage itself, Propertius seems not only to introduce a new kind of 'elegiac woman' but, in doing so, also to adopt a new elegiac voice that would align closely with the Augustan mainstream.

Nevertheless, just as with Cleopatra and Maecenas, there are further stories to be told here, too. To begin with, the discussion of *fides* upon which 3.12 pivots returns us once more to the cultural (and moral) challenge laid down by the arrival of Horace's *Odes* (on this occasion, especially *Odes* 3.7). But 3.12 looks inwards as well, revisiting Propertius' own generic conventions and presumptions. In terms of Book 3 itself, this central poem continues to unmask the role played by *fides* in elegy itself, a programmatic thread that began in 3.6, and which will continue in 3.20. In doing so, 3.12 reworks a pair of mismatching motifs from Propertius' earliest poetry. For a start, through the separation of Postumus and Galla 3.12 activates long-standing elegiac paranoia about erotic *in*fidelity (as well as the idea that 'Augustus' represents a public and dangerous intrusion into the private domain occupied especially by lovers); here we must think of the middle poem of Book 1, where Propertius obsesses in 1.11 about his own separation from Cynthia, or of his morbid assertion in 1.19 that even good girls will stray, eventually. But 3.12 also reprises a more overlooked motif from the earlier poetry concerning elegiac constancy, which is particularly effective now in pushing back a mainstream Horatian incursion. Here, through Galla's conspicuous fidelity, Propertius points out at the centre of his new book that the kind of *fides* that can transcend public interference in private affairs has in fact always informed the elegiac value system. As such, and for all her genuine novelty, the

---

[3] Heyworth & Morwood (2011) 21.

Setting (Us) Up

chastely married Galla will not offer any straightforwardly disruptive presence in Book 3, for she is still open to cooption as a properly elegiac symbol which restates the steadfastness that Propertius claims for himself (most of all: *Cynthia prima fuit, Cynthia finis erit*, 'Cynthia was the first and shall be the last', 1.12.20 – the elegiac *credo* from the middle of Book 1, forming a central palinode to the imagined inconstancy of 1.11),[4] as well as the matronly status that informs the way in which Propertius would view Cynthia (*semper amica mihi, semper et uxor eris*, 'You will always be mistress to me, and always wife too', 2.6.42).[5] 3.12 is a poem that begins, in fact, to resolve the narrative tension between the infidelity expected by elegiac characters of each other (and so, by us of them) and the actual fidelity they mostly display.[6] To the extent that Galla is indeed a 'new' character – and Propertius does proclaim her as such – much of her novelty lies in the way that she has taken what had been an elegiac subtext and promoted it now to the level of text itself.

Setting (Us) Up

This chapter begins with an examination of how 3.12 employs reminiscences of earlier poems (and other poets) in order to set up an expectation that this poem will follow a familiar course; this is a move which allows Propertius – precisely by thwarting such expectations – to mark out the *fides* that dominates the poem's central section as all the more conspicuous. 3.12 immediately introduces us to its addressee Postumus, and to the weeping Galla:[7]

---

[4] On the *constans fides* of the (male) elegiac lover, see Cairns (1995) 73, with examples and bibliography.
[5] On this general point, the observation of Nethercut (1970b) 102 is most apt: 'We should note that Propertius does not distinguish between the *fides* of married women and the straightforward interchange of affection all lovers ought to cultivate.'
[6] The supposed infidelity of (Propertian) elegiac women is seriously challenged by Cynthia's *apologia* in 4.7 and especially by the last elegiac woman of them all – the faithful Cornelia in 4.11.
[7] The names of the two characters are significant, though not in the way that much of the discussion about them would suggest. Cairns (1972) 16–20 speculates that Postumus might be the senator and proconsul C. Propertius Postumus, and thus

Marriage and the Elegiac Woman: Propertius 3.12

> Postume, plorantem potuisti linquere Gallam,
>   miles et Augusti fortia signa sequi?
> tantine ulla fuit spoliati gloria Parthi,
>   ne faceres Galla multa rogante tua?
> si fas est, omnes pariter pereatis auari   5
>   et quisquis fido praetulit arma toro!
> tu tamen iniecta tectus, uesane, lacerna
>   potabis galea fessus Araxis aquam.
> illa quidem interea fama tabescet inani,
>   haec tua ne uirtus fiat amara tibi,   10
> neue tua Medae laetentur caede sagittae,
>   ferreus armato neu cataphractus equo,
> neue aliquid de te flendum referatur in urna:
>   sic redeunt, illis qui cecidere locis.
>   3.12.1-14

Postumus, how could you leave Galla crying, to follow Augustus' brave standards, as a soldier? Was the glory of Parthia's spoils worth so much to you, with Galla repeatedly begging you not to do it? If it is permitted may all you greedy ones perish equally, and whoever else prefers his weapon to a faithful bed! You, you madman, wrapped in a cloak you have thrown on, weary, will drink Araxes' water from your helm. She in the meantime will pine away at each idle rumour, for fear your courage will cost you dear, or the arrows of Medes enjoy your death, or the iron-clad knight on an armoured horse, or some bit of you be brought back in an urn to be wept over. That is how they come back, those who fall in such places.

Against an inescapably Augustan backdrop (*Augusti fortia signa*, 3.12.2), these lines appeal to the familiar *topos* of the separation of lovers;[8] the theme is represented immediately in the poem's opening line, where Postumus and Galla are

---

a relative of Propertius; see also White (1995). But Heyworth & Morwood (2011) 222 are surely right in pointing out that both Postumus and Galla are common names typically used generically in literature – a seeming generality as the poem begins, then, which sets up the 'surprise' revelation of an apparently real identity when Galla becomes Aelia Galla in the poem's last line. Furthermore, both names Postumus and Galla bring with them literary associations. Galla suggests an elegiac connection through the Gallus of Propertius Book 1, (and) through Gallus the elegiac poet; Postumus, by contrast, directs attention outside elegy, not only through his participation in public Augustan affairs but also through a suggestion of the lyric Postumus who is addressed at Horace *Odes* 2.14 (on this connection, see again White (1995) and Keith (2008) 5–7)).

[8] For variations of this *topos* in the context of Propertius and Cynthia, see especially 1.6, 1.8, 1.11–12, 1.17, 1.19, 2.19.

Setting (Us) Up

thrown to opposite ends of the hexameter, just as the pursuit of Augustus' standards has sundered the couple to opposite ends of the known world. But Propertius also combines this motif with a concentration of other elegiac commonplaces which further imbue the poem's opening with a powerful sense of foreboding. The elegiac disdain for avarice is particularly prominent; indeed, it is Postumus' greed that has caused him to leave Galla behind in the first place. The presentation of avarice as a transgressive and ill-omened motif has already been prominent in Book 3: just recently the merchant Paetus has abandoned, not the tears of his *puella*, but the embrace of his *Penates* (3.7.33) in order to seek financial gain on the high seas – and with portentously disastrous results. Further, as he has already done in 3.4, Propertius here associates greed with military campaigning itself (which has been incompatible with elegy since 1.6) and presents both as a rejection of the erotic ideal of a faithful couch (*fido praetulit arma toro*, 3.12.6). In short, Propertius presents us with a Postumus who is simply asking for trouble in 3.12; and, by opening with a list of ominous *topoi*, Propertius has surely set us up with the expectation that something disastrous is about to occur. He makes Postumus break all of the elegiac rules at once: in the first four lines, Postumus abandons his girl for a military campaign, he abandons her for the allure of wealth and he does it all against her express wishes. And finally, if we needed further reminding, we need only think of poor Paetus, drowned just five poems ago, the last man to abandon elegiac values.

Of course, this will turn out to be a false lead: Galla's chastity will confound expectations, and Postumus will be rewarded, rather than punished, despite his apparent breaking of the elegiac code. This revelation occupies the second half of the chapter; but, first, it is useful to examine further the elegiac backstory concerning this particular *topos*, in order to draw out the elegiac belief in imminent infidelity that will inevitably shape readers' expectations as they come across the parting of Postumus and Galla in 3.12. It is important to note at the outset that the separation of lovers in Propertian elegy is accompanied not so much by actual infidelity as by an obsessive paranoia about infidelity; nevertheless, it is because of such paranoia that the mistress's desirable solitude during the lover's absence is constantly at issue. Just recently, in the programmatic third elegy of the collection, the poetry conjures up the idealised image of a loyal girl who might just foreshadow the kind of *puella* that Galla becomes, a girl who reads at home alone while awaiting the return of her lover:

> ut tuus in scamno iactetur saepe libellus,
>   quem legat exspectans sola puella uirum.
>   3.3.19–20

> your little book often thrown on the bench, read by a girl waiting alone for a lover.

But, even in this idealised portrait, the fact that the girl is actually alone – or rather, whether she is – is presented as a matter of great concern to the lover. Such is the case in 2.29, for instance, when the lover is moved (rather unwisely) to check that his mistress sleeps alone:[9]

> mane erat, et uolui, si sola quiesceret illa,
>   uisere: at in lecto Cynthia sola fuit.
>   2.29.23–4

> It was dawn; I wanted to see if she slept alone: and Cynthia was there, alone in her bed.

    The reason behind all this concern is, of course, that the lover believes he has good reason to doubt the *puella*'s fidelity whenever his back is turned. It is precisely this point that Propertius places at the heart of Book 1. 1.11 presents a thematic parallel to 3.12 in its focus on separated lovers. But it offers a significant structural parallel, too: as the eleventh poem of Book 1, it sits at exactly the same midpoint within the twenty-two poems of Book 1 as this twelfth poem does within the twenty-four poems of Book 3. In the middle of Book 1, Propertius worries obsessively about Cynthia's faithfulness to him during her stay at Baiae; yet, back in Rome, Propertius also takes advantage

---

[9] And his mistress is sleeping alone (2.29.24); we return to this at the end of the chapter.

Setting (Us) Up

of Cynthia's absence to present a foundational assimilation of erotic narrative and elegiac metapoetics:

> an te nescio quis simulatis ignibus hostis
>   sustulit e nostris, Cynthia, carminibus?
> atque utinam mage te, remis confisa minutis,
>   paruula Lucrina cumba moretur aqua,   10
> aut teneat clausam tenui Teuthrantis in unda,
>   alternae facilis cedere lympha manu,
> quam uacet alterius blandos audire susurros
>   molliter in tacito litore compositam,
> ut solet amota labi custode puella,   15
>   perfida communes nec meminisse deos:
> non quia perspecta non es mihi cognita fama,
>   sed quod in hac omnis parte timetur amor.
>   1.11.7–18

Or has some unknown rival with false pretence of passion drawn you, Cynthia, away from my songs? I would much rather some little craft, relying on feeble oars, entertained you on the Lucrine Lake, or that the waters, easily parting to alternating stroke, held you enclosed in the shallow waves of Teuthras, than that you be free to hear another's flattering whispers, as you lie arranged elegantly on the silent shore. Far from watching eyes a girl slips, faithlessly unmindful of the gods we share: it's not that your character is unknown to me, but that in this respect every love is afraid.

As is well noted,[10] here Cynthia is treated as a beloved girl as well as an erotic theme capable of being contained in song (1.11.7–8); Propertius' hypothetical adversary is figured as both a rival lover and as a competing poet, who whispers sweet nothings to Cynthia in just the same way that Propertius does himself (1.11.13–14). But the present significance of this passage lies in the second couplet, as quoted – that, without someone to watch over her (*amoto custode*, 1.11.15), then an elegiac *puella* will fall to infidelity, since she is faithless by nature (*perfida*, 1.11.16). Exactly this central fear from Book 1 underpins the poet's emphasis on his mistress's solitude in the subsequent extracts mentioned above. Such elegiac presumption of erotic susceptibility inevitably provides unspoken poignancy to Postumus' separation from Galla at the beginning of 3.12;

---

[10] See esp. Greene (1995) 313–18.

but it is also an old presumption, one about to be turned on its head at this latest Propertian midpoint here at the heart of Book 3.

Besides revisiting themes from earlier Propertian elegy, 3.12 also reveals a significant inter-generic connection. In particular, 3.12 shares its narrative construct with (in fact, given the closeness of the interaction, very probably derives it from) one of Horace's recently published *Odes* – the seventh poem of the third book, in which Horace offers consolation to Asterie, whose lover Gyges has gone overseas in search of wealth, just as Postumus has now done in the Propertian elegy.[11] The close engagement with Horace at *Odes* 3.7 provides a further thematic background for Propertius 3.12, and allows the elegist to interweave two distinct lines of significance. First, here in the middle of his third book he revisits and will soon reshape one of the central tensions from way back in Book 1 – a tension that stems from the mismatch between the everlasting loyalty he desires from his *puella* and the lack of loyalty he fears she will display should he ever be separated from her by distance, by death or by the overtures of another lover. At the same time, as we saw in chapter 1, the massive intervention of Horace's three books of lyric had mounted a challenge to the elegist to rearticulate the importance of his genre to the nascent Augustan literary scene: in this context, and taking Augustan *fides* as a battleground, 3.12 becomes one of the several poems in Book 3 where Propertius responds to external generic pressure with a poem that seeks to renegotiate a more expansive elegiac world view.

We come to the genre-play of both *Odes* 3.7 and Propertius 3.12 later in the chapter. For the moment, the significance of Horace's Asterie ode lies at its narrative level – in the way that Horace's poetic plot lays bare, with unerring insight, exactly the reasons why Postumus ought to worry about Galla's behaviour while he is away campaigning for Augustus. In other

---

[11] For treatments of Horace *Odes* 3.7 in the context of Propertius 3.12, see Pasquali (1920) 463–70, Davis (1991) 43–50, Cairns (1995).

Setting (Us) Up

words, Horace's Asterie ode offers a tendentious reading of elegy that privileges elegy's own paranoia about infidelity such as we have just seen in Propertius' earlier poetry.[12] Well before we meet Postumus and Galla, Horace had already contrived the separation of two lovers by an ocean: the merchant Gyges has left his lover Asterie in search of trade riches, while Asterie weeps at home for his absence:[13]

> Quid fles, Asterie, quem tibi candidi
> primo restituent uere Fauonii
> Thyna merce beatum,
>   constantis iuuenem fide,
> Gygen?
>
> *Od.* 3.7.1–5

Why are you crying, Asterie, for Gyges, whom at the first sign of Spring the bright zephyrs will restore to you, rich with Bithynian goods, a young man of constant faith?

Just as Propertius will later do, Horace here places significant emphasis on the fidelity of his characters. First, in the extract just quoted, he reassures Asterie of Gyges' faithfulness to her during his absence: Gyges is, says Horace, 'a young man of constant faith' (*Od.* 3.7.4). In turn, at the end of the poem the Horatian narrator also counsels Asterie to remain true to Gyges while he is away, in the face of erotic attention from a desirable suitor:

>   at tibi
> ne uicinus Enipeus
> plus iusto placeat caue;
>
> quamuis non alius flectere equum sciens   25
> aeque conspicitur gramine Martio,
> nec quisquam citus aeque
>   Tusco denatat alueo.

---

[12] Cairns (1995) 68–70.
[13] Harrison (1988) 187 points out that the oceanic separation of Asterie and Gyges brings the *Odyssey* into play – a parallel which becomes explicit later in Propertius 3.12 through the direct comparison of Postumus and Galla with Odysseus and Penelope, and through a (highly tendentious) paraphrase of Odysseus' wanderings at Prop. 3.12.24–37; on which see Brouwers (2006).

> prima nocte domum claude neque in uias
> sub cantu querelae despice tibiae,   30
>   et te saepe uocanti
>   duram difficilis mane.
>   *Od.* 3.7.21–32

But you take care, lest your neighbour Enipeus prove more pleasing to you than he should, though no one else is seen to be as skilled at guiding his horse over the grassy Campus Martius, nor does anyone swim so swiftly down the Tiber's channel. At night, shut up your house; don't look out into the street at the song from his sorrowful pipes; and, though he often call you cruel, remain unyielding.

Asterie is urged conspicuously in the poem's final line to 'remain unyielding' (*difficilis mane*, *Od.* 3.7.32). Thus the ode ends, just as it had begun, with an assertion of lyric constancy. But Horace's concluding imperative betrays a tension, one from which the poem as a whole gains its energy. This performance of Horatian *fides* gains its weightiness – or suggests its irony, depending on which approach you prefer[14] – by standing in the face of a powerful temptation to stray. In order to generate (and to emphasise) this tension within the poem's narrative, Horace grants each of the central lovers a tempting suitor. To Gyges he gives a hot-and-bothered hostess, Chloe:

> atqui sollicitae nuntius hospitae,
> suspirare Chloen et miseram tuis   10
>   dicens ignibus uri,
>   temptat mille uafer modis.
>   *Od.* 3.7.9–12

Yet the messenger of his love-struck hostess, relating that wretched Chloë sighs and burns with passion for your lover, trickily tempts him by a thousand means.

Chloe in fact receives three whole stanzas from Horace in which she attempts her seduction through a pliant messenger who

---

[14] See the (typically reserved) survey of varying approaches to *Odes* 3.7 at Nisbet & Rudd (2004) 113–15; see also the brief summary of approaches in Cairns (1995) 68–9. Some readers emphasise a tone of moral conservatism (e.g. Bradshaw (1978) 156–76, Santirocco (1986) 125–8); but others – adopting an approach firmly disapproved by Nisbet & Rudd – suggest that the Horatian narrator actually sympathises with the seducers, and especially with Enipeus (e.g. Owens (1992)).

Setting (Us) Up

tells Gyges fearful stories about the dangers of overchastity (*Od.* 3.7.9–20). Asterie receives in her turn handsome Enipeus, who spends the poem's final ten lines (*Od.* 3.7.23–32, quoted above) swimming the Tiber nakedly and racing his horse skilfully and playing his pipe mournfully beneath Asterie's window. The result of all this attempted seduction is that, in the end, Gyges' signature constancy does not remain figured for the simple morality it first suggests, but becomes represented as not being its opposite – as being, instead, a resistance to temptation.[15] Equally, Asterie is urged *difficilis mane* as the poem concludes, not simply because to act in this way is a good thing, but precisely because she is under threat of behaving *non difficile*. Looking at the poem as a whole, when the Horatian narrator emphasises *fides* in the case of his separated lovers in *Odes* 3.7, he is not so much mounting a positive case for the virtue of fidelity as he is staging a pointed rejection of infidelity as a vice. In doing so, the poem dwells – either circumspectly, or perhaps suggestively – on the threats to *fides* that crop up when lovers are separated.

Of course, there is a certain amount of literary gamesmanship here. As will be important when we come back to this poem shortly, the characters of Horace's poem are marked by conspicuously elegiac traits; here Horace is taking pot-shots at elegy in general for its seeming obsession with erotic clichés and for the tiresome inconstancy of its characters.[16] Nonetheless, in his perceptive prodding at elegy, Horace essentially reinforces for us a reading of what we might call 'elegiac norms': these represent the almost-caricature of elegiac behaviour that elegy itself has been complicit in creating. Here, drawing on the kind of material we examined earlier in Propertius' first two books, the point that Horace makes rather exquisitely in *Odes* 3.7 is that (elegiac) *puellae* seem ever on the point of yielding to the

---

[15] Davis (1991) 47.
[16] Cairns (1995), 68–75; Davis (1991) 45, 48. Cf. also Horace's poking at elegiac clichés in his ode addressed to Tibullus (1.33). Horace's use of conspicuously elegiac language is also important in terms of his own lyric project: in one sense, Horace appeals to elegiac symbols in *Odes* 3.7 in negotiating himself away from the excessive and weighty publicness of his 'Roman Odes' (3.1–6).

approaches of other lovers, whenever the current lover is not there to watch over them.

With this background now well flagged, we turn to the way that Propertius sets up Galla with the appearance (at least) of a chaste novelty in a Propertian poem, and as what must seem a pointed rejection of the fickle kind of elegiac woman we thought we had known. The first fourteen lines of 3.12 contain little to suggest to the poem's reader that Galla is significantly different from any other elegiac *puella* such as we have met many times before. In fact, we are encouraged to think that she is such a *puella*: even Galla's distress at the absence of Postumus in the poem's first line recalls Propertius telling us early in Book 1 that Cynthia herself was distraught then, as Galla is now, at the thought of him leaving town (1.6.5–6). But, if Galla (and her complicity in the *topos* of separated lovers) is set up to recall Cynthia from earlier poetry, then the revelation of Galla's faithfulness in 3.12 must surely come as a surprise. In fact, the middle section of the poem handles the transformation of Galla from a potential *puella perfida* into a third-book *casta coniunx* with quite a bit of panache:

>   ter quater in casta felix, o Postume, Galla!
>   moribus his alia coniuge dignus eras.
>   3.12.15–16

> O Postumus you are three or four times blessed by Galla's chastity! Your morals deserve a different wife.

For a start, as the extract opens husband and wife (we now learn!) have been reunited: Postumus now occupies the fifth foot of the hexameter, sitting side by side with Galla who has remained emblematically constant in the sixth foot – and this despite the following line asserting that Postumus is not worthy of the wife that the poem claims he will keep. Furthermore, at the moment that Galla's surprising constancy is made clear, Postumus too undergoes a transformation from the sort of avaricious man whom elegy would normally exclude, to one who reaps the kind of erotic reward that an elegiac poet usually desires for himself. We have already seen the way in which a reader might expect Postumus to become Book 3's second

Setting (Us) Up

Paetus for the fact that he had abandoned Galla for war and riches. But this proves to be exactly not the case – instead, we read *ter quater felix o Postume!* (3.12.15). It is worth noting that these very words – *ter quater*, which signal Postumus' good fortune in 3.12 – have already been used to count the three and four times that the raging sea overwhelmed the unlucky Paetus at 3.7.6 (*terque quaterque*). Reinforcing the apparent inversion of points of view within Book 3, it seems Postumus is now to be fortunate in exactly the same measure that Paetus had been unfortunate.[17]

Moreover, if elegiac paranoia about a woman's ability to remain faithful has so far sat largely implicitly behind the poem's opening *topos* of the separation of lovers, at 3.12.17–18 Propertius now calls upon such fears openly:

> quid faciet nullo munita puella marito,
>   cum sit luxuriae Roma magistra suae?
> sed securus eas: Gallam non munera uincent,
>   duritiaeque tuae non erit illa memor.
>   3.12.17–20

What shall a girl do with no husband to guard her, with Rome to instruct her in its voluptuousness? But go in safety: gifts will not win Galla, and she will not recall how harsh you were.

The first couplet here leads us to the midpoint of the poem, and significantly Propertius offers it to us as a question about the *puella*'s constancy. Given the elegiac background discussed above, we might have thought we surely know the answer. The phrase *nullo munita marito* ('with no husband to guard her', 3.12.17) recalls closely the kind of erotic licence that was granted to Cynthia through *amoto custode* in 1.11 ('while her guardian is absent', 1.11.15); and the inevitability that a girl will give in to temptation in just such a situation as this justifies Horace's warning to Asterie in *Odes* 3.7. But it turns out that Propertius has cited these fears only so as to show them up as now baseless: in direct contrast to the (hypothetically) perfidious Cynthia (we imagine) in Book 1, the Galla of Book

---

[17] It is also a significant connection that Paetus' death occurs in the context of a betrayal of *fides*, at Prop. 3.7.35–6.

Marriage and the Elegiac Woman: Propertius 3.12

3 will not be susceptible to seduction by others, despite being left to her own devices. And so Postumus – who, unlike Paetus, will not be made to pay for his transgression of elegy's ethic code through his neglect of Galla – may proceed safely into the second half of the poem (*sed securus eas*, 3.12.19; the first line past the poem's midpoint) precisely free from such fears about her loyalty, since Galla will prove incorruptible by the signature bribery of erotic elegy (*Gallam non munera uincent*, 'gifts will not win Galla', 3.12.19). We have here not only what seems to be a very new kind of elegiac creature but also one that is loudly proclaimed as such.

Yet it is hardly sufficient just to say that Galla simply does not fit. In a very basic sense she must fit, in that Propertius has placed her right at the centre of Book 3. Here we switch focus to the end of the poem. Galla's exceptionally chaste nature during her husband's absence has allowed Propertius to compare his married couple with Homer's paradigmatic Penelope and Odysseus (e.g. *Postumus alter erit miranda coniuge Vlixes*, 'Postumus will be another Ulysses with a wifely wonder', 3.12.23); but, by the poem's end, Homeric Penelope will have been surpassed by Propertian Galla:

> nec frustra, quia casta domi persederat uxor:
> uincit Penelopes Aelia Galla fidem.
> 3.12.37–8

> Not in vain [had Ulysses suffered], since his wife stayed chaste at home: Aelia Galla outdoes Penelope's loyalty.

Just as the basic scenario of Postumus leaving his Galla behind is common enough in love poetry, so the figure of Penelope is found frequently there as an *exemplum pudicitiae* (a model of chastity), and this is no different in 3.12.[18] But – unlike in 3.12 – the mythically chaste Penelope is usually drawn upon as the representation of an elegiac fantasy, as a way of describing the kind of female loyalty that the elegiac lover desires but finds

---

[18] See here Harrison (1988) 187 for both the relevance of the Odyssey to the poetic motif of separated lovers, and for the identification of this motif as particularly elegiac.

Setting (Us) Up

conspicuously lacking in his *puella*. In particular, Propertius makes the link (and distinction) between Penelope and the elegiac *puella* in 2.9, a further poem that will prove of significant relevance to 3.12:

> Penelope poterat bis denos salua per annos
>   uiuere, tam multis femina digna procis;
> coniugium falsa poterat differre Minerua,
>   nocturno soluens texta diurna dolo;
> uisura et quamuis numquam speraret Vlixem,   5
>   illum exspectando facta remansit anus.
>   2.9.3–8

Penelope was able to live untouched for twenty years, a woman worthy of so many suitors. She evaded marriage by her cunning weaving, unravelling each day's toil with night-time deceit; and though she never hoped to see her Ulysses again, she waited, growing old, for his return.

Here Penelope is foregrounded at the beginning of 2.9 for her customary faithfulness. But the point will turn out to be that such a Penelope acts in direct contrast to the poet's mistress; indeed, when Cynthia first appears towards the middle of the poem, she has been apparently unable to remain chaste even for one night in Propertius' absence (2.9.19–20). But what makes 2.9 a particularly useful poem for comparison with 3.12 (especially in setting up an association between Propertius–Cynthia and Postumus–Galla) is that Propertius goes on to wonder rhetorically just what would Cynthia get up to were he to go away at length on military service – just as Postumus has done in 3.12:

> quid si longinquos retinerer miles ad Indos,
>   aut mea si staret nauis in Oceano?
>   2.9.29–30

What if I were a soldier, detained in far-off India, or my ship was stationed on the Ocean?

To begin with, the precedent of 2.9 shows this third-book poem using a comparison with Penelope to promote Galla, once again, as an anti-Cynthia – in that Galla acts like a Penelope, rather than unlike one. But Galla does not therefore simply express some further kind of erotic fantasy. In fact, Propertius explicitly suggests the 'reality' of Galla in the poem's last line by suddenly giving her a specific name – Aelia Galla – and thus extracting her from what might have seemed her simply generic status within a generalising moral tale.[19] As such, Propertius' use in 3.12 of a symbolic Penelope – but now to characterise an apparently 'real' woman – establishes Galla as actually the real-world embodiment of a long-term elegiac desire; that is, as the flesh-and-blood incarnation of what has been, up till now, merely an insubstantial poetic dream of something unattainable.[20] Thus Galla represents both the antithesis of elegy's beloved and yet precisely what the elegiac lover desires above all else. And so an unenviable and highly unstable predicament results. Looking at elegy from one perspective, Galla is exactly the sort of woman that Propertius wants – hence the congratulations that he affords the fortunate Postumus at 3.12.15. But, from another perspective, Galla is exactly the sort of woman that an elegist cannot have. We have seen, for instance, that Propertius praises Galla for her loyalty in the face of erotic bribery: *Gallam non munera uincent* (3.12.19). But a girl who cannot be seduced by gifts is precisely a girl unattainable by an erotic elegist – whose poems *are* seductive *munera*, the only means through which he can exercise his erotic power, and in which he flaunts his erotic success.[21] Suggestively, in fact, the most recent edition of Propertius' text contrives to have exactly this Propertian crisis expressed succinctly early in Book 2 by relocating the final couplet of Propertius 2.6 into the midst of 2.7:

nos uxor numquam, numquam diducet amica:	6.41
semper amica mihi, semper et uxor eris.	6.42
nam citius paterer caput hoc discedere collo	7.7
quam possem nuptae perdere iure faces,	

---

[19] Heyworth & Morwood (2011) 229.
[20] Cf. Günther (2006) 368–9, with reference to Arethusa in 4.3.
[21] See esp. 1.9.9–12.

(Re-)claiming Augustan *Fides*

aut ego transirem tua limina clausa maritus,
respiciens udis prodita luminibus. 7.10
2.6.41-2-2.7.7-10

Never a wife, never a mistress shall part us: you will always be mistress to me, and always wife, too. For more swiftly would I allow my head to depart from this neck than I could squander marriage torches at the decree of a bride, or could pass by your sealed doorways as a husband, looking back at what I had betrayed with wet eyes.

Paradoxically, Propertius here would regard Cynthia as his wife – only then to renounce marriage itself in the very same breath. Looking at 3.12 in this light, it seems ironically the case that the more 'real' (Aelia) Galla becomes, the more she must slip back to being an unattainable fantasy. By placing a chaste and married woman in the middle of Book 3, Propertius has shown up an erotic impossibility that sits right at the heart of elegiac poetry.

(Re-)claiming Augustan *Fides*

Lastly, we turn from (un)elegiac characterisation to the metapoetic representation of genre, as this poem – in common with many others in Book 3 – offers comment upon the evolving nature of elegy. 3.12 opens with an immediate conflict and sense of contest between irreconcilable opposites. Postumus leaves the privacy of home for the public world of warfare (1–2); and to do so, he must overcome the force of Galla's tears – he must do what she explicitly asks him not to do (3–4):

Postume, plorantem potuisti linquere Gallam,
 miles et Augusti fortia signa sequi?
tantine ulla fuit spoliati gloria Parthi,
 ne faceres Galla multa rogante tua?
3.12.1-4

Postumus, how could you leave Galla crying, to follow Augustus' brave standards, as a soldier? Was the glory of Parthia's spoils worth so much to you, with Galla repeatedly begging you not to do it?

In Propertian poetry, all of these features are readily aligned with writing practices, and in particular with the ongoing defence and counter-defence of genre choice in poetic composition.[22] For instance, 1.6 – with its literary pair 1.7 – sets out early on a pervasive equivalence of lifestyle and poetic style that remains throughout Propertius' poetry:

> Non ego nunc Hadriae uereor mare noscere tecum,
>   Tulle, neque Aegaeo ducere uela salo,
> cum quo Rhipaeos possim conscendere montis
>   ulteriusque domos uadere Memnonias;
> sed me complexae remorantur uerba puellae   5
>   mutatoque graues saepe colore preces.
>   1.6.1–6

> I am not now afraid to discover the Adriatic with you, Tullus, nor to set my sail on the salty Aegean; with you I could climb the Rhipaean mountains, and go beyond the palace of Memnon. But the words and embraces of my girl hold me back, so too her oft-changing complexion and her painful prayers.

Here we see Propertius himself, in conspicuous contrast to Postumus in 3.12, very properly refusing a request to travel away on public business – and precisely because the entreaties of his *puella* forbid him (cf. 3.12.4). In essence, in 1.6 Propertius figures his literary decision in Book 1 to be and to remain an elegist, rebuffing requests for other, presumably more public forms of poetry. In the same way, Postumus' decision in 3.12 to follow the standards of Augustus is suggestive of a literary decision to embark on some manner of Augustan epic. In this vein Postumus is figured, Ennius-like, as drinking from an epicised water source (*potabis Araxis aquam*, 3.12.8);[23] Postumus will in fact transform into an epic character, an *alter Vlixes* (3.12.23); and in the second half of the poem he will even voice his own eroticised 'epic poem' – a retelling of the Odyssey that offers an equivalent to the tales Odysseus himself told about his own wanderings.[24] If

---

[22] See e.g. Kennedy (1993) 31–3, Sharrock (2000) 263–83 (esp. 270–1), Greene (2005).
[23] The widespread association of different types of (drinking) water with genres of writing is particularly prominent at the start of Book 3: see esp. 3.1.5–6 and 3.3.1–6, 51–2. On the potential generic symbolism of the Araxes (the Araxes is, significantly, depicted on Aeneas' emblematically epic shield at Virgil *Aen.* 8.728) see Richardson (1977) 369, Heyworth & Morwood (2011) 224.
[24] Cairns (1972) 201; see also Brouwers (2006) on the connections between this episode and the poem as a whole.

(Re-)claiming Augustan *Fides*

Postumus is thus suggestive of epic ambition, then the representation of Galla (just like Cynthia in 1.6) aligns closely with elegiac practice, as the poem begins. Here, not only does Galla's emblematic weeping in the poem's first line mark her as an elegiac character,[25] but so too does her aesthetically appropriate slightness, as she wastes away elegiacally during Postumus' absence (*illa quidem ... tabescet*, 3.12.9). Even her name, Galla, is well-steeped in elegiac symbolism, recalling the Gallus of Book 1 (and, through him, the elegiac poet of the same name).[26]

This initially simple generic dichotomy does not remain so; the epicised Postumus will receive an elegist's congratulations (rather than his disdain), and the elegiac Galla will shortly display a chastity worthy of epic. But one effect of the engagement here with a nebulous form of public poetry – not to mention the theme of marriage, and Galla's imminent faithfulness – is to move the poem's moral centre closer to the Augustan cultural mainstream.[27] It is significant that Postumus is a rare figure in elegy who is represented as successful (and who is handsomely rewarded) in the public choice he has made. Augustus appears prominently in the poem's second line, and the poem's apparent Augustan drift provides a context in which Galla's *fides* and the favour bestowed upon her marriage make best initial sense – especially, here, as a 'correction' of the polemic stance Propertius had adopted in 2.7.

But these Augustan associations bring us finally to the most significant interaction between lyric and elegy. 3.12 responds well to being read, above all, as a response to the generic challenge thrown down by the arrival of Horace's lyric collections, both in general terms and specifically in the case of *Od.* 3.7. But genre-play is already highly prominent in Horace's ode, as well.

---

[25] For weeping as an elegiac trait in both lover and beloved, cf. e.g. 1.3.46 (Cynthia) and 2.14.14 (Propertius). At 4.3.26 the weeping of Arethusa (whom Galla in many ways foreshadows) marks her too as an elegiac character. See here Heyworth & Morwood (2011) 222 on Prop. 3.12.1, and Cairns (1995) 73, with bibliography.

[26] On the significance of Gallus especially in Prop. Book 1, see now Cairns (2006) 104–45.

[27] Cf. Maltby (1981) 247 on the cultural value of representing marriage in Prop. 4.3: 'in her faithfulness to her openly acknowledged husband Arethusa, like Cornelia in 4,11, can be seen as representing the loyal wife of the Augustan ideal'.

Marriage and the Elegiac Woman: Propertius 3.12

The appropriation of especially elegiac language within *Od.* 3.7 has been well catalogued,[28] as have the elegiac credentials of the four characters in the poem as they take part in 'a programmatic discrimination of literary values'.[29] It is not necessary here to go into Horace's poem in detail on this point; but it is worth noting at least the way that Horace's poem seems to position the wholesome values of lyric verse at the heart of the Augustan cultural space, and that it does so especially at the expense of elegy.

In *Od.* 3.7 Horace takes on elegy on thematic ground that is common to both genres; erotic material is, of course, as much at home in lyric as it is in elegiac verse. At stake, however, is a value system when it comes to amatory matters. Elegy famously self-defines as a poetry of irrationality and extremity; Horatian lyric, on the other hand, identifies itself with control and the comfort of the middle course.[30] Love in Propertius is lovesickness; Propertian *amor* renders Propertius *amens*, 'out of his mind'. But love seems empowering for Horace – the poet's love song for Lalage in *Od.* 1.22 protects him from wild beasts as he walks in the woods; this is a poem in which Horace famously claims his lyric persona to be *integer vitae* ('wholesome in life', *Od.* 1.22.1).[31] In *Od.* 3.7 Horace appropriates and redeploys a series of elegiac clichés; but the point now is that he overwhelms any elegiac edginess with a timely measure of Horatian common sense. This is best demonstrated by the interaction of Chloe and Gyges. Chloe's methodology is strongly suggestive of the content and strategy of an elegiac poem:

> narrat paene datum Pelea Tartaro,
> Magnessam Hippolyten dum fugit abstinens;
>   et peccare docentes
>   fallax historias mouet.   20
>
> frustra: nam scopulis surdior Icari
> uoces audit adhuc integer.
>   Hor. *Od.* 3.7.17–22

---

[28] Syndikus (1972–3) vol. ii 98–102, Cairns (1995) 68–72.
[29] Davis (1991) 44.
[30] See generally Gibson (2007) for the characterisation of lyric and elegy along thematic lines of centrality and extremity, respectively.
[31] See the excellent discussion of Oliensis (1998) 110.

(Re-)claiming Augustan *Fides*

She speaks of Peleus, nearly condemned to Tartarus for fleeing in abstinence from Magnessian Hippolyte; and deceitfully she offers stories that teach faithlessness. Yet in vain, for deafer than the cliffs of Icaros he listens to her suit, but remains intact.

Chloe carries out her seduction through an intermediary (a technique much approved by an elegiac Ovid) and her approach is labelled elegiacally *fallax*, comprising mythic stories apt to encourage wrongdoing. But at this critical moment the lyric narrator intervenes with an emphatic *frustra* at the head of line 21: in the context of Horace's poem, Chloe's persuasive efforts will be 'in vain', since Gyges will prove a resistant lyric listener to the elegiac siren call. In a marvellous oxymoron, Gyges will 'listen deafly' (*surdior ... uoces audit*, *Od.* 3.7.21–2), and will remain 'wholesome' (*integer*, *Od.* 3.7.22), just like Horace himself. By aligning Horatian wholesomeness with Augustan *fides* through the faithful couple Gyges and Asterie, in small measure Horace both manoeuvers his lyric writing towards centre stage and relegates elegiac sentiment to the Augustan margins.

But in 3.12 Propertius responds in kind. In fact, Propertius' rebuttal is tellingly straightforward: he simply, yet firmly, reappropriates the representation of (marital) *fides* for elegy, using an approach similar to that which Horace had originally employed against elegy.[32] Propertius' approach here is to outdo Horace at playing Horace: Horace had intervened as narrator to warn Asterie off from listening to elegiac song, and so to assert lyric *fides*; but Propertius' retort is that Galla's elegiac *fides* is so securely founded that she has no need of Horace's intervention in the first place.[33] In fact, so wholehearted is Propertius' response in this comparative reading that, by contrast, it is Horace's poem that ends up looking a little deviously 'elegiac' in its tone, and more suggestive of an ironic reading that privileges the space Horace gives to the seductive

---

[32] Cairns (1995) 71.
[33] The way here in which elegy asserts a moral superiority over lyric in essence repeats a claim it has already made over epic: see Wiggers (1977).

attractions of Enipeus over the advice that he gives to Asterie to stay constant.[34]

There may yet lie one further Propertian riposte in this passage. At *Od.* 3.7.21–2 Horace presents a Gyges who will 'listen deafly' to Chloe's elegiac singing; and Harrison may be right to suggest that an allusion to Odysseus' encounter with the Sirens lies behind Horace's rebuffing of elegy at this point.[35] Propertius himself includes a swift summary of Odysseus' travels in 3.12, at the moment of Postumus' transformation into an *alter Vlixes* (3.12.24–37). Heyworth's 2007 *OCT* makes a suggestive emendation to the episode of the Sirens at 3.12.34, printing *lyras* in place of the transmitted *lacus*:[36]

> nigrantisque domos animarum intrasse silentum,
>   Sirenum surdo remige adisse lyras ...
>
>   3.12.33–4

> entering the black halls of the silent spirits; approaching the Sirens' lyres with deafened sailors ...

Heyworth's text thus contrives a Propertian hero who deafly approaches the lyres of the Sirens. If this is correct, then not only has Propertius completed a straightforward reappropriation of Horatian *fides*, but he has redeployed exactly the metaphor that Horace had used – in jabbing straight back at Horace.

The Unlikely Orthodoxy of Propertian Elegy

One means of dealing with the unparalleled presence of a married couple within a Propertian elegy has been to treat Aelia Galla's chastity with a kind of wry irony.[37] In such a reading, any lingering discomfort about the ways in which Galla does not 'fit' the elegiac value system is eased by treating her presence in any literal sense as an impossibility. Here the poem's final line (*uincit Penelopes Aelia Galla fidem*, 3.12.38) becomes

---

[34] Owens (1992).
[35] Harrison (1988) 191.
[36] See textual discussion at Heyworth (2007b) 346–7.
[37] See e.g. Fedeli (1985) 398.

The Unlikely Orthodoxy of Propertian Elegy

not elegiac conversion to a newly chaste ideal, but rather suggestive hyperbole. It is claimed that Galla will surpass the faithfulness of Penelope – but of course that is impossible, just as Postumus cannot really be Ulysses:[38] Penelope has always been the very pinnacle of literary loyalty, and to claim that Galla will surpass her in fidelity is as absurd as claiming that a girl will not give in to the gifts of a seductive poet. In fact, the elegiac world can return to order since we can assume that Galla will be deceiving her absent husband just as Penelope was probably cheating Odysseus and – as even our poem makes clear through his visit to Calypso at 3.12.31 – as Odysseus was cheating Penelope.[39] Ironic readings of this kind are encouraged by the somewhat easier way that *Od.* 3.7 yields to such an approach,[40] as well as by the belief that Propertius will only ever offer one particular point of view: as such, the faithfulness he claims to find in Galla must be ironic, since in the very next poem he declares that no Roman woman has faith (3.13.24); and in 3.20 (chapter 8), Propertius himself will suddenly play the disruptive role of Horace's seductive Enipeus, actively trying to lead astray a woman whose husband is away on business.

Then again 3.12 should alert us to the fact that the ideal of faithfulness, just the way we find it in this poem, has in fact always marked the elegiac ethos, despite the surface obsession about infidelity.[41] The strongest link of Prop. 3.12 to *Od.* 3.7 comes at the start of the last couplet of Propertius' poem, with the words *nec frustra*:

> nec frustra, quia casta domi persederat uxor.
> 3.12.37
>
> Not in vain, since his wife stayed chaste at home.

Horace had made the word *frustra* pivotal in his poem, at the moment of his lyric intervention to keep Gyges separate from

---

[38] E.g. Jacobson (1976) 162, Brouwers (2006) 220.
[39] The inevitability of infidelity in such situations will be reasserted once again at 3.20, when Propertius will cast himself as the successful seducer of a girl whose *uir* – like Postumus in 3.12 – has left her behind in pursuit of wealth abroad.
[40] See n. 14 above.
[41] E.g. Janan (2001) 103, writing rhetorically with reference to 4.7, uses in part elegy's reliance on a 'traditional' ideal of *fides* to undermine the apparent

Chloe (*Od.* 3.7.21). In this context, Propertius does more, in his poem, than comment upon the reward for Odysseus' labours; with the words <u>nec</u> *frustra* Propertius can be heard rejecting the very premise of Horace's elegiac parody. Propertius' point is – and Horace would have known very well – that the kind of *duritia* displayed by both Gyges and Asterie is actually very much at home in elegy. Horace had sought to thwart the elegiac project by urging his *puella* to ignore the lover singing out in the street.[42] But, in elegy, the girl *always* ignores the lover who sings out in the street. At the end of his ode, Horace urges Asterie *difficilis mane* – but, if she is truly an elegiac *puella*, she is already quite *difficilis* enough.[43] In fact, it is not hard to sustain a reading that elegy is essentially about loyalty, either that which the lover desires of the *puella* for himself or that which he laments of the *puella* for her husband. And, even then, perhaps Cynthia has an exaggerated reputation for disloyalty, in Propertius' case. When Propertius has come home late, as he does at the very beginning of the corpus at 1.3, he does find Cynthia there waiting for him (and spinning wool, indeed, Penelope-fashion); just so, at the other end of the collection, when Cynthia finally offers her own extensive version of elegiac history in 4.7, it is precisely her own wifely faithfulness that she chooses to assert. If *fides* is to be an Augustan theme, it will not take much tweaking on Propertius' part to demonstrate that elegy is (still) the vehicle through which to express it.

Perhaps the thematic palinode that best expresses the tension between elegiac paranoia and elegiac 'reality' comes in a pair of lines presented at the beginning of the chapter:

> mane erat, et uolui, si sola quiesceret illa,
>   uisere: at in lecto Cynthia sola fuit.
>   2.29.23–4

It was dawn; I wanted to see if she slept alone: and alone she was there, in her bed.

---

distinction between the elegiac *puella* and the kind of matronal woman symbolised by Galla: 'How different, in truth, is the elegiac ethos from the *mos maiorum*?'
[42] This perspective is well explained at Cairns (1995) 74.
[43] In Cynthia's own words, in fact: *non ego tam facilis*, 'I am not so easy' (2.29.33).

The Unlikely Orthodoxy of Propertian Elegy

When the paranoid Propertius arrives early that morning to check on Cynthia's bedroom, he finds that she is there, sleeping quite alone. Seen in this light, on the one hand Cynthia and Galla appear disconcertingly as simply different incarnations of the same character: Galla may not be won over by gifts; but then, neither was Cynthia. Yet – on the other hand – things must seem a little different now, all the same. In 2.29, the poem's weight had fallen on Propertius' distrust; now, in 3.12, it falls instead on the girl's *fides*.[44] This difference has consequence: it is of no small importance that the tension between erotic paranoia and amatory fidelity in 2.29 is instrumental in perpetuating the lover's signature unhappiness, even towards the end of Book 2 (Cynthia's displeasure at being investigated results in Propertius having 'no happy night since then', *ex illo felix nox mihi nulla fuit*, 2.29.42). In 3.12, by contrast, the unwavering focus on Galla's steadiness offers an early hint of an elegiac 'happily ever after', and the sense of closure for erotic poetry that this must bring with it.[45] Here, through a narrative that still belongs safely to others, we might catch a glimpse of the eventual union in perpetuity of Propertius and Cynthia that features morbidly in 4.7, and which is enacted finally by Cynthia's triumph at the end of 4.8.

We have seen that Galla provides a conspicuous moment of refocus at the heart of Book 3. By drawing renewed attention to the kind of patience already displayed by the elegiac mistress in 1.3, and even by foreshadowing Cornelia's matronliness in 4.11, Propertius reasserts elegy's relevance (for better or worse) to one of the emerging themes of the early Principate. But Galla also causes the poetry to take a step towards realising the truism that Propertius had prophesied back at 1.12.20: that 'Cynthia' will prove to have been both (at) the start and the end.

---

[44] In this way, the thematic pattern of 3.12 also reverses the pattern expressed back at 1.11.17–18: there, a concession that he believes Cynthia to be faithful gives way, all the same, to Propertius' fixation on infidelity; now, by contrast, the implicit suggestion of infidelity that underpins the opening of 3.12 is displaced by the emphatic example of faithfulness on Galla's part.

[45] So too with Catullus' emphasis on an 'eternal bond of sacred friendship' (*aeternum hoc sanctae foedus amicitiae*, 109.6) in his 'final' Lesbia poem; and with the sudden introduction of a married persona (and the theme of chastity) in Ovid *Am.* 3.13.

CHAPTER 5

DELAYS AND DESTINATIONS

Propertius 3.16

3.16 is Propertius' most sustained engagement with the theme of travel. Journeys of various kinds abound in Book 3, yet 3.16 promises us only the second literal expedition: in 3.7 the poet recounted the merchant Paetus' doomed attempt to cross the Mediterranean; now Propertius himself contemplates a dangerous night journey to Tibur, after receiving a midnight summons from his mistress. Inasmuch as the theme of travel sets up expectation of a destination,[1] in thematic terms Propertius' proposed journey in 3.16 teases the reader with the prospect of a path that leads once more to Cynthia. But we find instead a poem which resists a desire for conclusion, and which further displaces erotic narration by a continuing focus on elegiac poetics. Unexpectedly for erotic elegy, 3.16 narrates a journey to Cynthia which the poet wants not to end. The ending, when it does come, is not at Tibur with Cynthia but at the poet's idealised tomb, dressed up in Callimachean detail. In fact, in a basic sense this is a journey that never quite begins. For all that the poem springs from the poet's desire to get to Cynthia, 3.16 ends up revelling instead in the delays and diversions to which travel is subject. Ironically, this is a travel poem very much about not moving forwards.

This chapter examines the travel narrative in 3.16 first as an expression of the Propertian lover's (waning) desire for his mistress, and then more broadly as a symbol for the other 'journeys' made by the poet in Book 3, especially (but not only) towards an apparent renunciation of erotic elegy. In the context of the third book, 'travelling towards Cynthia' invites

---

[1] See too Hor. *Od.* 2.6.5–8 for Tibur itself as symbol of a desirable endpoint for one's travels.

In Medias Res

both amatory and closural approaches at the same time. 3.16 suggests its poet's switching focus from realist narrative, and yet a reluctance at the same time to abandon elegy's fundamental eroticism.

In Medias Res

Eschewing its destination, the poet's journey in 3.16 embraces instead the idea of the centre.[2] Each of the poem's three ten-line sections makes marked reference to the middle, placing the word *medius* either in its opening or concluding couplet (*nox media*, 1; *media uia*, 12; *media uia*, 30); and in each case the poet meditates on an aspect of centrality, in turn as an occasion for decision-making, as a shared space of safety, and in the end negatively as a space to be abandoned in preference for the exclusivity of the leafy fringe. Yet, in what announces itself as a love poem, the poet's fascination with the centre represents an elusive engagement with erotic themes. In one sense, Propertius celebrates middleness as the exclusive domain of lovers; in another sense, the lover's desire to remain in the centre ironically keeps him distant from Cynthia, and furthers a growing sense of disengagement from a personal erotic narrative. A similar ambivalence is present in the way that the poem's focus on 'middleness' acts against the narrative momentum implied by the poem's travel motif. At the heart of the poem (and in a collection which ends with erotic *renuntiatio*), the lover's contentment in the middle of the road (and the poem) suggests a reluctance to follow a journey to 'the end'; by contrast, the recovery of a Callimachean aesthetic as the poem ends – figured precisely as a symbolic move away from the centre – suggests the inevitability of conclusion. However, rather than finally hastening the lover on the path to his mistress, the poem's own ending leaves the path altogether

---

[2] For various perspectives on the significance of the literary middle in structural and more abstract terms, see Kyriakidis & De Martino (2004); see also Gibson (2007) for discussion of aesthetic moderation as negotiating a path between poetic extremes.

Delays and Destinations: Propertius 3.16

to find a new destination – and so, seemingly, the poet's diminishing interest in overtly erotic writing is further affirmed.

From the outset the poem's focus on centrality evokes elegy's eroticism while also suggesting a growing displacement of its erstwhile erotic focus. The first two words of the poem establish its temporal setting – midnight – and so plunge us into the middle of things:[3]

> Nox media, et dominae mihi uenit epistula nostrae:
>   Tibure me missa iussit adesse mora.
>   3.16.1–2

Midnight, and a letter has arrived for me from my mistress: she orders me to be at Tibur, and to dispense with delay.

For the Propertian lover night is the much-anticipated occasion for erotic encounters. At 3.8 – the corresponding poem to 3.16, concluding Book 3's opening set of elegies – nighttime provided the setting for a lengthy (and increasingly rare) erotic battle between poet and mistress. More recently at 3.10 Propertius looked forward to nightfall (and the lovemaking that comes with it) as the destination of a 'journey' through his mistress's birthday. But the current poem opens at midnight to reveal Propertius alone. The arrival of a letter from his mistress replaces the arrival of the mistress herself; her summons of the poet to Tibur promises but defers erotic activity (cf. 3.8) until the lover completes a new and now literal journey (cf. 3.10). And so, in 3.16, midnight becomes a time not for making love but for the lover to make a crucial choice.

To begin with, the explicit statement of the lover's dilemma emphasises the poem's engagement with structure as well as the ironic transformation of (mid)night from a time of sexual excitement to one of physical apprehension:

> quid faciam? obductis committam mene tenebris,
>   ut timeam audaces in mea membra manus?
> at si distulero haec nostro mandata timore,
>   nocturno fletus saeuior hoste mihi.
>   3.16.5–8

---

[3] The opening couplet also suggests the poem's sub-genre as a variation of a *komos*: see Cairns (2010) 79–83.

In Medias Res

What am I to do? Shall I trust myself to the shrouding darkness, so that I should fear reckless hands attacking my body? But if I put off these instructions due to my fear, my mistress's weeping will be more savage to me than a nocturnal enemy.

Symbolically, the poem's 'central' question *quid faciam?* comes in the fifth line, so beginning the middle couplet of the opening set of ten lines, and reinforcing the sense in the poem's opening words (*nox media*) that the midpoint now represents decision time for the lover. Further, whereas in 3.8 Propertius had welcomed his mistress's nocturnal assault on his body (*tu uero nostros audax inuade capillos|et mea formosis unguibus ora nota*, 'Indeed, boldly attack my hair, and mark my face with your shapely nails', 3.8.5–6), now darkness causes Propertius to fear 'reckless hands' assailing his limbs (*ut timeam audaces in mea membra manus*, 3.16.6). In fact, as the poem's opening section concludes, an ironic Propertius even comes to fearing (rather than desiring) the prospect of Cynthia raising 'ungentle' hands against him: *in me mansuetas non habet illa manus* (3.16.10).

The opening reference to time also sets the narrative clock ticking, and so plays up a basic tension between the poem's static theme of 'middleness' and the dynamic motifs associated with its 'travel' narrative. The lover's midnight deliberations betray his awareness that his journey towards Cynthia must begin.[4] Propertius does not consider refusing his mistress's demand; significantly, his midnight choice is established as being between 'committing' himself to the path (*committam me*, 5) or, at most, 'deferring' the mandated journey (*distulero haec mandata*, 7). The lover's knowledge that he must eventually accede to the wishes of his mistress complements an irresistible sense of forward motion provided by the poem's several pathways (*uia*, 12, 18, 30; *iter*, 15, 26);[5] the basic theme of progression is similarly reflected in the poem's final section, in the

---

[4] As Richardson (1977) 384 realises: 'He would like to defer going, but does not dare.'
[5] More broadly, see Clarke (2004) 140 for comment on the combined teleological pull of the several journeys represented in the latter half of Book 3.

living poet's knowledge of the inevitability of death (and, he hopes, immortality).[6] Yet the poem's metaphorical drive also serves to highlight the transience of 'middleness' in subjects as linear as life and poetry. As a result, the poem's simultaneous fascination with centrality attains a certain poignancy: idealised though it might be by a lover, it cannot remain midnight for long.[7]

Over the course of its remaining two sections, the poem affirms thematic passage from middle to end. In the first instance, it is unsurprising that, in a poem with overt focus on centrality, the middle sequence explores 'middleness' to the greatest extent. Given his early apprehension about travelling to Tibur, it comes as an epiphanic discovery for the narrator that the peculiar invulnerability of lovers to harm allows him to walk the middle of the road in safety:

> nec tamen est quisquam, sacros qui laedat amantis:
>   Scironis media sic licet ire uia.
> quisquis amator erit, Scythicis licet ambulet oris,
>   nemo adeo ut noceat barbarus esse uolet.
> luna ministrat iter, demonstrant astra salebras,   15
>   ipse Amor accensas percutit ante faces,
> saeua canum rabies morsus auertit hiantis:
>   huic generi quouis tempore tuta uia est.
> sanguine tam paruo quis enim spargatur amantis
>   improbus? exclusis fit comes ipsa Venus.   20
>   3.16.11–20

But there is not anyone who would harm sacred lovers: so it is permitted to travel down the middle of Sciron's highway. Whoever will be a lover, even though he walk on Scythian shores, no one will wish to be so barbarous as to harm him. The moon attends his path, the stars point out the rough places, Love himself shakes the blazing torch in front of him, the savage madness of dogs averts their gaping jaws: the highway is safe for this type of person at whatever time they please. For who is so cruel as to shed the meagre blood of a lover? Venus comes forth as companion for those lovers on their own.

---

[6] Putnam (1980) 104.
[7] Cf. the god Mercury's comic prolonging of night at Plaut. *Amph.* 112–14 in order to indulge Jupiter's amorous liaison with Alcumena.

In Medias Res

Here 3.16 furthers its ambivalent attitude to the familiar expression of Propertian elegy as 'erotic' poetry. On the one hand, Propertius' very fantasy about his own invincibility is a clear celebration of his amatory status. Here Propertius invokes the commonplace that 'lovers are sacred',[8] and his poem even flags the invulnerable lover as a 'genre' in his own right (*huic generi*, 18). On the other hand, in the middle of the poem Propertius seemingly forgets the erotic purpose of his journey. The sudden fascination of the Propertian lover with his own (literary) status further impedes the poem's progress towards Cynthia, and so towards the realisation of the poetry in its signature form as a personal narrative of lover and mistress. In structural terms, the exercise of the lover's invulnerability becomes a self-sustaining end in itself – the lover shows no desire to leave the road (nor the poem's middle) and in doing so threatens to finish the poem's journey halfway through.

Nonetheless, the central symbolism of 3.16 remains playfully awry and aesthetically provocative – and, ultimately, unsustainable. For a start, there is an ironic aspect to Propertius' engagement of motif of a lover's invulnerability. A useful point of contrast comes in Horace's 'Lalage' ode (1.22), a poem in which Horace claims his own love song once saved him from attack by a Sabine wolf. Horace's status as lover thereby enables the poet to wander carefree at the very fringes of his poetic world (*ultra|terminum curis uagor expeditis*, *Od.* 1.22.11–12);[9] by contrast, the Propertian lover is empowered to confront dangers in a conspicuously central space – mid-road at midnight. (Perhaps there is a satiric prod here in the direction of Horace in particular, whose poetic persona simultaneously inhabits the fringe (as in *Od.* 1.22) and famously shuns the common crowd (*Od.* 3.1.1), and yet advises his reader (*Od.* 2.10.5) to embrace

---

[8] E.g. Hor. *Od.* 1.22.9–16, Tib. 1.2.25–30. See also Richardson (1977) 385–6, on 3.16 lines 11 and 20; and generally Nisbet & Hubbard (1970) 262–3. For further special qualities of the lover in contrast to other men, see also Propertius 2.27.
[9] On Horace's (unelegiac) mastery of his own desire in this poem, see Oliensis (1998) 110.

the very middling *aurea mediocritas*.)¹⁰ Most of all, there is ironic amusement in finding the Propertian narrator – who, at the outset of the collection, had described the approach to the Muses as being 'not broad' (*non lata uia*, 3.1.14) and the path of his poetry as being 'untrod' (*intacta uia*, 3.1.18) – feeling so comfortable here in the middle of the common highroad.

In this context, the final section of the poem corrects the lover's position with a Callimachean move away from the centre.¹¹ Here the narrating lover prays that, should mortal injury befall him, his faithful mistress will establish his tomb in a remote location:

> quod si certa meos sequerentur funera casus,
>   talis mors pretio uel sit emenda mihi.
> afferet haec unguenta mihi sertisque sepulcrum
>   ornabit custos ad mea busta sedens.
> di faciant, mea ne terra locet ossa frequenti,   25
>   qua facit assiduo tramite uulgus iter!
> post mortem tumuli sic infamantur amantum.
> me tegat arborea deuia terra coma,
> aut humer ignotae cumulis uallatus harenae:
>   non iuuat in media nomen habere uia.   30
>   3.16.21–30

But if an assured funeral were to follow my demise, I would be obliged to purchase such a death whatever the price. My mistress will bring me perfumes, and adorn my tomb with wreaths, sitting watch as a guard at my grave. May the gods grant that she does not place my bones in a crowded place, where the common crowd makes its journey by the busy road! Thus, after death, the tombs of lovers are defamed. Let earth distant from the path cover me with arboreal foliage, else let me be buried walled in by heaps of unmarked sand: it does not please to have a name in the middle of the highway.

---

[10] See Gibson (2007) for discussion of the Horatian 'middle way' (esp. 17–19) and Propertian rejection of moderation (esp. 44–5); see 24–34 for the interaction between Propertius and Horace with regard to the aesthetics of 'the middle'.

[11] The trajectory of the poem in approaching its end represents not only a symbolic move away from the middle but also a reduction in scope. The text moves from a consideration of lovers as a 'class' to a more exclusive focus on the Propertian lover in particular, who is represented explicitly as being removed even from the generally exclusive class of lovers: 3.16.27–8, with Richardson (1977) 386.

In Medias Res

Highly stylised in its detail,[12] the portrait of the lover's resting place expresses the poet's literary desire as much as it does the lover's amatory and geographical sensibilities.[13] Here, as befits the epitaph of a poet whose current collection opens with an appeal to Callimachus, the narrator emphasises especially the exclusivity of his monument, placing it in good Callimachean fashion well away from the dust and noise of the crowd that traverses the middle of the road (25–6, 28–30),[14] just as in earlier depictions of his eventual funeral the narrator has focused on the similarly poetically appropriate values of brevity and narrowness (2.1.71–2, 2.13.31–4).[15] Of course, the poet's imagined death provides a suitably closural symbol for the poem's final section, in the same way that the lover's excitement at centrality marked the poem's middle. Yet, in the sense that 3.16 begins as a travel poem towards Cynthia, the literariness of the poem's ending continues a trend which began ostentatiously in 3.1 to prioritise a focus on poetics over the poetry's signature eroticism.[16] Here the remote (and so Callimachean) soil that would cover the poet's body (*deuia terra*, 28) explicitly marks the poem's departure from the road that leads to Cynthia; and, while the mistress is still a desired presence at the new destination for the poet's journey, she is less the object of erotic interest than the agent (*custos*, 24) responsible for ensuring the Alexandrian symbolism of the poet's burial.

---

[12] Putnam (1980) 104.
[13] Such an affinity between poetics and the materiality of an imagined tomb is common in elegy: see esp. Houghton (2007) 161.
[14] For Propertius' wider use of this imagery see Richardson (1977) 386, Houghton (2007) 161. It is interesting to note in passing that Houghton (166f.) links the unelegiac death and burial of Paetus in 3.7 with Paetus' rejection of elegiac values, including partly his rejection of poverty and pursuit instead of wealth; and yet the very elegiac tomb of Propertius in 3.16 comes as a result of a death for which the narrator would seemingly pay, possibly handsomely (*talis mors pretio uel sit emenda mihi*, 3.16.22: see Camps (1966) 131).
[15] Wilkinson (1966) 142–3, Houghton (2007) 168.
[16] As such, the depiction of the poet's tomb at 3.16.23–30 closely realises the explicitly *literary* predictions surrounding the poet's death at 3.1.35–8. Both these passages closely correct the terms of the poet's mortal pessimism at imagining his own (literal) death at 1.19.21–2: Houghton (2007) 162.

Postponing 'the End'

In a broader sense, the poem's early fascination with 'middleness' reflects an anxiety connected with the poem's position at the end of the book's central sequence. As the last 'middle' poem in the collection, 3.16 represents the final opportunity for poet and reader alike to defer confrontation with what must seem the end of Propertian elegy when an overtly closural group begins at 3.17 with Propertius' prayer to Bacchus for release from servitude to love.[17] In this context, the mooted journey towards Cynthia in 3.16 suggests in miniature the collection's overall movement towards (the climactic naming of) Cynthia in the book's final poems. Given that the book's journey ends with rejection of the mistress in 3.24, the poet's reluctance to leave 'the middle of the road', and even the poem's narrative move 'off course' in its closing section, suggest a wider disinclination to engage with the process of ending up. In this chapter's final section, such thematic synergy between 3.16 and Book 3 as a whole underpins two further approaches which briefly explore the way the poem's literal journey (especially its vacillation about onward movement) engages with more metaphorical journeys that a poet might pursue.

To begin with, the flamboyant enshrining of the poet's Callimachean reputation at the poem's 'destination' invites a metapoetic rereading of the poem's opening, precisely where the motif of the poet's journey originates. Here the lover's initial unease about setting foot on a dangerous road evokes closural anxiety of a more literary kind: a *topos* relating to authorial fear of finally releasing a text to an audience. Poetic concern with the dangers of publication is relatively commonplace. Propertius will later reveal more explicit interest in the publication of his work in 3.23, alluding at the end of that poem to the last line from Horace's first book of *Satires* in which Horace indicates that he has committed the collection

---

[17] For 3.17 as the first 'closural' poem in Book 3, see Courtney (1970) 48, Barsby (1974) 136–7, Hutchinson (1984) 106, Newman (2006) 346.

Postponing 'the End'

to the public.[18] Horace, Ovid and Martial all address cautionary poems to their emergent poetry books,[19] and, pertinently, a common feature is precisely the presentation of the publication of a text as 'travel' beyond the safety of its author's custody.[20] In this context, Propertius' equivocation about beginning his 'journey' suggestively evokes fear of assault on his *textual body*:[21]

> quid faciam? obductis committam mene tenebris,
> ut timeam audaces in mea membra manus?
> 3.16.5–6

> What am I to do? Shall I trust myself to the shrouding darkness, so that I should fear reckless hands attacking my body?

In as much as poets view publication as a loss of textual control, the verb *committere* (5) supports the sense of 'entrusting' or 'resigning' oneself to the care of others, as well as the narrative sense of 'undertaking' a journey. The term *membra* (6) can figure not only physical arms and legs but the individual parts of a poem or literary work.[22] More literally, the hands (*manus*, 6) of a text's readers are indeed seen as having the potential to cause damage to the physical text itself; in *Epistles* 1.20, for instance, Horace playfully warns his poetry book that it risks grubby disfigurement when it passes into the *hands* of the common

---

[18] Propertius 3.23.23: *i, puer, et citus haec aliqua propone columna* ('Go, boy, and quickly set forth these words on some column'); recalling Horace *Satires* 1.10.92: *i, puer, atque meo citus haec subscribe libello* ('Go, boy, and quickly append these words to my little book'). See Comber (1998) 51, Pelling (2002) 173; also Cairns (1972) 76f.
[19] Hor. *Epist.* 1.20; Ovid *Trist.* 1.1, Martial 1.3, 11.1.
[20] Horace, for instance, expresses concern at the text passing beyond the author's control once it is published: *A.P.* 390–1: *delere licebit|quod non edideris; nescit uox missa reuerti* ('You can destroy what you haven't published; once it has been sent forth, the word knows not how to return'); similarly at Hor. *Epist.* 1.20.5–6: *fuge quo descendere gestis.|non erit emisso reditus tibi* ('Then flee, my book, to where you long to descend. There will be no returning for you, once you've been let loose').
[21] At *Trist.* 1.1.3–14 Ovid similarly blurs the distinction between his own physical wellbeing and the physical condition of his book; see Hinds (1985) 13, and generally Tissol (2005), but esp. 99–102.
[22] E.g. Pliny *Epist.* 8.4.7: *itaque a me ... spectabuntur ut membra* ('I will look upon your work as fragments'); cf. also Cic. *Partitiones Oratoriae* 118: *haec accusationis fere membra sunt* ('These are, in general, the constituent parts of an accusation').

crowd (*contrectatus ubi <u>manibus</u> sordescere uolgi\coeperis*, 1.20.11–12).[23]

Similarly, when setting the programme for the poem's middle section Propertius' epiphany is that there is none who would 'wound' him (*qui laedat*, 3.16.11) on his journey. Again, underpinned by the motif of travel, Propertius' language combines a narrative of physical harm with evocation of literary reception: Ovid, addressing his poetry book as it sets off for Rome in the first poem of his *Tristia,* describes the capacity of poetry both to cause and receive wounds (*ne te mea carmina laedant*, *Tr.* 1.1.63); in the same vein, Horace warns his own book that it runs the risk of physical injury (*te laeserit*, 1.20.7) in its desire to reach actual readers. More strikingly still, Propertius' vivid image of rabid dogs averting the 'gaping bitings' (*morsus hiantis,* 17) of their jaws calls closely upon the language of (literary) criticism: the noun *morsus* ('a biting') and its cognate verb *mordere* ('to bite') are employed commonly in literary contexts to describe the envious gnawing of carping critics.[24] These echoes highlight 3.16's metapoetic engagement with centrality as an aspect of the collection's structure. The freedom from physical assault experienced by the lover as he strides the middle of the highroad reflects the sanctuary from criticism enjoyed by the poet, so long as he lingers in the middle of the work.

One further approach to the poem as a whole appeals paradoxically to an overarching eroticism in 3.16 in a way that binds together the mortal fears of the lover and the literary concerns of the poet. 3.16 plays with a tension it generates between the essentially static motif of 'middleness' and the teleological drive of its travel imagery, where in various senses the 'central' poem seeks to postpone the acknowledged inevitability of yielding eventually to an ending. Here the fundamental theme of the poem is apparent neither in the motifs of centrality nor travel themselves; instead, the poem becomes a

---

[23] Cf. also the wearing effect of hands on the physical book (here, *tabellae*) at Prop. 3.23.3: *has quondam <u>nostris</u> <u>manibus</u> detriuerat usus* ('Use at my hands has long since worn these tablets down').
[24] E.g. Hor. *Od.* 4.3.16; Hor. *Epist.* 1.14.38; Ovid *Trist.* 1.1.25; Martial 5.80.13.

Postponing 'the End'

performance of the very theme which the mistress's letter seeks to proscribe in the poem's opening couplet – the essentially erotic motif of delay.

The opening of 3.16 announces the arrival of the letter and the summons to Tibur, but it also introduces (only to dismiss) the concept of *mora*:[25]

> Nox media, et dominae mihi uenit epistula nostrae:
> Tibure me missa iussit adesse mora.
>
> 3.16.1–2
>
> Midnight, and a letter has arrived for me from my mistress: she orders me to be at Tibur, and to dispense with delay.

These opening lines purport both to give the poem a destination and to hasten the reader towards it – the use of *adesse* (even more so than *missa mora*) actually seeks to omit the necessary journey altogether, instead uniting lover and mistress at Tibur in an instant.[26] But, as Ovid demonstrates in *Amores* 1.5 (*quis cetera nescit?*), the destination itself makes a poor subject for amatory poetry. Lingering on the delights and diversions of the journey – that is, actively deferring the climax – makes for more 'erotic' writing, and reading too.[27] In a general sense the erotics of deferral even underpins the broader seductive elusiveness of elegy.[28] It is within this framework that the various poetic narratives of 3.16 actually subvert the expectations created by the poem's opening couplet. As the poem begins the narrating lover seems aware that he *must* travel, and that the demands of his mistress (the requirements of his Muse, the needs of the poem, the inevitability of the completed book and of his own *fama*) cannot be put off. As such, the poem invites the belief that 'the path of love ends in Tibur'.[29] Yet by the poem's end the lover's journey has not led there – indeed,

---

[25] Cf. Cairns (2010) 73, speculating that Propertius includes *mora* as an anagram of *Roma* as 'an elegant verbal sophistication'.
[26] Richardson (1977) 385.
[27] Sharrock (1995) 152.
[28] E.g. Connolly (2000) 75. It is suggestive to note the presence of 'delay' in Propertius' programmatic defence of elegy at 3.9.36: *tota sub exiguo flumine nostra mora est*.
[29] Putnam (1980) 104.

it is not even certain that he has set out.[30] To put it another way, the poem opens with the lover considering two possible courses of action, and encourages its reader to believe that the narrator opts for the first of these – to 'commit' himself (*committam me*, 5) to the road to Tibur. But the poem's second and third sections prove the journey actually to be a diversion from its stated destination, first towards a celebration of the lover's especial generic qualities, and then to a statement of the poet's assured and exclusive immortality. As the poem's paradoxically static narrative demonstrates, the reader's expectation of an erotic destination is set up – only to be frustrated.[31]

In the end the poem has adopted as its programme the lover's second course, that of deferral (*distulero*, 7), leaving both reader and narrator effectively as remote from Tibur at the end of the poem as they were at the beginning. In a basic sense, 3.16 contrives once more to keep the lover apart from his mistress, deferring still further the possibility of their happy union that would threaten the need for the existence of elegiac lament;[32] in a broader sense, the wandering narrative of this avowedly central poem avoids engaging with any wider implication of closure, preferring instead to make the most of erotic verse's time in the spotlight. But the Propertian narrator also knows that deferral only lasts so long. For all that 3.16 delights in the safety of centrality, we will see in the following chapter that the very next poem (3.17) finds Propertius praying to Bacchus for release from servitude to love – and suddenly he and we are staring directly, not at closure in the happy union of poet and mistress, but at what seems the bitter breaking up of Propertian erotic elegy.

---

[30] E.g. Richardson (1977) 384.
[31] Cf. Prop. 2.15, with Connolly (2000) 78–9.
[32] Cf. Tib. 1.2, where similarly the narrator takes advantage of a lover's invulnerability to travel through the inhospitable night to his mistress's house – only there to be blocked still by a locked door.

CHAPTER 6

A HYMN TO BACCHUS

Propertius 3.17

Augustan literature gives particular prominence to Bacchus.[1] At 3.17, Propertius makes his most substantial contribution, a full-length Bacchic hymn in which he pleads for relief from the pain of love, and for inspiration to rise above the lowly poetry he writes. In terms of love elegy, 3.17 presents itself as an ostentatiously closural poem that points the way to the poet's attempt to dismiss Cynthia once and for all as the book comes to a close; yet it is also a densely allusive poem that builds upon a rich and fundamentally ambiguous cultural narrative so as to call into question the poet's desire actually to leave elegy behind.

A number of Augustan literary Bacchuses in different genres provide an essential backdrop to Propertius 3.17. Reflecting the enigmatic nature of the god himself, we find here a pair of clashing motifs. In one sense, Bacchus offers teasingly to cohere with an Augustan narrative of revitalisation and rebirth. So Virgil had turned to a verdant Bacchus at the start of his second book of *Georgics* as a way of leaving behind the portentous chaos which concludes the first book. Horace – who addresses Bacchus in his *Odes* more than he does any other god – affirms Bacchus' positive role as (lyric) music-maker and bringer of merriment; in fact, in his final ode Horace aligns his own poetic task with Augustus' imperial project, uniting the two under 'amid the cheerful gifts of Bacchus' (*inter iocosi munera Liberi*, *Od.* 4.15.26). Even Tibullus, in only his second elegy, adapts the lyric poet's symposiastic appeal to Bacchus in the hope of easing the pain of an elegist's signature vigil outside his mistress's locked door. At the same time, however, Bacchus is an infamously capricious god, whose favour

---
[1] Troxler-Keller (1964) 56–64; Nisbet & Hubbard (1978) 314–17.

A Hymn to Bacchus: Propertius 3.17

is sought at the risk of unwanted and often ruinous consequences. For Tibullus, appealing to Bacchus only compounds his elegiac solitude, making his lonely vigil worse. And Horace devotes his more substantial Bacchic poems to exploring Bacchus' potent flip-side as a dangerous and turbulent influence: in *Odes* 2.19 and 3.25, Bacchic inspiration dramatically overwhelms the moderate poet, driving him towards a scale of poetic and political ambition that sits seemingly against the poet's better judgement.

As Horace's poetry in particular makes clear, the presence of Bacchus in Augustan literature inevitably interacts – often tensely – with the reorganisation of political symbols during the early Augustan period, when the divisiveness of triumviral imagery was still potent.[2] Most significantly, here, Mark Antony had adopted Dionysus as his political avatar (and Antony's political biography captures well the double-edged nature of Bacchic contact). No doubt Antony intended to associate himself with Bacchus' populist side as a harbinger of song and pleasure; but Antony's fateful decision allowed Octavian, in the guise of Apollo, to tarnish him with Bacchus' edgier aspect as an intemperate, tyrannical and (therefore) un-Roman deity.[3] As we will see, one effect of Bacchus' Augustan prominence – especially in the poetry of Horace and Propertius – is to expose the *princeps* to the Bacchic immoderation that Octavian had turned against Antony in the decade before, to devastating effect.

Propertius himself turns to Bacchus at a crucial stage in his collection. Within the book's triadic structure, 3.17 is the third of three elegies which introduce broad sequences of eight poems. An address to Callimachus in 3.1 heralds a progressive meditation on the evolving connections between style and content in elegiac writing; then, in 3.9, an elegy for Maecenas

---

[2] For the independence of Horace's stance regarding 'Augustan ideology', see Santirocco (1995).
[3] Both these sides of Bacchus are on tense display in Horace *Odes* 1.37, where Horace reclaims for Rome the celebratory aspects of (moderate) drinking and dancing, while pinning to Cleopatra (and implicitly to Antony) the disorder of unrestrained drunkenness and sexual licence.

Bacchic Oppositions

initiates a variety of approaches to (notably Augustan) morality and its relevance to erotic poetry. Now, an appeal to the liberating nature of Bacchic celebration introduces a final set of elegies which flirt with bringing elegy into alignment with an Augustan mainstream.[4] But here Propertius offers an audacious and ostentatiously self-defeating poem that unwrites the poet's rededication to erotic elegy in 3.1 and promises an imminent end to love poetry – and which yet frames the very idea of abandoning elegy for a higher genre as the deluded raving of a poet who is clearly out of his mind. Both these aspects of 3.17 are important; the poem derives its energy and its humour from the ironic mismatch between the poet's intention and the means by which he hopes to realise it. Moreover, 3.17 revives a playful programmatic game that we have seen elegy perform before. In a very real sense, Propertius' promise here to write 'unhumble' poetry in honour of Bacchus returns us to the programmatic world of 3.9, where Propertius had promised Maecenas to write elevated Augustan epic if only his self-effacing patron would lead the way. Now, as then, Propertius floats the possibility of writing in new modes largely as a way of exploring the developing capacity of elegy itself, rather than as a gesture towards any unelegiac writing that does not (and would never) appear.

Bacchic Oppositions

In a narrative sense, 3.17 begins with the poet's desire to free himself from love's slavery, and so foreshadows the dramatic *renuntiatio* with which the book ends. (Here 3.17 binds with 3.24 in framing Book 3's final eight poems as an outwardly closural set.) As the poem opens, Propertius abases himself before Bacchus' altar in search of erotic guidance:

> nunc, o Bacche, tuis humiles aduoluimur aris:
> da mihi pacatus uela secunda, pater!

---

[4] See Mader (1994) 380–5 for the closural role of 3.17 within the thematic architecture of Book 3.

A Hymn to Bacchus: Propertius 3.17

> tu potes insanae Veneris compescere fastus,
>   curarumque tuo fit medicina mero.
> per te iunguntur, per te soluuntur amantes: 5
>   tu uitium ex animo dilue, Bacche, meo!
> te quoque enim non esse rudem testatur in astris
>   lyncibus ad caelum uecta Ariadna tuis.
> hoc mihi, quod ueteres custodit in ossibus ignis,
>   funera sanabunt aut tua uina malum.   10
>   3.17.1–10

Now, O Bacchus, I humbly prostrate myself before your altar: peacefully, father, grant me favouring sails! You are able to restrain the pride of maddened Venus, and a cure for passion is contained in your wine. Through you lovers are joined, through you they are separated: Bacchus, wash this failing from my heart! That you too are not unskilled in love, there is a witness among the stars in Ariadne carried heavenward by your lynxes. This evil of mine, which watches over the old fires burning in my bones, death will cure – or your wine.

The sacral context (and structural parallel with 3.1) prompts comparison with Propertius' initial appeal for poetic guidance in the grove of Callimachus and Philetas at the beginning of the book. Now Bacchus is set up to offer thematic advice, based on his own particular expertise in amatory matters (*te non rudem*, 3.17.7). Yet here there is also a first hint of the way Bacchus will offer a lesson other than that which the poet claims to be seeking; the credentials that Propertius cites for the god point to his success with women, rather than his empathy with those less blessed with erotic favour.[5] Indeed, at this point 3.17 leaves open the possibility that the desired way of removing the pain of the poet's lovesickness is to bring about the transformation of Cynthia into Propertius' Ariadne (3.17.8).

For the moment, however, another matter is more pressing. One lesson in the poet's midnight summons from Cynthia in

---

[5] Heyworth (2007a) may well be right to move lines 7–8 (the *exemplum* of Ariadne, suggesting Bacchus' erotic affinity with Propertius himself) to after the poem's opening couplet, where they are less intrusive for the general description of Bacchus' powers: see discussion at Heyworth (2007b) 375. In this case, the poem's opening emphasis on erotic success (rather than on successful liberation from love) would be even more marked.

Bacchic Oppositions

3.16 is that Amor will not let Propertius sleep.[6] Accordingly, in 3.17 Propertius prays for the wine god's gift of repose, and promises in return to compose panegyric in Bacchus' honour:

> quod si, Bacche, tuis per feruida tempora donis
> accersitus erit somnus in ossa mea,
> ipse seram uitis pangamque ex ordine collis,   15
> quos carpant nullae me uigilante ferae.
> dum modo purpureo tumeant mihi dolia musto
> et noua pressantis inquinet uua pedes,
> quod superest uitae per te et tua cornua uiuam,
> uirtutisque tuae, Bacche, poeta ferar.   20
> dicam ego maternos Aetnaeo fulmine partus ...
> 3.17.13–21

But if, Bacchus, by your gifts sleep is summoned through my fervid temples into my bones, I myself shall sow vines and plant the hillsides in rows which, under my watchful eye, no wild beasts will plunder. Provided that my vats swell over with purple must and the new grape stain the feet that tread it, I shall live what remains of my life through you and your horns, and I shall be called a poet of your good qualities, Bacchus. I shall speak of your maternal birth by an Aetnan thunderbolt ...

Here life and poetry combine with complementary effect. The lover's closural plea for sleep as relief from amatory distress finds a parallel at a literary level in the poet's declared intention to take up distinctly unelegiac modes and subjects;[7] the pressing feet (*pressantis pedes*) which would be stained by a new bunch of grapes (*noua uua*) in line 18 surely symbolise as much the freedom of movement granted the newly unshackled ex-lover as the urgency with which the poet's metre seeks to be coloured by new and juicy *materia*. At the end of the poem, this dual gesture away from love and elegy seems confirmed:

> haec ego non humili referam memoranda cothurno,
>   qualis Pindarico spiritus ore tonat: 40
> tu modo seruitio uacuum me siste superbo,
>   atque hoc sollicitum uince sopore caput.
> 3.17.39–42

---

[6] The poet's night-long battle with his mistress offers the same lesson in 3.8 – a poem that likewise precedes the poet's promise to write about something else (here a promise to Maecenas in 3.9).

[7] Thus Mader (1994) 380–1 links Propertius' 'biotic' role as *amator* with his aesthetic role as *poeta*; also Keith (2008) 65.

A Hymn to Bacchus: Propertius 3.17

> I shall tell these things, fit to be celebrated in no humble buskin, with such breath as thunders from Pindar's mouth. Do you only set me free from tyrannical slavery, and conquer this troubled head with sleep.

Propertius makes clear the terms of his (generic) bargain with Bacchus: free me from a life of erotic slavery and as poet I will turn to the elevated modes of tragedy (*non humili cothurno*, 39) and lyric in the manner of Pindar (40).[8] Or so the captivated poet claims, at least.

When we read the poem in this closural sense, Propertius appeals to Bacchus in his role as a transformative god, endowed with an ability to grant release and escape (including, importantly, from one's senses).[9] The conspicuously hymnic form in which Propertius makes his appeal to Bacchus already initiates a sense of difference from the love elegy that Propertius ought to be writing.[10] Moreover, an invocation of Bacchus in this context signals a thematic turning point, just as it had for Virgil at the outset of *Georgics* 2. In 3.17, Propertius uses Bacchus to bring about what seems a pertinent series of inversions and reversals of previous statements of poetic identity – particularly those (re)stated vehemently in markedly Callimachean language at the beginning of Book 3. Propertius' proffered allegiance to Bacchus also signals an intention to abandon elegy's signature lowliness and to produce more elevated styles of poetry (pointedly, *non humili cothurno* negates the elegiacally humble pose adopted at the beginning of the poem – *nunc, o Bacche, tuis humiles aduoluimur aris*, 3.17.1). Symbolically, here, Bacchus will give a transcendant Propertius the capacity to 'thunder' like Pindar himself (*qualis Pindarico spiritus ore tonat*, 3.17.40). As commentators point out, Propertius appears to reject his previous association with Callimachean control, which has been figured already as an explicit rejection of 'thundering' as a poetic mode (e.g. *neque ... intonat angusto*

---

[8] Fedeli (1985) 537–9.
[9] This is Bacchus *Lyaeus*, the 'unbinder' – a role hinted at etymologically by the verbs *soluuntur* and *dilue* at 3.17.5–6: Heyworth & Morwood (2011) 276.
[10] Keith (2008) 65.

pectore Callimachus, 'nor does Callimachus thunder from his narrow chest', 2.1.39–40).[11]

In a broader sense, the shift away from the poetics of Callimachus and Apollo in 3.1 towards Pindar and Bacchus in 3.17 maps the trajectory of Book 3 directly onto the terms of the hoary literary 'contest' between *ars* (technical skill) and *ingenium* (innate ability). Propertius effectively figures a move away from elegiac writing as a switch between symbols of artistry and inspiration in defining the nature of his poetic endeavour. Thus, at a symbolic level, 3.1 and 3.17 make their appeals to opposite ends of an aesthetic spectrum: in 3.1 Propertius asks after symbolic water in a poem addressed to Callimachus that ends by citing the approval of Apollo; in 3.17 Propertius seeks inspiration in wine that will permit him to emulate Pindar in a hymn addressed to Bacchus.[12]

But we should recognise here a poet having a bit of fun at the expense of his credulous reader, all the same. Even as he sets his collection on its way to an impending erotic crisis, both in his text and by allusion Propertius puts on display a certain knowingness of the self-defeating potential in seeking amatory assistance from Bacchus – and in this doubleness lies much of the poem's playfulness. For a start, the elegist acknowledges early on that Bacchus has the power to unite lovers as much as to separate them (*per te iunguntur, per te soluuntur amantes*, 3.17.5)[13] – not to mention that drinking can make the pain of love worse.[14] More tellingly, the role the poem claims in setting up Propertius' emancipation from love in 3.24 rests on a series of amusing absurdities that are missed completely by most readers. In 3.17 Propertius will repay Bacchus for the gift

[11] Miller (1991) 79, Mader (1994) 382, Heyworth & Morwood (2011) 282.
[12] For the use of water and wine as symbols for (supposedly) opposed poetic value systems, see the seminal discussion of Crowther (1979); cf. Knox (1985). Fowler (2002) usefully extends the same contrast to include many more (and especially gendered) oppositions. For the symbolic opposition of Pindaric and Callimachean modes in Latin poetry, see Newman (1985) – especially, in the current context, for the use of Pindar as a paradoxical 'impulse ... towards epic' (189).
[13] Littlewood (1975) 665–6. More generally, Griffin (1985) 70 locates such appeals to Bacchus at the Roman *conuiuium* ('the realm of Bacchus'), where initiating and forgetting erotic encounters form part of an ongoing 'life of love'.
[14] Tib. 1.5.37–8, Hor. *Epod.* 11.8–14.

A Hymn to Bacchus: Propertius 3.17

of sleep by promising to stay awake (*me uigilante*, 3.17.16). It makes only comic sense for a poet to seek escape from a love he describes as 'insane' (*insanae Veneris*, 3.17.3) by appealing to the god of ritualised madness. In much the same vein, in no reasonable way might a visit to Dionysus – of all gods – be considered an effective strategy in guiding a person into the sober sanctuary of *Mens Bona*, a feat Propertius will attempt symbolically at 3.24.19. Finally, in a very basic sense, there is more than a little comedy on offer when a love poet appeals to the wine god for release from erotic passion in the first place.[15] Notwithstanding that 3.17 purports to draw the poet away from elegiac poetry, the poem's overall premise – that wine is an effective *remedium amoris* – is so familiar as a (failed) amatory convention that any potential departure from love asks to be read with immediate irony.[16]

Moreover, even as Propertian elegy promises once more to switch to other genres, 3.17 makes a show of failing to depart from an elegiac erotic tradition. Here Propertius frames his poem suggestively by recalling the beginning of an early love elegy by Tibullus:[17]

>adde merum uinoque nouos *compesce* dolores,
>occupet ut fessi lumina *uicta sopor*.
>
>Tib. 1.2.1–2

Add liquor, and rein in unaccustomed pains with wine, so that sleep might seize my eyes, overcome through weariness.

>tu potes insanae Veneris *compescere* flatus
>Prop. 3.17.3

>atque hoc sollicitum *uince sopore* caput.
>Prop. 3.17.42

Like Tibullus before him, in 3.17 Propertius certainly expresses a wish for release from love (and so from elegy); yet the opening

---

[15] Lyne (1980) 138, Fedeli (1985) 514–15.
[16] Indeed, Neumeister (1983) reads 3.17 as fundamentally a love poem (rather than a meaningful movement away from love).
[17] Miller (1991) 82–5.

contact with Tibullus 1.2 acknowledges, at the same time, that such desire 'to rein in' (*compescere*) the generic storms of Venus is embedded at the very beginning of erotic and elegiac discourse. Moreover, by returning to Tibullus in his poem's final line Propertius does not so much offer a successful development away from Tibullus' starting point as confine his hymn within the limits of Tibullus' opening couplet; Propertius ends his prayer for elegiac escape by returning to where Tibullus begins his elegy and, in fact, his elegiac collection. The suspicion that Propertius might well end up back where he started is furthered by an ironic juxtaposition of imagery in the final couplet: Propertius asks to be liberated from haughty servitude (*seruitio uacuum me siste superbo*, 3.17.41), only to finish the poem still using language of defeat and enslavement (*uince caput*, 3.17.42) that recalls the poet's initial submission at the feet of Amor at the start of Book 1 (*caput impositis pressit Amor pedibus*, 1.1.4). Here, at the outset of Book 3's final sequence, Propertius' Bacchic hymn not only sets up the final rejection of Cynthia but also hints at Cynthia's rejection being tantamount to a generic impossibility that would then provide Book 3 with a false ending (so 3.24 and chapter 9).

Bacchic Integration

The tendency to regard Propertius' Bacchus primarily as a gesture that points to the symbolic break with Cynthia at the end of Book 3 (Keith, for instance, writes that '[i]n this way alone does it seem possible to assimilate elegy 3.17 to Propertius' overarching elegiac project'[18]) means that Bacchus' wider role especially within the collection has been crucially undervalued. In this section, an analysis of Horace's Bacchic lyric and its thematisation of Caesar provides a crucial backdrop for Propertius' own Bacchic inspiration, in a poem that leads directly into a 'public' lament for Marcellus at 3.18. Horace's *Odes* highlight the embeddedness of Bacchus in Augustan

---

[18] Keith (2008) 65.

A Hymn to Bacchus: Propertius 3.17

poetry – but in such a way that maintains Bacchus' disruptive vigour, and that resists appropriation for political ends.

Bacchus comes to Augustan culture as an already complex and politically marginalised figure. Triumviral politics had rendered Dionysus and Apollo lethally incompatible. Octavian had worked hard to stabilise Dionysus' meaning as (only) that of a Romanly inappropriate drunken, excessive and exotic deity as part of his propaganda campaign against Antony.[19] This political opposition proved an important element in the way early Propertian elegy fashioned its own identity, and so took up its position in the Augustan cultural landscape; in particular, the potent imagery that attended Octavian's campaign against Antony provided earlier Propertian poetry with rhetorical clothing in which he might further dress up elegy's protestant voice. The two short elegies which close Propertius' first book had already married the youthful voice of an alienated and unfulfilled lover with that of a socially disenfranchised young man whose family had fought on the wrong side of the civil war.[20] But, in the middle of Book 2, Propertius seemingly further implicates his poetic persona in the 'Bacchic' imagery that came to define the political struggle between Octavian and Antony:

> qualem si cuncti cuperent decurrere uitam
> et pressi multo membra iacere mero,
> non ferrum crudele neque esset bellica nauis
> nec nostra Actiacum uerteret ossa mare
> 2.15.41–4

If everyone should desire to run through a life like mine and to lay down their limbs weighed down by much wine, there would be no cruel iron nor ship for war, and the Actian sea would not turn over our bones.

Here Propertius places the leisured lifestyle of a sympotic poet (41–2) in explicit opposition to the fighting that dominated the final years of the Republic (43) and which had

---

[19] Recently Miller (2009) 26–8; also Zanker (1988) 57–65.
[20] Prop. 1.21–2. Johnson (2009) 1–26 persuasively connects the rise of poetic interest in the figure of the 'erotic madman' with the collapse of traditional social and political structures in the final decades of the Roman Republic.

come to a head with Octavian's victory at Actium (44). But the Actian context suggestively aligns the poet's symposiatic drinking with the bibulous Bacchic avatar that Antony had adopted, and which Octavian's propaganda had then turned against him; provocatively, in 2.15 wine-drinking unites the elegist with Antony in opposition to Octavian's aggression – even as Propertius too further 'condemns' Antony with the drunken caricature that Octavian had developed precisely for this purpose.[21]

After the social and institutional fragmentation of the civil war years, it is unsurprising that the early Augustan period is marked by officially sponsored efforts at cultural reintegration. Significant aspects of Augustan art toy with a practice of bringing together disparate symbols in service of a newly cohesive central narrative (typically associated with Augustus himself) – even if such art frequently refused to toe wholeheartedly any official line that there might have been.[22] As with other central symbols (Apollo especially),[23] no doubt Bacchus would have felt similar pressure to mobilise in support of the new regime. After Actium, Octavian – now Augustus – would himself find a use for those more congenial aspects of Dionysus that had appealed to Antony in the first

---

[21] Griffin (1977) and (1985) 32–47 are classic arguments for the association of Propertius and (the legend of) Antony. Griffin's position should be read in light of Miller (2001) 128–30, for cautionary advice against accepting elegiac identification with Antony 'at face value' (129); and Johnson (2009) 15–19, for the crucial observation that it was not Antony himself but rather Octavian's pejorative characterisation of Antony as 'Mad Lover' that had appealed to Propertius. The prompt to regard Antony as a 'real world' incarnation of an oppositional elegiac lifestyle returns in Book 3, when at 3.11 Propertius cites Cleopatra as a parallel for the dominating elegiac mistress.

[22] Anchises' organisation in *Aeneid* 6 of divergent Republican icons into an Augustan teleology is a famous instance of such integration – notwithstanding Virgil's choice, via Aeneas' interjection, to have Anchises end his catalogue with youthful Marcellus' destined death, so diverting attention at the end from Augustan triumphs (cf. Marcellus in Prop. 3.18, chapter 7). In architectural terms, the Forum of Augustus (Zanker (1988) 210–15) provides a powerful example of the coordination of art, myth and history in service of a unified story; yet cf. Barchiesi (2005) for the way that tendentious art such as this contains within it a prompt for resistant interpretation.

[23] See the full-scale treatment of Apollo as a site of interaction between Augustan religion, politics and literature in Miller (2009).

A Hymn to Bacchus: Propertius 3.17

place.[24] Besides Dionysus' populist connections with pleasure and communal revelry, the guise of a Dionysian 'Liberator' cohered well with the narrative Augustus would promote that had 'freed' the Republic from the tyranny of his political opponents;[25] and Dionysus as successful conqueror and *triumphator* would have provided a powerful symbol for Augustus' new and unparalleled position as Roman *princeps*.[26]

Superficially, at least, Propertius' Bacchic hymn now offers to align elegy with such Augustan integration (or disarming) of cultural symbols. For some readers, when Propertius appeals to Bacchus now as a remedy for lovesickness in a closural context for love elegy, the loudest voice to be heard is that of a poet reversing his earlier subversive preference for an 'Antonian' and explicitly anti-Actian lifestyle, so bringing elegiac Bacchus now into alignment with mainstream Augustan moderation.[27] The self-defeating nature of Propertius' hymn should already give some pause to such readings. More significantly, however, Propertius' continued engagement with Horace's *Odes* – in particular his 'Bacchic' odes 2.19 and 3.25 – reveals a competing programme which relies on maintaining the kind of perilous opposition between Bacchus and Apollo that had marked the divisive triumviral years, and which Augustus was now striving to smooth over.[28]

Horace's poetry exemplifies a wider trend in Augustan poetry that explores the combination of Bacchic *ingenium* and Apolline *ars*, frequently even as the individual poet narrates encounters with one or other source of inspiration.[29] Yet this

---

[24] Castriota (1995) 87–123 discusses at length the integration of Dionysian symbols of fertility and prosperity on the friezes of the *Ara Pacis Augustae*; see esp. 106–23 for broader Augustan attempts to *unite* Bacchus and Apollo.

[25] Aug. *RG* 1 (*a dominatione ... in libertatem uindicaui*), with Hunter (2006) 50.

[26] Cairns (2006) 367–9 goes so far as to speculate – though on little evidence – that much Augustan Bacchic poetry (including Propertius 3.17) might have been written expressly for performance at an officially supported poetic festival supposed to have been held annually at the shrine of Bacchus on the Palatine.

[27] So Heyworth & Morwood (2011) 272, Cairns (2006) 366–7.

[28] Miller (1991) reads 3.17 as establishing a competitive relationship with both Horace and Tibullus. Keith (2008) 63–5 regards 3.17 as further expressing elegy's 'contamination' with lyric in Book 3. Also Hubbard (1974) 72, Littlewood (1975) 674.

[29] E.g. Hor. *Od.* 1.7.3; Tib. 1.4.37, 3.4.44, 3.7.7–8; Prop. 3.2.9; Ovid *Am.* 1.14.31–2, *Ars Am.* 3.347–8, *Met.* 3.421.

is hardly a simplistic willingness on the poets' part to help with 'the regime's programme to rehabilitate Bacchus'[30] by rendering Bacchus indistinguishable from Apollo. Rather (albeit, ironically, perhaps like Augustus himself)[31] these poets mobilise the divergent natures of these symbols in support of their own capacity and (literary) *auctoritas*. As the Roman inheritor of a lyric tradition, Horace explicitly rejects the dichotomous approach of his predecessors to the symbols of poetic inspiration;[32] instead, Horatian poetry will derive its authority precisely from hitching the Callimachean control of Apollo to the ferocious potency of Bacchus. Importantly, Horace does not seek to water down Bacchus' vigour – much of the attraction of Bacchus to Horace comes from *eschewing* the kind of control associated with Apolline inspiration.

The antithesis between these poetic gods comes out most clearly in Horace's *Odes*, and here Bacchus' tendency to resist assimilation is marked. Symbolically, Horace frames his initial three books of *Odes* with references to the emblematic ivy of Bacchus (*Od.* 1.1.29–30) and the laurel of Apollo (*Od.* 3.30.15–16).[33] Within this doubled system of Horace's three-book collection, Bacchus appears in a guise very different from the genial god whose pleasant gifts close out the poet's final collection of *Odes*, amid other fertile symbols of Augustus' golden age (*inter iocosi munera Liberi*, *Od.* 4.15.26). Certainly, in *Odes* 1–3 Horace does include a musical and merry Bacchus whose wine enhances honest *otium* when sipped in moderation. But in two substantial odes Horace also depicts encounters with an ecstatic, transgressive and wholly more dangerous version of Bacchus, who compels the enthralled poet to abandon his customary lyric control.[34] In *Odes* 2.19, the first of his two

---

[30] Cairns (2006) 369.
[31] See Batinski (1991) 374 on the parallelism in Horace's poetry between poetic and political systems in terms of Apollo and Bacchus; in more general terms, see Oliensis (1998) 102–5.
[32] Hor. *A.P.* 408–11, with Batinski (1991) 361.
[33] Putnam (1973), Batinski (1991) 362.
[34] In highlighting the literal artifice of Horace's poem, Nisbet & Hubbard (1978) 317 are far too cynical; but their comment on *Od.* 2.19 is remarkable for the way it too calls upon a symbolic distinction between *ars* and *ingenium*, and for the way it

A Hymn to Bacchus: Propertius 3.17

full-length Bacchic odes, Horace narrates a seemingly chance sighting of Bacchus in the poetic wilderness that comes with immense consequences for the poet:

> Bacchum in remotis carmina rupibus
> uidi docentem, credite posteri,
>   Nymphasque discentis et auris
>   capripedum Satyrorum acutas.
>
> euhoe, recenti mens trepidat metu   5
> plenoque Bacchi pectore turbidum
>   laetatur: euhoe, parce Liber,
>   parce graui metuende thyrso!
>   Hor. *Od.* 2.19.1–8

I saw Bacchus on far-off cliffs – believe me, O posterity – teaching songs to studious Nymphs and goat-footed Satyrs with pricked-up ears. Euhoe! my mind trembles with fresh fear and, my breast full of Bacchus, rejoices wildly. Euhoe! spare me, spare me, Liber, dreaded for your mighty thyrsus.

As the poem opens Horace foregrounds the externalised and prodigious nature of his Bacchic contact by directing our attention to the incredible sight (*credite posteri*, 2) of Bacchus teaching songs on remote hilltops to nymphs and goat-footed satyrs. But the moment that the second strophe begins, Horace himself is driven suddenly to the expression of frenzied excess perhaps best caught by the poet's repeated *euhoe* (5, 7): for the eloquent Horace, this is the *in*articulate cry of the poetically possessed.[35] *Odes* 2.19 does not offer an amiable depiction of Bacchus the music-maker, but rather an encounter with 'the ill-defined terror of the thyrsus'.[36]

Such a tyrannical incarnation of Bacchus must have sat uneasily with any concurrent Augustan reinvention of Bacchus/ Dionysus as a symbol for carefully controlled abundance.[37] Yet

---

privileges Apollo over Bacchus: 'The *craftsman* who *moulded* the Ode to Bacchus was an *Apollonian* not a *Dionysiac* ... his *controlled ecstasy* implied no commitment but was contrived with *calculating deliberation*' (my emphasis).

[35] Here the inexplicable remark of Castriota (1995) 97 regarding *Od.* 2.19 misses the point entirely: 'But there is nothing wild or frenetic about this ... No one is to pass the bounds of moderation in enjoying Liber's gifts.'

[36] Nisbet & Hubbard (1978) 315.

[37] Cf. Cairns (2006) 366–9; Castriota (1995) 97–101.

Bacchic Integration

any such uneasiness seems exactly what Horace has in his sights in his Bacchic poetry, since each of his odes to Bacchus sets the poet on a thematic collision course with Rome, and with Augustus himself. In 3.25 Horace is 'filled with Bacchus' (*quo me Bacche rapis tui | plenum?* 3.25.1–2; cf. *plenoque Bacchi pectore*, 2.19.6) and, possessed by a voice that seems not his own, is driven headlong by the god towards the most hyperbolic of subjects, and so the most lyrically problematic: the 'undying glory of unrivalled Caesar' himself (3.25.1–6).[38] And a similar aesthetic tension is already on display – but on a grander scale – as 2.19 sets up the end of *Odes* 2 and the beginning of *Odes* 3. Possessed and transformed by Bacchus in Book 2's penultimate poem, Horace closes the collection by assuming a double aspect (*biformis ... uates*, *Odes* 2.20.2–3) before opening his third book with a grand sequence of six 'Roman' odes in a newly unified sacral voice that marks a significant departure from the ostentatiously lyric *uariatio* with which Horace had begun Book 1.[39]

No doubt Jasper Griffin has a point when he comments that, in one sense at least, an appeal to Bacchic ecstasy in these poems provided Horace 'with a suitable mask'[40] in which he could praise the greatness of Rome and Augustus without compromising his lyric attachment to ephemera – and without the ephemerality of lyric compromising the grandeur of the praise he offered. But there is surely more to it than this. Even if it is a poetic pose, Horace presents praise of the *princeps* as coming not from his better mind, as being something he must

---

[38] There is far more at stake here than the blunt observation of Santirocco (1995) 233 would allow: 'C. 3.25 ... conveys the excitement of writing political poetry through Bacchic imagery.'

[39] The first six poems of *Odes* 3 are each in Alcaic stanzas, while *Odes* 1 begins with nine poems each in a different lyric metre (the so-called Parade Odes). Oliensis (1998) 132 observes that, in *Od.* 3.1–6, Horace pointedly abandons a regular variation of metre (and so recurrent moments of metrical stoppage) that had so far enabled lyric to resist the stichic form and ambitious scope of an epic project. Horace's Alcaic streak at this point actually numbers eight consecutive poems, including 2.19–20 – thus linking the elevated odes at the beginning of Book 3 to the transgressive Bacchic ode at the end of Book 2.

[40] Griffin (1985) 74.

A Hymn to Bacchus: Propertius 3.17

take leave of his senses to produce;[41] Horace's imperial acclamation is delivered (almost) against the poet's will, as it were, and performed quite literally under compulsion.

More significantly, the mannered excess and peril that attend Horace's movement towards Roman themes risk contaminating Augustus himself, as subject, with precisely those extremes that Augustan moderation was seeking to control. This is especially so since Horace furthers a broader strategy that seeks to align the *princeps* with the (possessed) poet himself through a series of symbolically literary settings. When Horace places Caesar in the Muses' grotto at 3.4.37–42, ostensibly Augustus-as-poet receives calm counsel (*lene consilium*, 41) from Calliope that teaches the triumph of reason over violence; but the suggestive association with Horace's own experience in a poetic grotto (cf. esp. 3.25.4f.) implies that Augustus risks simultaneous exposure to a kind of overwhelming inspiration that eschews rational thinking (and which, in 2.19, has released the poet to begin the mad task of addressing Augustus in the first place). In 3.3, Horace flatters Augustus in a setting that is vividly sympotic:

> hac arte Pollux et uagus Hercules
> enisus arces attigit igneas,   10
>   quos inter Augustus recumbens
>   purpureo bibet ore nectar;
>
> hac te merentem, Bacche pater, tuae
> uexere tigres indocili iugum
>   collo trahentes;   15
>   Hor. *Od.* 3.3.9–15

By these means Pollux and roving Hercules strove for and reached the fiery citadels, reclining between whom Augustus shall drink nectar with empurpled lips. By these means, Father Bacchus, your tigers conveyed you deservedly, drawing the yoke on untamed necks;

Like 3.4, this poem celebrates Roman control in the face of disruptive passion, a message that maps favourably on to

---

[41] A point conceded implicitly at Nisbet & Rudd (2004) 299: 'a Maenad's ecstasy makes an odd analogy for political commitment, however fervid'.

Bacchic Integration

Augustus' political imagery of the decade before Actium. The depiction of Augustus himself lavishly evokes the peace that the *princeps* claimed to have brought to Rome by ending the war with Antony; here Caesar reclines at ease, in eternal leisure, with decadently empurpled lips (11–12). Yet, in their very turn towards luxuriousness, these lines come very close to conjuring up for Augustus the kind of pejorative imagery that Augustus had used just recently against Antony. Indeed, by placing Augustus right between Hercules and Bacchus, Horace opens his flattering portrait of the *princeps* to ambiguous interpretation.[42] The poem's syntax certainly links Augustus most directly with a deified Hercules who, along with Pollux, offers a flattering paradigm of divine reward in return for heroic service on earth (9–11);[43] and, of course, Augustus lips are stained, not by wine, but by divine nectar. Yet the poem's juxtaposition of Augustus' purple lips with an immediate address to Bacchus (12–13) lends Augustus' nectar-sipping a distinctly Dionysian colouring, and even threatens to reposition Hercules in a way that evokes his earthy Antonian incarnation as a bibulous god with Bacchic connections.[44] It is certainly possible that, in 3.4, Horace's association of Augustus with Bacchus and Hercules responds to an Augustan attempt to enlist these figures in support of Augustus himself,[45] something Antony had already attempted in the decade before. But Horace's devastating contact with Bacchus in 2.19 – not to mention Antony's own – provides broader precedent that this is a god more given to controlling than being controlled.

Propertius is rather more direct – even ostentatious – in the way that he too structures and instils his third book with an uneasy

---

[42] The potential for ambiguity is evident in the clear concern at Nisbet & Rudd (2004) 41–2 to dismiss unflattering associations for Augustus in these lines – including an uncomfortableness about Horace's willingness to predict Augustus' deification and apotheosis.
[43] Fraenkel (1957) 384–5, Nisbet & Rudd (2004) 41.
[44] Zanker (1988) 44–6.
[45] Engaging a similar trope, at *Aen.* 6.791–805 Virgil will present Augustus as surpassing the deeds both of Hercules and Bacchus.

A Hymn to Bacchus: Propertius 3.17

synthesis of Apolline and Bacchic inspiration.[46] In narrative terms, Propertius calls upon Bacchus in 3.17 in order to invert his Callimachean programme from 3.1. But in structural terms, just as Horace had framed his three books of *Odes* with symbolic references to Bacchus' ivy and Apollo's laurel, Propertius simultaneously balances his third book with opposed sequences of poems that stem from seeking inspiration first in poetic water, and then in wine. In other words, Horace's precedent helps to demonstrate that Propertius' appeal to the wine god to allow him to thunder in a louder voice – for all that it is open to a reader to interpret this as (in)sincere on its own terms – works within a larger, doubled system that contains, too, a dedication to Apolline restraint.

In fact, Bacchus is already deeply embedded, well before we reach 3.17. Propertius already infuses the book's opening Callimachean/Apolline sequence with flourishes of Bacchic language, and so foreshadows the doubled inspiration of the collection's structure as a whole, as well as the poetic pay-off that derives from it. Right at the start of the book Propertius enters as Callimachean priest performing Bacchic ritual:

> primus ego ingredior *puro de fonte* sacerdos
> Itala per Graios *orgia* ferre choros.
>
> 3.1.3–4

> I enter as the first priest from the pure spring to bring Italian mysteries by means of Greek music.

The clear water implied by *puro de fonte* (3) certainly links Propertius' entrance with the Apolline ideal of poetic purity.[47] Yet with the word *orgia* in the accompanying pentameter Propertius imports the disparate sonority of Dionysian mysteries to the same couplet.[48] In a sense, this couplet makes a programmatic virtue out of the paradox in 3.1 that Propertius

---

[46] Propertius has already concluded his second book by bringing together Bacchus and Apollo: at the end of 2.30 Propertius submits explicitly to Bacchic authority, claiming that 'without you my talent is nothing' (*sine te nostrum non ualet ingenium*, 2.30.40), while 2.31 is a celebration of Augustus' temple of Apollo.
[47] Wimmel (1960) 225.
[48] Hunter (2006) 8.

Bacchic Integration

both rejects military themes in the name of Apollo (3.1.7) and yet seeks association in the poem's second half with the immortal subjects and legacy of the *Iliad*: the priest's clear water suggests the aesthetic principles that underpin the Callimachean *recusatio*, while his Bacchic rites permit poetic contact with Homer, one of the most infamous 'wine-drinking' poets of them all.[49]

A similar collision of symbols can be seen in 3.3, the companion piece for 3.1 that rounds off the first three elegies of Book 3 as a programmatic set. Here, in a dream, Propertius' misguided ambition to write historical epic in the manner of Ennius is brought short by the intervention of Apollo, who reminds the erring poet of the Callimachean littleness that constrains his poetry (3.3.15–24). Apollo then directs Propertius to a poetic grotto in which Calliope anoints the elegist with Philetan water (3.3.51–2). But the cave to which Apollo directs Propertius is conspicuously Bacchic in its decor:

> hic erat affixis uiridis spelunca lapillis,
>   pendebantque cauis *tympana* pumicibus,
> *orgia* Musarum et *Sileni patris* imago
>   fictilis et calami, Pan Tegeaee, tui;   30
> ...
> haec *hederas* legit in *thyrsos*, haec carmina neruis   35
>   aptat, at illa manu texit utraque rosam.
>
> 3.3.27–30, 35–6

Here there was a green grotto studded with pebbles, and drums hanging from the hollow pumice, the mystery objects of the Muses and a clay image of father Silenus and your pipes, Tegean Pan ... One (of the Muses) picks ivy for the thyrsi, another fits her songs to her lyre strings and a third weaves roses with either hand.

These lines describe the crucial location in which Propertius receives his elegiac reinitiation at the outset of the new collection – and, importantly, they extend the same rich confluence of symbols with which the collection begins. Calliope's cave at the end of 3.3 itself balances the Callimachean grove that

---

[49] E.g. *uinosus Homerus*, 'Homer the wine-drinker', Hor. *Ep.* 1.19.6: Wimmel (1960) 225, Crowther (1979) 9–10, and esp. Fowler (2002) 146–7.

149

A Hymn to Bacchus: Propertius 3.17

opens 3.1; like the *nemus* at 3.1–4, the *spelunca* in 3.3 contain both water font and *orgia*, now with Bacchus' own ivy-clad thyrsus thrown in for good measure. On this occasion, however, the programmatic fusion of symbols also foreshadows more clearly an ongoing tension within Book 3. These lines convey the 'Callimachean' ideal of poetic restraint (as Calliope draws Philetan water that would restrict Propertius to erotic subjects and prevent him from writing epic),[50] yet they also embed at the moment of Propertius' reinitiation the dissonant instrumentation (the *tympana* and *calami* in particular) that will reappear in 3.17 as Propertius narrates a Bacchic procession that claims to represent his triumphant escape from the thematic *seruitium* of amatory verse.

But it is in 3.2 – the central poem of the opening triptych – that Propertius most fully envisages the potency of his new project, through its Apolline capacity to harness wilder sorts of material and bring it into the service of a reinvigorated form of (love) elegy. Of course, it is here that Propertius attributes his unique authority as a poet explicitly to the presence of both Bacchus and Apollo at his right side (*et Baccho et Apolline dextro*, 3.2.9). But immediately before he claims the favour of both gods, Propertius employs three mythic *exempla* to explore the sway that song allows a singer to exert over his audience:

> Orphea detinuisse feras et concita dicunt
>   flumina Threicia sustinuisse lyra;
> saxa Cithaeronis Thebanam agitata per artem   5
>   sponte sua in muri membra coisse ferunt;
> quin etiam, Polypheme, fera Galatea sub Aetna
>   ad tua rorantes carmina flexit equos:
> miremur, nobis et Baccho et Apolline dextro,
>   turba puellarum si mea uerba colit?   10
>   3.2.3–10

They say that Orpheus restrained the wild beasts and held back the rushing rivers with his Thracian lyre; they tell that Cithaeron's rocks, driven to Thebes by the singer's skill, of their own accord came together to form parts of a wall; what is more, Polyphemus, even Galatea below wild Aetna turned her dewy horses at your songs. Why be amazed, with

---

[50] Wimmel (1960) 247–8; cf. Crowther (1979) 6–7.

Bacchic Integration

both Bacchus and Apollo at my right, that a crowd of girls should cherish my words?

Orpheus (3–4) and Amphion (5–6) appear here as typical examples of powerful singers.[51] Yet the implicit clash of modes that underpins Propertius' description of their art is significant. Orpheus is said to have 'restrained the wild beasts' and 'stopped the rushing rivers' (1–2); here Orpheus' music manifests precisely as a taming influence over irrepressible nature, anticipating the crucial moderation that Apolline control might bring to the wild force of Bacchic inspiration. More tellingly, Amphion contrives to bring together two opposing effects at the same time; by means of his skill (*per artem*) the rocks of Cithaeron are both 'roused up' in a frenzied manner (*saxa agitata*) and yet 'brought together' in ordered fashion (*coisse*) to form the walls of Thebes. In the third *exemplum*, Polyphemus (7–8) is conspicuous for the way that Propertius portrays him as successful in his wooing of Galatea – surely in Propertius' unique cyclops we should see wild nature (Polyphemus' seduction occurs *fera sub Aetna*) and civilising song (*carmina*) coming together in unparalleled and persuasive combination. Within the argument of 3.2, these complex *exempla* seek to bolster Propertius' claim to success as an amatory poet, an achievement that Propertius represents at the end of the sequence by gesturing to the crowd of girls hanging upon the poet's every word (9–10). But, at the outset of Book 3 as a whole, these ultimately destructive myths also hint at the volatility of the forces that the *exempla* seek to combine. Mention of Polyphemus cannot but bring to mind the cyclops' more common story of poetic (and erotic) failure. In particular, the bloody death that will come to Orpheus – Apollo's son – at the hands of frenzied Bacchants glosses a decidedly less congenial relationship between the gods whom Propertius unites by his shoulder in 3.2.9; and it highlights especially the devastating power of Bacchic inspiration (actually more violent than in Horace) to overwhelm those whom it encounters. In this way, Propertius'

---

[51] Both appear widely (and frequently together) as exemplary poetic figures: Fedeli (1985) 93–5.

A Hymn to Bacchus: Propertius 3.17

choice of myths at the outset of 3.2 articulates the potency of his elegiac *ingenium* and yet anticipates the ill-omened subjects of the book's more pessimistic elegies, such as Paetus' portentous drowning in 3.7, the unrealised potential symbolised by Marcellus' early death in 3.18 and the loss of Cynthia herself in 3.24.

When we return to Propertius' Bacchic hymn at 3.17, we find a poem not only engaging the symbolism of Augustan cultural politics, but also in dialogue with a complex Horatian background, and implicated in a fraught elegiac binary of Propertius' own making. To begin with, the penultimate couplet of 3.17 signals the poem's wider engagement with Horace's Bacchic poetics by offering clear reference to *Odes* 3.25 (targeting Horace's poem also four lines from its end):[52]

>   *nil* paruum aut *humili modo*,
> nil mortale *loquar*.
> Hor. Od. 3.25.17–18

I will speak nothing trivial or in humble manner, nothing mortal.

>   haec ego *non humili referam* memoranda *cothurno*,
>   qualis Pindarico spiritus ore tonat:
> 3.17.39–40

We have already seen Propertius' *non humili cothurno* flagging an aesthetic move upwards from elegiac lowliness, but the allusion to Horace just at this moment gives Propertius' gesture considerably more focus.[53] Certainly, in *Odes* 3.25 Horace has similarly called upon Bacchus for the opportunity the god provides of escape from emblematic lyric modesty;[54] but, more pertinently, ecstatic Bacchic possession 'liberates' Horace to address Augustus in lyric metre. In this context, Propertius' allusion to Horace in the climactic lines of 3.17

---

[52] Miller (1991) 78–9, Lefèvre (1991) 1003–4.
[53] Several critics suggest that Propertius' *Pindarico ore* (3.17.40) is in fact a flag for an allusion to a 'lyric' Horace in the previous line: e.g. Miller (1991) 78, Lefèvre (1991) 1004. Cairns (2006) 368 links the two poets not by allusion but by a common device: 'Propertius, like Horace, understood the value of Pindaric poetry as a cultural matrix for the glorification of the *princeps*.'
[54] Mader (1994) 383.

Bacchic Integration

performs a double role that highlights a tension between these two aspects. In a basic sense, Propertius foreshadows his own thematic collision with Augustus when, at 3.18, he will turn his promised Pindaric manner towards his most 'Augustan' elegy yet – an egregious lament for Marcellus, Augustus' nephew and adopted son, who had died at Baiae in 23 BCE.[55] Yet Propertius' reference also targets the moment when the lyric poet's revelling in the poetic authority Bacchus grants him effectively displaces focus on the glory that lyric poetry might grant Caesar, and so when the poet's Bacchic voice rises in support of his own agenda, ahead of any official programme.[56]

For Propertius, these resistant Horatian reverberations are highly suggestive. Reference to *Odes* 3.25 serves as closing 'authorisation' (and so a prompt to read) for the way that Propertius's prayer for Bacchic relief in fact withstands Augustan appropriation and, indeed, even outdoes Horace in affirming the elegist's long-standing literary authority. In structural terms, the Bacchic procession that sits at the heart of Propertius' poem corresponds to the imperialising triumph that opens the first poem of the collection (3.1.9–12). In 3.1, Propertius' role as *triumphator* characterises the poet's lofty status by seeking comparison with Augustus himself – even by seeking to dislodge Augustus from his position of imperial authority;[57] similarly, in 3.17 Propertius effectively harnesses the chaotic energy of a Dionysian *thiasos* to serve the moment of his (imagined) consecration as an un-humble poet in a Pindaric mode. But here Propertius sets up a pejorative comparison not only with Augustus but with Horace, too. For all that Propertius' gesture towards *Odes* 3.25 signals that the elegist is making a stylistic move like the one Horace has made,

---

[55] Lefèvre (1991) 1004. Miller (1991) 79 effectively denies the juxtaposition of Bacchus in 3.17 and Marcellus in 3.18, writing that, *unlike* Horace, Propertius 'will sing of Bacchus, not Caesar'.
[56] Commager (1962) 347. See too the discussion of Horace's realisation of Bacchic potency in 3.25 at Connor (1971), esp. 269–72; cf. Fraenkel (1957) 259, Williams (1968) 70, where the poet's stylistic elevation connects more closely with promised Roman themes than with Bacchic inspiration in itself.
[57] Fowler (2002) 154–5.

A Hymn to Bacchus: Propertius 3.17

the resulting comparison of the two poems shows up the extent to which each poet's experience of Bacchus is fundamentally different. Horace submits himself to a mind-boggling Bacchic thrall that robs him of responsibility even as it enables him to countenance (Roman) greatness as a lyric subject. In contrast, Propertius strikingly maintains control of his Bacchic hymn in a way that belies his ostentatiously grovelling approach to Bacchus' altar in the hymn's opening verse – Propertius even uses his promised elevated manner as a tit-for-tat bargaining tool with the god in return for the gift of sleep.[58] Meanwhile, if we read 3.17 against a cultural background in which Bacchic allegiance is contested, then it is conspicuous that Propertius' Bacchic performance occurs in a poem that repeatedly undermines its supposedly closural narrative of seeking to leave elegy behind. Indeed, if we follow the poem's prompts towards an ironic reading in which 3.17 enacts a humorous failure to abandon elegy, then we find a poem that in fact subsumes Bacchic capacity within elegy as very much still a going concern – in effect, elegy here reclaims Bacchus for itself, to the exclusion of other claims upon the god.

But this should hardly be surprising. Quite apart from plotting a closural path towards Augustan redemption, the cacophanous Bacchic procession has been an ostentatious emblem for elegiac otherness – and in 3.17 Bacchus threatens to return to type. Most famously there is elegy's early cultural identification with Antony's divergent 'new Dionysus'. In 1.16, a similar friction between 'Roman' and elegiac symbols is framed in Bacchic terms when Propertius' sententious house door offers a pejorative comparison between the chaste triumphs for which it had once stood open, and the noisy revelry of garlanded lovers that it must now shut out; here, 'inspired Bacchic song' is (already) the inebriated and exaggerated *carmina* of the excluded elegiac

---

[58] A key difference between the poets is that Propertius remains a narrator of Bacchic frenzy rather than a participant in it. A comparison of verbs used by each poet to introduce his Bacchic manner reveals the elegist's emphasis on his own authority in contrast to the lyricist's relative passivity (active syntax underlined): Hor. *Od.* 3.25.1–6: *quo me ... rapis, agor, audiar, dicam*; Prop. 3.17.15–21: *ipse seram ... pangamque, uiuam, ferar, dicam*.

Bacchic Integration

poet seeking access to his mistress. In 1.3, Propertius' very first Bacchic 'procession' (*ebria cum multo traherem uestigia Baccho*, 'When I was dragging footsteps unsteadied by much Bacchus', 1.3.9) inspires the poet to elevate Cynthia to mythic status, and yet leads directly to the erotic failure that characterises the impotence of Propertian seduction thereafter.

Moreover, the opening poems of Book 3 itself make a point of highlighting the extent to which Bacchus and Bacchic poetics are deeply embedded, with Apollo, in a two-pronged elegiac pantheon. As such, when Propertius turns from Apollo to Bacchus as the book's final sequence begins, he makes a gesture that he has made many times before; but the novelty in 3.17 lies in the fusion of Propertius' Bacchic turn with elegy's latest attempt to engineer its own demise. Insofar as 3.17 states its poet's desire to compose a (higher) poetry other than elegy, it echoes a motif Propertius has used regularly,[59] and perhaps most famously in the sequence 2.10–13. The irony now is that Propertius attempts to turn away from elegy by turning to a god who has served precisely as a symbol for elegy's subversive vigour and independence: in other words, Propertius gestures away from, and towards, elegy at the same time.[60] Set in a broader cultural context, the teasing ambivalence of the poet's redemptive strategy in 3.17 does not so much affirm a new programme as bait its audience with ongoing uncertainty about its author's generic allegiance. On the one hand, 3.17 flirts with an Augustan narrative that would align Bacchus with a healthful recovery of sleep and mainstream common sense. On the other

---

[59] Wilson (2009) 197.
[60] A similar elegiac doublespeak can be heard even in Propertius' climactic *non humili cothurno* at 3.17.39. In one sense, here the poem purports to look ahead to an elevated 'tragic/Bacchic' mode which humble elegy does not yet possess; at the same time, it affirms the presence of a tragic manner that elegy already claims: on the slippage between a future tense and present tense claim here, Phillips (2011) 124–5. Importantly, just two poems previously at 3.15, Propertius already demonstrates elegy's affinity with tragic narrative by appropriating at length the story of Dirce – who reappears as part of the Bacchic procession at 3.17.33 – from a (mostly lost) tragedy by Euripides: Heyworth & Morwood (2011) 255–6; on Propertius' sources, see too Butrica (1994) 147–8, Fedeli (1985) 470–1. Alfonsi (1961) argues that Propertius follows a Latin translation of Euripides by the Roman tragedian Pacuvius.

A Hymn to Bacchus: Propertius 3.17

hand, the poem's ironic play with its own Bacchic history (and its competitive game with Horace) leaves it open to a reader to hear a poet not redeeming but rather reviving Antony's subversive *thiasos* just as his poetry comes into closest contact with Augustus.

Looking Ahead to Caesar

Reading 3.17 as an unwitting celebration of elegiac potency which overwhelms its poet's desire to depart from elegy's constraints underscores the way that Propertius employs Bacchus to explore the genre's increasing scope. Most directly, for instance, Propertius' Bacchic singing heralds (and implicitly facilitates) the radical inclusion of Caesarian celebration in elegiac couplets at 3.18, even if it establishes a degree of distance and ambivalence as it does so. In this chapter's final section we see Propertius using framing allusions to Virgil's *Georgics* in order to unite 3.17 with 3.1 and 3.9 in bedding down such thematic expansion within the programme of Book 3 as a whole. The *Georgics* have already proved an essential intertext in this regard: the proem to *Georgics* 3 provides 3.1 with its triumph metaphor, while the favourable voyage that Virgil asks Maecenas to grant him at the outset of *Georgics* 2 provides the metaphor of ocean travel for Propertius' own address to Maecenas in 3.9. At first glance, Propertius' promise at 3.17.15–16 to plant vines in honour of Bacchus must itself evoke the viticultural didactic of Virgil's second *Georgic* (even if the elegiac connection with Virgil is mediated by Tibullus' vine-planting at 1.1.7–8);[61] and, as introductory poem for the collection's final set of elegies, 3.17's thematic evocation of

---

[61] Newman (1997) 263, Keith (2008) 64. Cf. Fedeli (1985) 524, who cites Virgilian precedent at *Ecl.* 1.73 (*pone ordine uites*, 'plant the vines in rows') – intriguingly at the end of a poem that launches a collection by Virgil which Propertius feels capable of describing as 'erotic' poetry (e.g. 2.34.71–2), even if love is necessarily more carefree in Virgil's pastoral world than in Propertius' elegiac construct: O'Rourke (2011) 476–81. For the 'rustic' connection of vine-planting in Tibullus, see Littlewood (1975) 667.

Looking Ahead to Caesar

Georgics 2 foreshadows Propertius' coming dialogue in 3.22 with Virgil's *laudes Italiae* (*Geo.* 2.136–75). Rounding off a pattern established by its counterparts, 3.17 also alludes specifically to Virgil's programmatic language in its opening and closing sequences. Here Virgilian mediation offers insight into the role played by Bacchus (and by the Pindaric voice that Bacchus inspires) in augmenting rather than undermining Propertius' Callimachean credentials. To begin with, the opening couplet of 3.17 offers reference to the famous double proem of *Georgics* 2:

> *nunc, o Bacche*, tuis humiles aduoluimur aris:
> *da* mihi pacato *uela* secunda, pater.
> 3.17.1–2

> *nunc te, Bacche*, canam ...
> Maecenas, pelagoque uolans *da uela* patenti.
> Virg. *Geo.* 2.2, 41

Now I will sing you, O Bacchus ...
Maecenas, (and) spread your sails as you fly over the open sea.

Propertius' direct appeal to Bacchus in his first verse certainly reprises conventional hymnic language,[62] but when combined with a clearer reference to Virgil's invocation of Maecenas in the elegy's second line, Propertius seems to compress the weight of Virgil's two addressees – Bacchus and Maecenas – into the two lines which begin his elegy; and the result is significant. The presence of Virgil's book opening in the words *nunc, o Bacche* already reinforces the sense that 3.17 marks a new beginning within the course of Book 3. But the echo of Virgil's complex request of Maecenas for poetic sails at the end of the *Georgics* proem considerably enriches the nature of the 'new start' that Propertius proclaims. At *Geo.* 2.39–46 Virgil represents his project through his patron as a remarkable fusion of epic and Callimachean principles: Maecenas is asked both to fly upon the open sea and yet to keep the land within sight;[63] the poet's

---

[62] Miller (1991) 80 thus argues that verbal similarities between Bacchic hymns 'remain coincidental'.
[63] Mynors (1990) 106 very soberly points out that ancient sea voyages usually followed a coastal route, such that 'V. makes two different, but not inconsistent points' – but

task is an epicising *labor* (2.39), yet he eschews the bombast that comes with a voice of iron (*ferrea uox*, 2.44). As a result, Propertius' gesture to Virgil's paradoxical programme anticipates the ironic opposition that we have seen 3.17 maintain. As the poem begins, Propertius seeks from Bacchus the kind of (epic) sails that Propertius had told Maecenas he was lacking in 3.9, and which Apollo had forbidden him in 3.3. But instead of simply inverting still further the programmatic symbols from earlier in the book, the metaphorical sails that Propertius asks Bacchus to bestow come to elegy coloured by a Virgilian background which depicts a poet seeking to bring together disparate literary modes as a way of driving genre forward.

With this in mind, Propertius' second allusion to Virgil's *Georgic* programme – at the end of the poem – offers the chance to unite the conflicting lines of interpretation that 3.17 has so far invited. Here we return to the emotional heart of the poem: the cacophonous Bacchic procession that drives the poem to its climax (3.17.29–36).[64] Significantly, the procession leads Propertius to the doors of a temple, outside which the elegist makes a priestly offering of wine from a golden bowl:[65]

> ante fores templi cratere antistes et auro
> libatum fundens in tua sacra merum ...
> 3.17.37–8

Before the doors of the temple, as a priest pouring out a libation of your wine from a golden bowl in service of your rites ...

These overtly programmatic lines mark the Propertius' consecration as a Bacchic poet, and so, seemingly, his

---

the effect of such common sense is to normalise what Virgil presents as a bold collision of literary values. Thomas (1999) 111–12 describes Virgil as 'changing his mind' – flirting initially with abandoning Callimachean values before, finally, 'the "correct" stance prevails'.

[64] Littlewood (1975) 668–9.
[65] Heyworth (2007a) gives the wine-pouring to a Bacchic priest other than Propertius by emending *libatum* to *libabit*, and marking the end of a sentence after *merum* (3.17.37): see discussion at Heyworth (2007b) 380. If this is correct, the libation occurs as the final act of the Bacchic procession which Propertius imagines, and the poet himself re-enters the poem as he promises that he will 'tell these things' (*haec ego ... referam*, 3.17.39) as the final quatrain begins.

repudiation of his initial recommitment to Callimachean elegy. The poet's arrival at the Bacchic temple with a bowl of wine reframes his entrance to the Callimachean grove seeking a font of water in 3.1 (indeed, the Bacchic procession as a whole reworks the metaphor of an imperial triumph that opens 3.1); and this couplet immediately precedes Propertius' Horatian promise now to thunder in an un-Callimachean Pindaric voice, should only Bacchus reward him with the gift of sleep, and thus with escape from elegiac *seruitium*. Yet, when Propertius reaches a poetic temple in a programmatic elegy that begins with allusion to *Georgics* 2, inevitably he arrives at a further programmatic site for Virgil at the same moment: the Caesarian temple that sits at the heart of the proem to *Georgics* 3.[66] As at the beginning of 3.17, here too Virgil's precedent invites a reading of Propertius' Bacchic conversion that emphasises a fundamental embrace of conflicting themes, even as an inspired Propertius seeks ostensibly to flee from one to the other.

Even more so than the introduction to his second book, Virgil's proem to *Georgics* 3 presents a complex conflation of principles:[67]

> primus ego in patriam mecum, modo uita supersit,   10
> Aonio rediens *deducam* uertice Musas;
> primus Idumaeas referam tibi, Mantua, palmas,
> et uiridi in campo *templum de marmore ponam* ...
> Virg. *Geo.* 3.10–13

I first, should only life remain, shall return to my country, leading down with me the Muses in triumph from the Aonian peak. I first shall bring back to you, Mantua, the Idumaean palms, and on the green plain I will establish a temple in marble ...

As he 'leads down' the Muses from the Aonian peak, Virgil pointedly employs a programmatic verb (*deducere*) that signals his background in the refined Alexandrian aesthetic associated

---

[66] Heyworth & Morwood (2011) 281.
[67] Gale (2000) 14 emphasises the way that the *Georgics* 3 proem – as distinct especially from like passages in *Georgics* 2 – fashions disparate influences into 'a harmonious whole', where paradoxical combinations are presented as 'a solution rather than a problem'. See too Newman (1985) 189.

A Hymn to Bacchus: Propertius 3.17

especially with Callimachus.[68] Yet Virgil proceeds from here to announce the construction of an extravagant literary temple that will house Caesar himself, and which offers an irresistible metaphor for the eventual composition of the poet's Augustan epic.[69] From a Propertian perspective, it is pertinent that Virgil calls upon pervasively Pindaric imagery[70] – the motif of a victorious procession that subsumes Virgil's Callimachean 'leading down' of the Muses, and the architectural metaphor itself – to negotiate (and to annotate) his ambition to engage a personal and disengaged Hellenistic aesthetic in service of overtly public poetry.[71] In this context, Propertius' promise at 3.17.40 to thunder like Pindar is not (only) a gloss for his allusion to Horace but (also) an acknowledgement that the poetic temple he attains in his Bacchic hymn represents an important

---

[68] Thomas (1988) vol. 2, 40 (Thomas argues that Virgil explicitly rejects Callimachean style at this moment; for a response, cf. Gale (2000) 14). In one sense Virgil's *deducam* coheres with the proem's triumphal imagery: Nappa (2005) 117; also Wilkinson (1969) 168, Buchheit (1972) 100–3, Boyle (1986) 46. Yet the word *deducere* – coming in a programmatic passage just into the second half of the *Georgics* – must also recall Apollo's instruction to Tityrus to produce a Callimachean *deductum carmen* at *Ecl.* 6.5, with which Virgil had begun the second half of the *Eclogues*. See Ross (1975) 26–7 on *Ecl.* 6.3–5; 65–6 on *deductae, ducere* at Prop. 1.1.19, 24; 134–5 on *deduxisse* at Hor. *Od.* 3.30.14; Hinds (1987) 19–20, Heyworth (1994) 72–5 on *deducite* at Ov. *Met.* 1.4. On programmatic use of *deducere* generally in Latin poetry, see Reitzenstein (1931) 49–51, Wimmel (1960) 6 and *passim*.

[69] The discrepancy between the Augustan historical epic that *Georgics* 3 'seems' to announce and the nature of the eventual *Aeneid* (a mythological epic that projects Augustan 'history' into the prophetic future) has been well noted: e.g. Boyle (1986) 46–7, Thomas (1988) vol. 2, 41–7, Kraggerud (1998) 1–20, Miller (2009) 140. But by embedding Augustus explicitly within a broad gesture towards future Virgilian writing, the *Georgics* 3 proem inevitably serves up a vivid prompt for interpreting (and, especially, for anticipating) the project that would turn out *as* the *Aeneid*: Schauer (2007) 48–56. Moreover, the architectural metaphor for poetry that the *Georgics* establishes is picked up pervasively within the *Aeneid*, such that the epic opens *itself* to being read 'as a metaphorical temple celebrating Augustus' triumphs': Kirichenko (2013) 2 and *passim*.

[70] Wilkinson (1969) 165–72 and (1970), Balot (1998). Most intertextual discussion of the *Georgics* 3 proem has sought to establish either Pindar or Callimachus as the primary influence on these lines; yet Gale (2000) 11–14 is surely right to hear (and to point out that nothing prevents readers from hearing) the influence of both Greek poets. For the presence of Callimachus rather than Pindar, see esp. Thomas (1983) and (1998).

[71] For the *Georgics* 3 proem as an explicit model for 'the fusion of the poetic and politico-military worlds', see Boyle (1986) 46. Meban (2008) 167–9 reads Virgil's construction metaphor as emphasising the 'public utility' of his coming poetry, by seeking comparison with the building projects of various *uiri triumphales*.

Looking Ahead to Caesar

moment of synergy with Virgil, too. For all that Propertius' Bacchic temple and 'Pindaric voice' must work, at one level, to symbolise a *claimed* departure from the lowliness of love elegy, Virgil provides literary authority for the way that a Pindaric mode, duly reconfigured for its new Roman context, might make a paradoxically productive partnership with a 'Callimachean' manifesto.[72]

The incorporation of a Virgilian background at the poem's climax, alongside references to Tibullus, Horace and Pindar, invites a reader to take stock of where Propertius has positioned his own development as an elegist precisely by comparing it with the ways in which other writers have expressed their own literary evolution. Aligning himself momentarily with Horace and Virgil, Propertius too gestures in outline towards topics for future writing which (if we take up the invitation to read him closely with his two contemporaries) will seemingly effect closer interaction with Roman subjects; this is a programme that will be tested immediately in Propertius' egregious but evasive lament for Marcellus at 3.18. But, inevitably, Propertius also marks out difference from his peers. The procession in 3.17 from *humiles* to *non humili cothurno* (and so to the thematic elevation represented by Marcellus, and eventually by Actium in 4.6) certainly tracks a potent development in the declared capacity of Propertian elegy – but it does not align elegy uncomplicatedly with Virgil's generic ascent, nor with any new centrist way of looking at things. Even as he arrives at his poetic shrine, Propertius maintains the fundamentally 'excluded' viewpoint of the elegiac poet: Propertius enacts his Bacchic consecration still positioned 'outside the doors' of the temple (*ante fores templi*, 3.17.37). Indeed, as Propertius makes his offering of wine in front of the building to which his sympotic procession has delivered him, we return once more to the elegiac commonplace expressed by the opening of Tibullus 1.2, where the Tibullan lover calls for more wine while locked outside Delia's door (esp. Tib. 1.2.5–6; also 1.2.95 *stare nec ante fores puduit*, 'nor did it shame [him] to

---
[72] Gale (2000) 13–14.

A Hymn to Bacchus: Propertius 3.17

stand before the doors [of his girl]' – providing a closural ring-reference six lines from the end of the poem).

But the effect of all these poetic collisions on Propertian verse is not the poem's most surprising aspect. The influential presence of Virgil and Horace would always result in the development of an elegiac identity for which Tibullus serves here as exemplar, rather than the abandonment of it entirely (as always, when the elegist claims his emancipation from elegy, he has overstated his case). But what does remain remarkable about 3.17 is the way it offers a vivid annotation of this moment at a crucial stage within the poet's new collection. Notwithstanding his Bacchic transformation, Propertius remains an outsider looking in; but the imperious metaphor that elegy's *puella* has always offered now takes on an edgy transparency. In 3.17 the dwelling outside which he will sing contains not Cynthia but – if we hear *Georgics* 3 clearly enough – just possibly Caesar himself (Virg. *Geo.* 3.16, *in medio mihi Caesar erit templumque tenebit*, 'and Caesar will dwell in the middle of my temple'): *dominus* has replaced *domina*. More broadly still, we might hear Propertius taking up the stance he must inevitably adopt with regard to Virgil's imminent *Aeneid*. In the proem to *Georgics* 3, Virgil foreshadows the possible epic narratives he will come to write by inscribing these as images precisely 'on the doors' of his programmatic temple (*in foribus ... faciam*, *Geo.* 3.26–39). When Propertius then imagines himself *ante fores templi*, at an intertextual level he occupies a position from where – like all Roman poets who write after Virgil – he will view, interpret and critique the literary edifice that will soon lodge at the heart of the Augustan cultural landscape.

The richly allusive final couplets of 3.17 acknowledge that the thematic pull of the Principate has a similar influence in shaping elegy's future direction to the effect it has (already had) on other Augustan genres; but also that Propertius will retain an elegist's perspective, all the same. Under Augustus, writes Alessandro Barchiesi, 'The epic author is now the maker of monuments, while elegiac poets (Propertius, Ovid) will have to invent the new poetics of the *flaneur*, the roving male viewer

Looking Ahead to Caesar

who approaches official monuments at an oblique angle.'[73] We have seen this elegiac 'invention' developing directly from existing elegiac dynamics – and that 3.17 offers an allusive commentary on just such transitions even as they are under way.

---

[73] Barchiesi (2005) 300.

CHAPTER 7

IN LAMENT FOR MARCELLUS

Propertius 3.18

M. Claudius Marcellus – Augustus' nephew, son-in-law, very possibly his adopted son and most likely his intended successor – died prematurely in 23 BCE, at the age of eighteen.[1] Marcellus' death was mourned at an extravagant public funeral outside Augustus' new Mausoleum. Extraordinarily for a figure comparatively so young, his short life was also celebrated widely in contemporary literature, a phenomenon surely reflecting Marcellus' unique distinction in Roman public life: Rome had not before experienced what amounts to a crown prince. Seneca – after offering his own praise for Marcellus in his *De consolatione ad Marciam* – refers to a number of poems written to celebrate Marcellus' memory that Octavia, the dead man's grieving mother, refused to hear.[2] We have Propertius' elegy; in addition, Horace had already carefully positioned a Marcellus at the climax of his Pindaric catalogue of Roman heroes in *Odes* 1.12 – probably the elder Marcellus, third winner of the *spolia optima* and captor of Syracuse in 211 BCE,[3] but doubtless evoking the marriage of the younger Marcellus to Augustus' daughter Julia, by means of a climactic juxtaposition where Horace hitches the rising fame of 'Marcellus' to the Julian star of Augustus' own family.[4] Most famously of all, Virgil afforded Marcellus extraordinary prominence by restaging the young man's funeral right at the end of *Aeneid* 6.[5] In

---

[1] Marcellus was the son of Augustus' sister Octavia, and married Augustus' daughter Julia in 25 BCE – giving rise to an popular expectation that Marcellus was the Principate's heir apparent (Dio 53.30). Plutarch (*Ant.* 87.2) claims additionally that Augustus adopted Marcellus as his own son.
[2] [*Octauia*] *carmina celebrandae Marcelli memoriae composita aliosque studiorum honores reiecit* (Sen. *Cons. Marc.* 2.5), with Falkner (1977) 11.
[3] Nisbet & Hubbard (1970) 161–2.
[4] Hor. *Od.* 1.12.45–8: Schmidt (1984) 144–6, Williams (1974) 150–1.
[5] Skard (1965) 64, Putnam (1998) 95.

In Lament for Marcellus: Propertius 3.18

the Roman programme of Virgil's epic as a whole, the young Marcellus provides a central focal point for Rome's Trojan destiny, and encapsulates in his short life not only the received virtues of Roman history but the promise of – and perhaps fears for – the emergent Augustan Principate.[6]

That Marcellus had indeed been marked out as Augustus' successor is a crucial implication that these (extant) texts have in common. Yet, notoriously, this was a sort of dynastic narrative with which Augustus himself was careful not to become associated too directly. While refraining from an overt (and obviously fantastic) claim that the old Republic constitution had been restored,[7] Augustus was clearly concerned to ensure that his own public behaviour during this period were seen, at least, to respect traditional sources of authority under republican government – the Senate and the Roman people (*Res Gestae* 34.1). At times, Augustus' methods were openly theatrical, as when he begged release from a popular appeal that he assume a dictatorship by falling to his knees and baring his chest (Suet. *Aug.* 52; cf. *Res Gestae* 5.1).[8] And we might suspect a similar theatricality behind Augustus' offer, after his illness in 23 BCE, to read aloud his will in the Senate to prove that he had not anointed a successor (and especially not *Marcellus*, who, as a member now of Augustus' family, would give rise to thoughts of monarchy);[9] the Senate, of course, respectfully declined to hear the document, which remained sealed. In this context, the prominence that contemporary literary texts give to Marcellus suggests not only a very different but – for Augustus – an equally important narrative, in which Marcellus was promoted as (having been) an attractively promising face for an evolving process of rather deeper constitutional change.

---

[6] For readings of Marcellus in the context of Virgil's exploration of Roman history in *Aeneid* 6, see esp. R. D. Williams (1964) 59–63, Burke (1979), Horsfall (1982) and (1991), Feeney (1986) 5–16, Zetzel (1989) 282–4. For Marcellus as a poignant embodiment of both promise and (Augustan) pessimism, see Johnson (1976) 107, Putnam (1998) 95.
[7] Gruen (2005) 34–5.
[8] E.g. Gruen (2005) 35: 'The histrionics were calculated but meaningful.'
[9] For contextualisation of 'Augustus the actor' here, see Eder (2005) 25; for the apparent marginalisation of Marcellus in particular, see Gruen (2005) 41.

In Lament for Marcellus: Propertius 3.18

In the broadest sense, this reflects a strategic subtext that Augustus was compelled to leave to artists to shape for him (indeed, such art would have helped create the popular perception of Marcellus as heir apparent which Augustus could then reject so dramatically); it would be reflected, too, in later artwork more closely influenced by the *princeps*'s input – the Ara Pacis Augustae and the Forum Augustum, which both contribute powerfully to the identification of Augustus' family with the Roman state as a whole, and which prepare the way for Augustus' eventual role and rule as the nation's 'father' (*pater patriae*: *Res Gestae* 35.1; cf. Suet. *Aug.* 58). This chapter addresses just such artistic abstraction of a practical reality behind the founding of Rome's first imperial family. In particular, the interaction between Propertius 3.18 and *Aeneid* 6 shows that, even as Propertius offers outwardly 'genuine' lament for the death of Augustus' son(-in-law), his poem exposes specious myth-making within the Trojan narratives that underwrite the authority of the *princeps* himself – the framing stories about Augustan dynasty that Augustus could not tell himself.

In terms of elegy itself, Propertius' choice to write a lament for Marcellus remains a remarkable one at a number of levels.[10] In a basic sense, 3.18 represents a generic paradox: as an epicedium, the poem coheres very naturally with an ancient belief that elegy began as funeral song (in this sense 'Propertius is in effect taking elegy back to its roots'[11]); at the same time, a poem that offers empathy for the death of Augustus' protégé is the very last thing you would expect from an Augustan love poet, whose seeming disrespect for the symbols of imperial authority was notorious (and for Ovid, soon enough, disastrous). Moreover, the fact that the cultural phenomenon of Marcellus' death results in Propertius joining numerous others in a communal act of poetic lament is difficult to reconcile with the love elegist's proud singularity and proverbial solitude (for which Propertius 1.17–18 is paradigmatic). Here, the 'public' nature

---

[10] The uncritical assessment at Cairns (2006) 347 simply that 3.18 is a 'clearly commissioned piece' from Augustus himself does not remotely do justice to the poem's literary and political complexities.
[11] Clarke (2004) 136 n. 25; see too Luck (1969) 26.

of 3.18 – both in theme and production – is highly suggestive, given the poem's place within the structure of Book 3. In 3.17 Propertius had prayed for release from the strictures of love elegy, and for the capacity to produce a higher form of poetry; now, in 3.18, we might expect Propertius either to affirm a new direction for elegy or to reject it once again, as so often in the past. As it turns out, the programmatic commentary of 3.18 very knowingly takes note of both extremes. As the discussion begins below, we will see Propertius positioning his poem on Marcellus as precisely the departure from elegiac norms that it must represent – an expansion of the elegiac compass from a singular focus on Cynthia to a more upfront engagement with mainstream public life. But, as we move to Propertius' treatment of Marcellus as an elegiac subject (in conspicuous contrast to the epic Marcellus of *Aeneid* 6), we will find that an old elegiac recalcitrance remains alive and well. In the end, Propertius' Marcellus does affirm the poet's generic transition, but not necessarily in the way we might have expected. Above all, in 3.18 we get a glimpse of the kind of oblique presentation of Roman symbols that appears eventually in Propertius' fourth book.

Returning to Baiae

3.18 opens in Baiae, which in Propertian elegy is richly evocative terrain.[12] In effect, Propertius delays the announcement of Marcellus' death by beginning his poem with a crescendo of apostrophes that frame the site of the prince's death in significant ways for the epicedium that follows:

> Clausus ab umbroso qua ludit pontus Auerno,
>   fumida Baiarum stagna tepentis aquae,
> qua iacet et Troiae tubicen Misenus harena,
>   et sonat Herculeo structa labore uia,
> hic ubi, mortalis dexter cum quaereret urbes,
>   cymbala Thebano concrepuere deo,

---

[12] Falkner (1977) 13–16.

In Lament for Marcellus: Propertius 3.18

(at nunc, inuisae magno cum crimine Baiae,
   quis deus in uestra constitit hostis aqua?)
hic pressus Stygias uultum demisit in undas,
   errat et inferno spiritus ille lacu.
                        3.18.1–10

Where the sea plays, enclosed by shadowy Avernus, Baiae's steaming pools of warm water; and where Troy's trumpeter Misenus lies in the sand, and the road constructed by Hercules' labour resounds; here where, when he propitiously sought out mortal cities, cymbals clashed for the Theban god (but now, Baiae, hateful along with your great crime, what hostile god has settled in your water?); here he was overcome, sinking his face into the Stygian waters, and his spirit wanders by the infernal lake.

Unexpectedly, the poem's first couplet recasts Baiae's Avernus and Lucrine lakes in their civil war guise as the *portus Iulius*:[13] in 37 BCE, at the height of confrontation with the fleets of Sextus Pompey, Octavian's general Agrippa established a concealed naval station at Baiae by means of radical canal works that linked its two lakes with each other,[14] and with the open sea. Propertius' striking opening with the *portus Iulius* will prove significant later in the chapter, but for the moment it is worthwhile noting the way in which the harbour's mingled waters are pressed into artistic service. In particular, Agrippa's disruptive digging opens the way for Propertius' ensuing depiction of Marcellus' death in the fifth couplet – the poem's first climax, and the moment that unifies the poem's opening ten lines as a set.[15] Marcellus had died while no doubt seeking the restorative minerals found in the Lucrine's volcanic lagoon.[16] Yet Propertius vividly depicts the young man drowning in the

---

[13] Cf. Virg. *Geo.* 2.161–4, Strabo 5.4.5.
[14] As the text is transmitted, 3.18.1 (describing Avernus) and 3.18.2 (describing the Lucrine) are most likely equated in apposition: Fedeli (1985) 547, following Shackleton Bailey (1956) 194; cf. Camps (1966) 138, Richardson (1977) 391, who treat these lines as vocative constructions. Heyworth (2007b) argues against apposition in the opening couplet (and so emends his text) on the basis that the two lines refer to different bodies of water.
[15] Falkner (1977) 12 points out that the simple structure of the transmitted text (in three sections of ten lines, with a coda of four lines) 'argues against the presence of lacunae in the text'; for discussion of this structure, see too Fedeli (1985) 544.
[16] Dio 53.30.4 records that Marcellus received hydropathic treatment similar to that which had revived Augustus during his illness in 23 BCE; Strabo 5.4.5 mentions Baiae's Lucrine specifically in terms of its ability to 'cure disease'.

Returning to Baiae

waters of the Styx (*Stygias uultum dimisit in undas*, 9). At the moment of Marcellus' death, the poem reprises the mingling of waters at its beginning; we return to Avernus, a lake supposedly fed directly by the rivers of the underworld (e.g. Strabo 5.4.5), and now linked physically with the Lucrine where we are to presume an ailing Marcellus went to bathe. But here mythic and manmade topography joins up with sinister effect – in conspicuous contrast to Bacchus' divinely propitious visit to 'mortal cities' (*mortalis dexter cum quaereret urbes*, 5)[17] right in the middle of this opening passage. By the time we reach Marcellus' watery demise, the steaming pools of the Lucrine, the shady waters of Avernus, and (therefore) the fateful currents of the Styx, have been interlinked in parallel ways: not only by a dramatic leap of the poet's imagination, but by Agrippa's wartime tunnelling for Octavian, as well.[18]

The most immediate connection set up in these opening lines by their focus on the landscape around Baiae is surely with the first of a pair of poems that sits right in the middle of Book 1. Prominent details in the description of Baiae in 3.18 recall those in 1.11:[19]

> Ecquid te mediis cessantem, Cynthia, Bais,
>   qua iacet Herculeis semita litoribus,
> et modo Thesproti mirantem subdita regno
>   proxima Misenis aequora nobilibus,
> nostri cura subit memores adducere noctes?
>   ecquis in extremo restat amore locus?
>   ...
> tu modo quam primum corruptas desere Baias:
>   multis ista dabunt litora discidium,
> litora quae fuerunt castis inimica puellis:
>   a pereant Baiae, crimen amoris, aquae!
>   1.11.1–6, 27–30

While you idle in Baiae's midst, Cynthia, where Hercules' causeway lies by the shore, gazing now at waves nearest renowned Misenum that

---

[17] The presence of cymbals (*cymbala*, 6) identify 'the Theban god' as Bacchus: Shackleton Bailey (1956) 195–6.
[18] In fact, Propertius' Baiae is marked generally as a site for blurring and crossing boundary lines: see the excellent discussion at M. F. Williams (1996) 152–3.
[19] Barsby (1974) 136, Falkner (1977) 13–16, M. F. Williams (1996) 154–6.

wash Thesprotus' kingdom, does any thought strike you bringing nights mindful of me? Does any place linger at the fringes of your love? ... Only leave corrupt Baiae as soon as possible: those shores will bring rupture to many lovers – shores which have been hostile to girls' chastity: perish the waters of Baiae, crime against love!

At a basic level, Propertius activates the ominous symbolism that Baiae possesses in the private elegiac world and amplifies it for the unprecedented public context of his new poem. Back in the midst of the first book, Baiae was the place above all that threatened erotic prosperity. For Propertius, the opportunities for perfidy provided at Baiae rendered its fashionable waters a *crimen amoris*, a 'crime against love' (1.11.30). Now, in 3.18, Propertius revives the 'great crime of Baiae' (*magno ... crimine Baiae*, 3.18.7) as its complicity in Marcellus' demise; the inevitable *discidium* of which Propertius warned at 1.11.28 – that final sundering of lovers that is tantamount to elegiac death – becomes realised now in the death of a prince.[20]

But the most remarkable new use to which Propertius puts 1.11 lies not in fashioning a melancholy proem for Marcellus but in focusing attention on the transgressive moment that arises with the presence of Marcellus in a Propertian elegy in the first place. At this thematic level, 3.18 represents an important juncture within the generic trajectory of Book 3. The crashing cymbals that attend Bacchus' (otherwise unattested) tour of Campania at 3.18.5–6 provide a crucial link between 3.18 and Propertius' raucous Bacchic *thiasos* in 3.17, where we have just seen the elegist seek relief from erotic servitude, and promise to write instead an elevated sort of poetry that just might include a lament for the *princeps*'s adopted son; and, significantly, 3.18 turns out to be the first (though, in fact, the only) poem in Book 3 to offer no immediate connection with love as a theme, or with the poet's mistress, or with love poetry itself. In this context, the opening reminiscence of 1.11 sets itself up as a red herring. By returning the reader to Baiae and to Book 1, it creates expectation of the appearance, at last, of Cynthia herself, who gave her name unofficially to the first

---

[20] Barsby (1974) 136, Falkner (1977) 14, M. F. Williams (1996) 155, Clarke (2004) 136.

book and yet who has remained unnamed through seventeen poems in Book 3. Indeed, one might even read the beginning of 3.18 with a familiar sense of recognition that Propertius' promise to abandon love in 3.17 has turned out, once again, to be false.[21] But such a reader falls for the poet's double bluff: as it turns out, recollection of 1.11 serves rather poignantly to highlight Cynthia's *absence* from 3.18. Where we should find mistress, we find instead Marcellus.

Moreover, the background presence of 1.11 provides astonishingly apt commentary on a shift seemingly underway in Propertian poetics. To begin with, back at the heart of the Cynthia book Propertius had obsessed precisely over the possibility that his elegiac verse might lose its amatory muse – and the effect of looking back to Baiae as 3.18 introduces Marcellus is to pose the very question a reader might have now as to whether Propertius really is on the point of abandoning erotic writing:

> an te nescio quis simulatis ignibus hostis
> sustulit e nostris, Cynthia, carminibus?
> 1.11.7–8

Or has some unknown rival with false pretence of passion drawn you, Cynthia, away from my songs?

The *hostis* (7) who would remove Cynthia in the fourth couplet of 1.11 reappears in the fourth couplet of 3.18 as the *deus hostis* (3.18.8) who has occasioned Marcellus' death,[22] and so provided the reason for Marcellus' presence in Propertian elegy. In other words, the intratextual dialogue between the two poems flags the appearance of Marcellus in elegy as the moment when the third book's gradual drift away from erotic themes arrives at the point of no return: the moment when 'Cynthia *has* been removed from Propertian poetry' (1.11.8). More broadly, 3.18 begins by reviving an implicitly closural sequence from the first book of Propertian elegy that established Baiae as a place to address the possibility that erotic life might well come to an

---

[21] Falkner (1977) 13.
[22] Falkner (1977) 14.

end (*multis ista dabunt litora discidium*, 'those shores will bring about the end for many lovers', 1.11.28) – even if the point was, back then, that Propertius would put such an end firmly on hold. Now, when we return to Baiae in Book 3 (and when Marcellus appears to displace Cynthia and *amor* itself) erotic closure suddenly seems very much at hand. In this context, recalling the forewarned *discidium* of 1.11 not only colours our reading of Marcellus' death-in-elegy but prepares us for the end of elegy itself, as well: the climax at the end of Book 3, when Propertius will claim to part from Cynthia for good. In other words, the allusive opening lines invest the poem with a programmatic double valency. Propertius' lament for Marcellus rests on the suggestion of (impending) lament for Propertian love poetry at the same time.[23]

Building on this point, the dialogue between these two poems also annotates the apparent movement in Propertian elegy, not only away from its exclusive early focus on private material but towards a more public and especially Augustan interaction at the same time (a phenomenon that is already figured in the marked transition of subjects from Cynthia to Marcellus). In the first collection, 1.11 forms a key central palinode with 1.12. Across these two poems Propertius develops a programmatic promise of elegiac stasis: balancing his fears about losing Cynthia in 1.11, Propertius resolves epigrammatically at the end of 1.12 that things will never change (*Cynthia prima fuit, Cynthia finis erit*, 'Cynthia was the beginning, Cynthia shall be the end', 1.12.20). So Propertius begins the second half of Book 1 by asserting the certainty of his own (thematic) affections; but he ends the first half of the collection expressing his wishful desire always to be able to control Cynthia, too – a rather less secure task, especially in the face of Baiae's seductions:

---

[23] The link between Marcellus' death and erotic (literary) closure seems confirmed by a pre-echo in the middle of 3.18 of the 'death' of Propertius' writing tablets in 3.23: *tot bona tam paruo clausit in orbe dies* ('that day enclosed *so many goods* in so small a circle', 3.18.16); *scripta quibus pariter tot periere bona* ('[my tablets have perished,] on which *so many good writings* have perished as well').

Returning to Baiae

> atque utinam mage te, remis confisa minutis,
> paruula Lucrina cumba moretur aqua,
> aut teneat clausam tenui Teuthrantis in unda
> alternae facilis cedere lympha manu ...
> 1.11.9–12

> I would much rather some little craft, relying on feeble oars, entertained you on the Lucrine Lake, or that the waters, easily parting to alternating stroke, held you enclosed in the shallow waves of Teuthras ...

As metapoetry, this fantasised sketch of Cynthia reaches after an elegiac ideal in which mistress and poetry remain indivisible.[24] The physical aspect of this alternative Baiae repeatedly evokes the diminutive aesthetic of elegy itself: Cynthia's boat and its oars are 'small' (*paruula ... cumba*, 10; *remis ... minutis*, 9),[25] the water in which Cynthia swims is 'shallow' (or literally, 'slender': *tenui ... in unda*)[26] – even the alternation of Cynthia's arms as she swims suggests the alternating verses of an elegiac couplet (*alternae ... manu*, 12); and the poet would have Cynthia embedded (*clausam*, 11) within this elegiac landscape for as long as possible (*te ... cumba moretur*, 9–10). Yet it is precisely this idealised depiction of elegiac stasis that Propertius manipulates in tracking the elegiac development brought about – and symbolised – by Marcellus' appearance in 3.18. Here the intratextual dialogue emphasises the manner in which Marcellus serves as a pointed replacement for Cynthia in 3.18. In very general terms, of course, it is now Marcellus who seeks the waters of the Lucrine where Cynthia once swam. More specifically, it is now the day of Marcellus' death that expresses an elegiac ideal that used to pertain to Cynthia and the boat that carried her in Book 1:

> occidit, et misero steterat uicesimus annus:
> tot bona tam *paruo clausit* in orbe dies.
> 3.18.15–16

---

[24] Greene (1995) 310–17.
[25] The (small) boat is itself a regular metaphor for elegiac poetry: cf. 3.3.21–4.
[26] For *tenuis* as a programmatic characteristic of elegiac writing, cf. 1.2.2, 3.1.8; for its use with water, see Shackleton Bailey (1956) 33.

In Lament for Marcellus: Propertius 3.18

He died, and the twentieth year stood still for the poor boy: that day enclosed so much good in so small a compass.

More significantly still, the elegiac skiff – Cynthia's *paruula cumba*, pointedly so small in 1.11 as to fit only one occupant – resurfaces in 3.18,[27] but reinvented now as the infernal boatman's capacious raft that will carry not only Marcellus' shade but the shades of all mortals across the river Styx:

> scandenda est torui *publica cumba* senis.
> 3.18.24
>
> Everyone must climb aboard the grim old man's communal raft.

The outward movement from *paruula* to *publica* neatly glosses a thematic shift that has taken place between Book 1 and Book 3, such that when Propertius returns belatedly to Baiae he finds himself lamenting the death of a prince along with other poets of the Augustan court, rather than burdening merely his own ears with worries about his mistress's promiscuity (1.12.13–14). (This development even comes tinged with a weary sense of inevitability: the 'public raft' is one that everyone must climb aboard, sooner or later: *cunctis ... scandenda est*, 22–4.)[28] At the same time, Propertius' subtextual gesture to a more communally Roman orientation continues to reverse quite flamboyantly the stylistic advertisements he offers in earlier poetry. At the end of 3.17, we saw the poet's desire to thunder in a Pindaric voice threaten to recant his prior allegiance to Callimachean restraint; now the crowded ferry at 3.18.24 opposes the lightly loaded dinghy (the only other appearance of the word *cumba* in Book 3) that Apollo commended to Propertius in 3.3 as part

---

[27] M. F. Williams (1996) 156.
[28] Propertius' general observations in 3.18 (esp. 19–28) about the inevitability and equalising nature of death in connection with Marcellus are closely linked with earlier meditations on his own poetic career and legacy (esp. in 3.5 and 3.7): Boucher (1965) 78–9, M. F. Williams (1996) 159–60. The imagery that Propertius employs in this sequence also draws suggestively upon the poet's own programmatic language. In particular, death is figured as a 'pathway' (*uia*, 3.18.22 – a conventional image, but significant in a book that repeatedly figures poetry itself as a journey; cf. 1.1.18, 3.1.14, 3.1.18, 3.24.15–16) that must be 'worn down' (*terenda*, 3.18.22; cf. 1.7.9, 2.1.46, 2.30.14).

of an elaborate (and Callimachean) metaphor for a poetry that should not be burdened by 'weighty' themes:[29]

> non est ingenii cumba grauanda tui.
> 3.3.22
> The little boat of your talent must not bear a heavy load.

In symbolic terms, the sheer capacity of Charon's communal ferry in 3.18 transgresses the stylistic limitations that came with Apollo's literary craft in 3.3, and the thematic limitations that attended Cynthia's solitary dinghy in 1.11. In other words, the poet's embrace of a 'public' poetry – both in subject and its attendant symbolism – is signalled precisely as a departure from the programmatic strictures of earlier elegy.

Marcellus and the *Gens Claudia*

Virgil's expansive lament for Marcellus (*Aen.* 6.860–86) provides a famously melancholic end note for the triumphant pageant of future Roman heroes that Anchises commends to Aeneas during his journey through the underworld. In a Virgilian context, Marcellus is well recognised as an integral part of the book as a whole.[30] Yet when readers approach Virgil's lament from a Propertian perspective, there is a tendency to excerpt the Virgilian passage on the basis of its raw Augustan emotion – effectively, to treat the passage as that short *epicidium* remembered out of context especially for causing Marcellus' mother Octavia to faint;[31] and here Propertius 3.18 (certainly a more emotionally evasive poem) has suffered in critical opinion by comparison with the 'genuine' pathos that Virgil is seen

---

[29] 3.18.24 recalls 3.3.22 not only by repetition of *cumba* but also by the mannered gerundive construction used in each instance (*non est … cumba grauanda|scandenda est … cumba*). The resulting conceit that Propertius' *cumba* might now seem 'burdened' by the weightless shades of the dead might well develop ironically from Virg. *Aen.* 6.413 (*gemuit sub pondere cumba*, 'the boat groaned at the weight') – where the ferry that usually carries ghosts without difficulty suddenly takes on water when the living Aeneas steps on board.
[30] E.g. Otis (1963) 303–4, Johnson (1976) 107, Putnam (1998) 95.
[31] The famous story found at *Vita Suetonii-Donati* 32 records that Octavia fainted when this passage was read to her by Virgil himself; that this story is most likely a post-Virgilian invention, see Horsfall (2001).

to generate for Marcellus.[32] For some readers this is simply because the tone of Propertius' poem has been fundamentally misunderstood: Johnson, for instance, argues that in 3.18 we should hear 'the voice not of a eulogist but of a satirist'.[33] More likely, it is because Propertius' poem demands to be read not just against Virgil's closing epicedium but against the progression of *Aeneid* 6 more fully; here, Propertius too begins his poem at Avernus and the tomb of Misenus (cf. *Aen.* 6.124–9, 232–5), and moves through central focus on the underworld (indeed, following Aeneas, an infernal journey on foot). In this larger context, the position of Virgil's Marcellus at the business end of an awesome sweep through Roman family history foregrounds – for Propertius – the ironies of calling upon the dignity of Republican bloodlines to explain the authority of a new imperial class, whose numbers spring as much as ever from politically adept intermarriage and adoption.

Two pervasive concerns of *Aeneid* 6 are generational succession from father to son, and (thereby) the creation of dynasty. The family unit at the heart of the story places the book's interest in patrilineal continuity front and centre: Anchises is concerned above all to pass onto his son his unique foreknowledge of dynastic glory, before joining at last a line of family ancestors whom the future Roman heroes he describes already resemble;[34] and the importance of the paternal line that links Aeneas' own son Iulus to the realisation of Anchises' glorious Roman vision is emphasised early on by the ghost of Palinurus, who appeals to Aeneas with the words 'by your father, by the hope of rising Iulus' (*per genitorem oro, per spes surgentis Iuli*, 6.364).[35] This framing focus on succession within the immediate family finds greater resonance in the parade of heroes that closes out the *Aeneid*'s first half. Significantly, here

---

[32] E.g. Austin (1977) 269. See too Falkner (1977) 11, with a telling survey of opinion at n. 1.
[33] Johnson (2009) 118, a point of view based explicitly on a contrast to 'the voice that informs the grief for Marcellus toward the end of *Aeneid* 6'. For a similar juxtaposition of Propertius and Virgil, see Nethercut (1970a) 398–9.
[34] Burke (1979) 227.
[35] Reed (2001) 154.

Marcellus and the *Gens Claudia*

Anchises' narration focuses on the centrality of family lines in the transmission of Roman greatness (and, indeed, infamy).[36] The luminous individuals of the Roman future/past are ultimately subordinated to the organising presence of the great Republican *gentes* that shape the parade and, seemingly, the character of the Roman nation.[37]

In these instances Virgil's Anchises pays respect to the gentilicial dignity of the Roman Republic. But, reflecting the poem's composition in the early Principate, the focalising presence of Aeneas as the primary audience for the heroic pageant has the conscious effect of promoting one *gens* above the others. Once the procession of early kings has reached Romulus and Rome itself, Anchises asks his son to turn his gaze at what is effectively the elevation of his bloodline into a *gens Romana*:

> huc geminas nunc flecte acies, hanc aspice gentem
> Romanosque tuos. hic Caesar et omnis Iuli
> progenies magnum caeli uentura sub axem.
> Virg. *Aen.* 6.788–90

Now bend your twinned gaze here, behold this family, and your own Romans. Here is Caesar and all the offspring of Iulus, destined to venture beneath the great arch of heaven.

The promotion of (Augustus) Caesar at this point – the first dramatically unchronological moment in the procession – juxtaposes Augustus with Romulus as founder and re-founder of Rome,[38] and simultaneously establishes the *princeps* as the destined end point for the narrative's most immediate patrilineal succession, the line from Anchises to Aeneas to Iulus to the Iulii. More importantly, Anchises elides the difference between the *gens Iulia* and the Roman race as a whole: in line 789, not only does Anchises invite Aeneas to consider the Romans 'his' (*tuos*), the balancing of *Romanos* and *Iuli*

---

[36] Horsfall (1991) 204.
[37] Feeney (1986) 5. Burke (1979) draws upon the focus on family groups to argue that the pageant of heroes is characterised as a *pompa funebris* (a funeral parade) which recalls the procession of ancestral *imagines* worn by actors that took place at noble Roman funerals.
[38] Austin (1977) 242, note on 788f.

In Lament for Marcellus: Propertius 3.18

at each end of the hexameter strongly suggests the equivalence of the two groups, to the extent that the *Iuli progenies* at which Aeneas now gazes becomes effectively a metaphor for a greater Roman 'family' comprising the many *gentes* that follow.[39]

If Augustus marks the beginning of the properly Roman part of the procession, then its ending is marked by Marcellus; these two figures thus form a (nearly)[40] balanced frame for the heroes that pass between them. In this larger context, the figure of Marcellus at the climax to the pageant aptly demonstrates the kind of fluidity between family and nation that underpins Anchises' vision of a pan-Roman *gens Iulia* at Rome's founding. Importantly, it is Aeneas who draws attention to Marcellus, pointing out the young man as one of the Claudian *gens* with whom he stands (6.863–6), and so indicating that he has learned the gentilicial lesson his father would impart. But Anchises' expansive response (and his final words in the *Aeneid*) in fact avoids overt classification by family, and instead depicts Marcellus broadly as an idealised embodiment of Roman (that is, *Julian*) virtues.[41] At the same time, the similarity of the sweeping 'national' praise Marcellus receives, at the end of the pageant, to that Augustus had received at its beginning reinforces Marcellus' framing association with the *princeps*, and so with the Julian *gens*. Here Virgil evokes not only Marcellus' (otherwise unremarked) adoption by the *princeps*, but also his likely status as heir to the Principate itself – and Anchises' reference to funeral rites for Marcellus at Augustus' Mausoleum (the 'new-built tomb', *tumulum ... recentem*, 6.874) furthers

---

[39] Reed (2001) 153–4. Cf. Burke (1979) 223: '[A]lthough the emphasis is clearly on the *gens Iulia*, the scope of the procession has been expanded to include many non-Julian participants. That is, Virgil's *pompa* is an event which implicitly treats all Roman heroes as members of one immense, extremely ancient family.'

[40] Augustus and Marcellus conspicuously receive the two longest accolades, at eighteen and fifteen lines, respectively.

[41] Indeed, Anchises' references to Marcellus as a 'boy of the Trojan race' (*puer Iliaca ... de gente*, 6.875) and vividly as his 'grandson' (*nepotis*, 6.884) serve to link Marcellus' unrivalled potential with that of Iulus himself.

Marcellus and the *Gens Claudia*

both points.[42] In this way Marcellus ends *Aeneid* 6 as at once a Claudian but yet a (dead) son in Rome's first dynastic family.[43]

A glance at the importance Virgil places on one's family and patrilineal ancestry highlights the extent to which, in 3.18, Propertius does precisely the opposite. In fact, Propertius pointedly questions the value of gentilicial identity – and he positions Marcellus less in context of his paternal line than in connection with his mother:

> quid genus aut uirtus aut optima profuit illi
> mater, et amplexum Caesaris esse focos?
> aut modo tam pleno fluitantia uela theatro,
> et per maternas omnia gesta manus?
> 3.18.11–14

What did his noble birth avail him, or his virtue, or the best of mothers – or to have embraced the house of Caesar? Or the billowing sails just recently on his crowded theatre, and everything brought about by his mother's hands?

Here Propertius offers a notoriously nihilistic perspective on points that Virgil presents as a poignant climax.[44] But the real sting in these lines comes from exposing an irony at the heart of the Virgilian narrative of meaningful bloodlines and Julian pre-destiny. Virgil allows the implication that Marcellus was destined as the latest in the line of succession from Aeneas himself, an ancient lineage whose authority is legitimised in Anchises' narration by juxtaposition with the many noble *gentes* of Roman history (only the Iulii are more so). On the other hand, Propertius in his poem makes it unavoidable that to consider Marcellus a Julian heir means acknowledging not a bloodline but a failed political adoption: *quid ... profuit illi ...*

---

[42] Dio 53.30.5 records Marcellus as the first occupant in the Mausoleum. For the likelihood that Virgil evokes Marcellus' actual funeral, see Skard (1965) 64, Burke (1979) 222–8. See too the brief remarks at Putnam (1998) 95.
[43] Reed (2001) 153.
[44] The rhetoric in Propertius' focus on the futility of rank and wealth is not out of place in an epicedium: see McKeown (1998) 118–20 on Ov. *Am.* 2.6.17–20, with numerous parallels. Yet Propertius' ironic, even sarcastic manner in the central section of 3.18 has frequently been felt to offer insufficient consolation to a

amplexum Caesaris esse focos? (11–12; and we will remember at this point that 'embracing Caesar's hearth' is a dynastic move already made by Augustus himself, adopted posthumously in the will of Julius Caesar).[45] More provocatively still, Propertius' poem emphasises that celebration of Marcellus as a *de facto* Julian is precisely not a salute to patrilineal succession but praise of his maternal family instead:[46] that Marcellus' mother Octavia is Augustus' sister surely underpins the marked enjambment of *mater* into the pentameter that references Caesar's household (12); and the conspicuous repetition in *per maternas ... manus* (14) then reinforces the point.[47]

In fact, an interrogation of the kind of multi-family relations that represents the dynastic 'reality' behind the Virgilian narrative – but not its gentilicial rhetoric – persists right through Propertius 3.18, and is especially prominent at the poem's beginning and end. We have seen that Propertius' remarkable opening couplet evokes Baiae as Octavian's wartime harbour that had admitted the sea into the enclosed waters of the Lucrine and Avernus lakes:

> Clausus ab umbroso qua ludit pontus Auerno,
> fumida Baiarum stagna tepentis aquae
> 3.18.1–2

Given that the ensuing poem will develop against a Virgilian background that underlines the importance of gentilicial identity, it is significant that Propertius opens with a striking reference to the naval station that Octavian had named *portus Iulius*, in honour of the family of his adoptive father. But it is far more significant that the poem's opening word – *clausus* – surely

---

grieving family – indeed, to a grieving nation: e.g. Nethercut (1970a) 401, Johnson (2009) 118.

[45] That 3.18.12 refers to Marcellus' adoption by Augustus and not his marriage to Augustus' daughter Julia see Richardson (1977) 392, revising the interpretation of Camps (1966) 140.

[46] A further suggestive parallel here, especially in juxtaposition with the name 'Caesar' at 3.18.12: Treggiari (2005) 140 points out Augustus' own reliance on his maternal lineage for access to power in the first place – as the grandson of Caesar's sister, and son of Caesar's niece.

[47] Heyworth (2007a) emends *maternas* to *maturas* (in the sense of 'precocious') precisely because the transmitted adjective is 'repetitious', and 'unsuited to the

Marcellus and the *Gens Claudia*

evokes Marcellus' gentilicial name *Claudius* at just the same moment;[48] at the very outset of the poem, it seems Propertius himself marries Claudius with Julius at the site of Marcellus' death, in anticipation of the (failed) political union that ushers in the poem's central sequence.[49]

Seemingly to reinforce the fusion of family names embedded in the opening two lines, the poem's final couplet restates the point more explicitly. As the poem ends, Propertius wishes Marcellus an unexpected apotheosis that would see Marcellus follow the footsteps of his ancestors in what are now two distinct lines:[50]

> at tibi nauta pias hominum qui traicit umbras
> hac animae portet corpus inane tuae
> qua Siculae uictor telluris *Claudius* et qua
> *Caesar* ab humana cessit in astra uia.
> 3.18.31–4[51]

> But may the sailor who conveys the shades of pious men carry your body empty of its soul on that route by which Claudius, victor in Sicilian territory, and by which Caesar left from the human road to the stars.

The text and meaning of these lines are subject to long-standing controversy that rises from Propertius' peculiar vision of an afterlife: here, not only do body and soul enjoy eternity in different locations, but the route that Marcellus will follow seems to pass across the Styx and towards the heavens

---

encomiastic context' in that it praises Marcellus' mother rather than the young man himself: see Heyworth (2007b) 384.

[48] Falkner (1977) 14 n. 7 attributes the observation that *clausus* (and *clausit*, 16) provide a pre-echo of the name *Claudius* to an unpublished manucript by Leo C. Curran (and wonders, 'Is this why Marcellus is nowhere *named* in the elegy?'). See too Richardson (1977) 391, and Heyworth & Morwood (2011) 291.

[49] Here Propertius echoes Horace's union of 'Marcellus' and the Julian clan at Hor. *Od.* 1.12.45–8; but while Horace appears to mark the wedding of Marcellus to Julia, Propertius raises the union in the context of Marcellus' death.

[50] For the ending of 3.18 as a 'surprise', see Falkner (1977) 13, Johnson (2009) 118. Adding to the novelty, the elder Marcellus is not attributed a catasterism before Propertius.

[51] In these four lines I follow the emendations and (absence of) punctuation presented by Heyworth (2007a). In particular, Heyworth makes *tibi* (31) refer to Marcellus rather than to Charon; and the verb *cessit* (34) becomes shared by Claudius and Caesar, rather than having an implied Marcellus (or his *anima*) as subject.

In Lament for Marcellus: Propertius 3.18

simultaneously.[52] But the significance of Propertius' fantastical flourish in the final lines comes out once again in a Virgilian dialogue. In an intertextual sense, Propertius' coda brings us full circle: by sending Marcellus back to the underworld after his death, Propertius returns us to where Virgil had introduced Marcellus before he was born, and in this context Propertius pointedly 'resolves' the careful gentilicial fudge that sits at the end of *Aeneid* 6. Virgil presents the parade of unborn heroes as a grand procession of Roman clans. But which of these family lines should Marcellus (re)join, now? – now that his ashes lie sealed in a Julian tomb? In the *Aeneid*, Marcellus walks with the Claudian family, and his potent but implicit association with the *gens Iulia* is subtle enough not to overpower the gentilicial logic of the preceding parade (the logic which of course underpins Augustus' mythic authority, and which, ironically, would presumably have come to bear on any future accession for Marcellus, too). But in 3.18, we see Propertius framing his lament for Marcellus in terms of a political 'reality' that rests on the miscibility of bloodlines when it comes to the exercise of imperial (and even republican) power. And so Propertius sends Marcellus back to the underworld readied for a flattering but faintly ridiculous double catasterism. As in Virgil, he lines up behind M. Claudius Marcellus, the victor at Syracuse – but now he also follows the celestial footsteps of G. Julius Caesar, at the same time (*qua ... Claudius et qua Caesar*, 33–4). The idealised republican logic that would keep the two figures walking separately in Virgil is displaced in Propertius by an imperial *Realpolitik* embodied in Marcellus himself that shows Claudius and Julius sharing a singular verb and proceeding together along the very same path (*ab humana cessit in astra uia*, 34).[53]

---

[52] The textual and interpretive issues are discussed thoroughly at Heyworth (2007b) 386–7; see too Falkner (1977) 13.

[53] Notwithstanding Augustus' protestations to the Senate that he had no interest in establishing a familial dynasty akin to a monarchy, his actions behind the scenes point to a long-standing intent to link the Iulii with the Claudii, beginning with his own marriage to Livia in 38 BCE, and including the marriage of Marcellus to his own daughter Julia.

Propertius' Roman Elegy

Propertius 3.18 offers us two parallel narratives. At a symbolic level, the poem seems to affirm that Propertius is making good on the desire he expressed in 3.17 to cease writing erotic elegy. The opening remembrance of Baiae returns to a crucial diptych at the centre of Book 1 where Propertius had offset an obsessive fear of inevitable amatory failure (1.11) with an assertion of thematic permanence (1.12); now a return to Baiae reprises that early unease, and seemingly binds the death of Marcellus to an impending demise for erotic poetry itself. Here, too, 3.18 appears to annotate precisely the tonal elevation for which Propertius prays at the end of 3.17: as elegiac subject, Marcellus is framed ostentatiously as a transition from early elegy's introspection to a newly Roman orientation. Meanwhile, at a thematic level, 3.18 offers a glance at just how ambitious Propertian 'public' elegy might prove to be. At its first outing, Propertius' newly Roman attitude is realised in observing the powerful dynastic hybridity that stems inevitably from Marcellus' position as Claudian heir to a Julian *princeps*: by opening his poem in the en*clos*ed waters of the *Julian* harbour, by ending it in the ancestral footsteps of both Claudius and Caesar, Propertius effectively (and very presciently) subordinates Marcellus' death as but a small false step within the framework of an evolving imperial super-family known to subsequent history as the Julio-Claudian dynasty.

And yet, when we bring the poem's two narratives together like this, an ironic recapitulation comes to light. 3.18 certainly presents itself as a radical departure for Propertian elegy, yet the obstinacy of its politics retains a striking familiarity. 3.18 annotates a conscious transition away from the self-imposed (and always disingenuous) narrow focus of early elegy – a transition that has been under way for some time; but the resulting poetry seems to indulge a new freedom to interrogate public material more than it shows the presence of such material as a novelty in itself. More significantly, participation with other poets in a public celebration of Marcellus hardly results in a newly integrated elegiac voice. Rather, Propertius makes use of

In Lament for Marcellus: Propertius 3.18

a public platform to amplify a poetic voice that remains notably individual, and elusively dissident in the best elegiac manner. To reiterate one case in point: Propertius offers a lament that does indeed celebrate Marcellus' young life[54] – but which undermines Marcellus' role in nation-building myth precisely when the poem is brought to bear on the community of texts of which it forms a part. When 3.18 is read against *Aeneid* 6, in particular, the effect is dramatic: to champion Marcellus as a destined heir-in-law to the Principate – to inter the ashes of an adopted son as the first occupant of the family mausoleum – now highlights not the centrality but the profound irrelevance of *gens* to the establishment of an Augustan dynasty. Moreover, behind this Augustan barb lies the reinvention of an early elegiac shibboleth that symbolised Propertius' disengagement from public life. Propertius has maintained an active disinterest in bloodlines – and especially in the politicisation of children – since early in Book 2. Dynasty is the challenge (especially for Augustus) of creating sons; but, as 2.7.5–14 makes clear, Cynthia is about *not* having babies.[55]

Perhaps the double bluff in 3.18 is not that where we expect to find Cynthia we find Marcellus instead; but rather that a poem which sets up Marcellus as a pivotal thematic movement away from Cynthia finally resists delivering Marcellus in the way we expect. In fact, the absence of Marcellus' name from 3.18[56] helps to emphasise the way that Propertius ultimately subsumes the young man's individuality beneath the symbolism of a broader story. Framed by the myths of an emergent Augustan regime, the dead youth matters less to Propertius

---

[54] Falkner (1977) 11 rightly points out that '[t]he elegy is *essentially* a tribute to the youth and a consolation to his family, not a parody of the *epicedion*'.
[55] Until 3.22, at least – a poem I discuss below as an Epilogue.
[56] Unsurprisingly, many commentators note that Marcellus' name is not mentioned in 3.18. For Camps (1966) 140, 'Marcellus does not need to be named'; for Fedeli (1985) 542, the occasion of the poem is too close to Marcellus' death for his name to be used in good taste; while M. F. Williams (1996) 159 reads the absence of a name as a suggestive elision: 'The contrast between names and non-names, the famous and the unmentioned is striking – Marcellus is now one of the forgotten.' By contrast, Heyworth (2007a) prints a lacuna prior to the couplet 9–10 in which he presumes Marcellus' name was given and his illness accounted for: see discussion at Heyworth (2007b) 381–2.

Propertius' Roman Elegy

as Marcellus than as member of the Claudii; here, instead of Marcellus' cognomen, the poem offers us *clausus – clausit – Claudius* at regular intervals (in the first, eighth and sixteenth couplet, respectively).[57] But what a seditious story this is, for an elegist who still teases with the promise of Augustan conversion! If *Aeneid* 6 presents Marcellus at the apex of a Julian celebration and triumph of a Trojan *gens*, then Propertius 3.18 laments Marcellus throughout as a Claudian – the latest of a famously Sabine clan incorporated into the make-up of Romulus' Rome.[58] Where Virgil narrates a patrilineal progression from Iulus to Iulius, Propertius presents instead an etymologising transition from (Attius) Clausus to Claudius (3.18.1–33).[59]

In closing we return to Falkner's provocative suggestion that, at the beginning of 3.18, a reader 'might well imagine that he is reading a love-elegy dealing with the poet's mistress at Baiae'.[60] In essence, Falkner opens up a second metamorphosis for elegy alongside its transition in scope since 1.11 from *paruula* to *publica*: listening to 3.18's initial couplets as a *love* elegy set at Baiae highlights a parallel gendered transition from *clausa* to *clausus*. In 1.11, the adjective *clausa* conveys the lover–poet's fantasised containment and control of his mistress; but more typically it provides the impulse to elegiac song itself, since the beloved is 'enclosed' behind locked doors (1.16.18, 3.3.49, 3.13.9, 3.14.23). As the first word of 3.18, *clausus* describes the sea enclosed by Lake Avernus. Yet it also evokes Marcellus' name – and it captures very well Marcellus' current 'enclosure'

---

[57] The even spacing of these allusions to Marcellus' cognomen supports the omission of the lines transmitted as 3.18.29–30 as a misplaced couplet (Richardson (1977) 394, Heyworth (2007b) 385), while also suggesting against the presence of a lacuna before 3.18.9–10 (for which, see Heyworth (2007b) 383–4).

[58] Livy *A.V.C.* 2.16 links the origins of the *gens Claudia* with the arrival in Rome of a Sabine refugee, one Attius Clausus, accompanied by a large number of supporters. Clausus took the Roman name Appius Claudius, and together with his followers became known as the 'old Claudian tribe' (*uetus Claudia tribus*, 2.16.5).

[59] See note 58. Here the Marcellus elegy most provocatively presents a model for a strategy that Propertius will employ frequently in the aetiological poems of Book 4 – a sideline in etymological play, such as with the name of the god Vertumnus in 4.2 (on which see O'Neill (2000) 260–1).

[60] Falkner (1977) 13.

In Lament for Marcellus: Propertius 3.18

behind the sealed doors of Augustus' new Mausoleum. If, with Falkner, we hear Propertius here reinventing an amatory trope for an Augustan prince, then the poet might just conjure a fleeting moment when elegiac lament becomes a national song, a split second when a locked-up Marcellus does not displace Cynthia so much as become her.

Here 3.18 furthers an ironic realisation of the agenda Propertius announced in the previous poem. In 3.17, with Virgil's proem to *Georgics* 3 resounding in the background, Propertius consecrated his newly elevated Bacchic/Pindaric programme while standing outside an intertextual temple that just might contain 'Caesar' (*ante fores templi*, 3.17.37; *in medio mihi Caesar erit*, Virg. *Geo.* 3.16).[61] In a sense, this vision comes to pass. In the very next poem, as he offers one of the consolatory *carmina* that Seneca will later recall, Propertius performs funereal song outside a monument that contains Augustus' heir.[62] As 3.17 passes to 3.18, does the patriotic promise of Caesar's temple find ironic expression in Marcellus' tomb? At least, by choosing to join a public chorus of lament outside the doors of the Mausoleum in which Marcellus has been sealed up, just possibly Propertius intimates that the death of Augustus' adopted son has briefly made love elegists of us all.

---

[61] See the discussion in chapter 6 (pp. 158–63).
[62] Cf. Virg. *Aen.* 6.873–4: *uel quae, Tiberine, uidebis|funera, cum tumulum praeterlabere recentem* ('And what funeral rites you will see, O Tiber, as you glide past the newly built tomb').

CHAPTER 8

RENEWING AN ELEGIAC CONTRACT

Propertius 3.20

3.20 narrates Propertius' attempt to seduce an unnamed *puella* whose lover has abandoned her in order to seek wealth overseas. The poet's seductive strategy rests on making a clear distinction between fidelity and infidelity, an antithesis reflected in the poem's three-part structure.[1] The poem's opening (1–6) appeals to lovers' generic lack of faith, as Propertius urges the girl to break her union with her current lover, arguing that he has already broken his pledge to her. In the central section (7–24) Propertius pledges his own good faith instead, seeking to enshrine his *fides* in an erotic contract which draws on the legal apparatus of the Roman marriage ceremony.[2] The final section (25–30) returns to the opening theme of infidelity, as Propertius outlines the penalty that should apply to anyone breaking the terms of love's contract.

Inasmuch as Propertius seemingly seeks a new mistress in 3.20, the poem foreshadows the poet's imminent break-up with Cynthia in 3.24, and affirms the outwardly closural gestures for erotic elegy in 3.17 and 3.18. At the same time, the late return of the poet's own erotic narrative in 3.20 – conspicuous by its absence in Book 3 – provides an unexpected reinvigoration of amatory verse even as the ending of the collection looms. This proves especially the case when the poem is read with two earlier third-book poems which overtly engage the theme of

---

[1] Fedeli (1985) 584. For a detailed structural analysis, see Lieberg (2006) 958–60. All recent editors rightly regard 3.20 as a single elegy: Richardson (1977), Fedeli (1984), Goold (1990), Heyworth (2007a); for discussion, see Fedeli (1985) 583–4, Heyworth (2007b) 391. For an appeal to 1.8 in terms of precedent for dividing 3.20, see Courtney (1970) 49–51; on this point, cf. Williams (1968) 414–15, and Cairns (1972) 148–52. For 3.20 as a 'reaction' poem see Cairns (1972) 138–57, Barsby (1975) 31; for the poem's coherence in terms of vocabulary and allusion, see Racette-Campbell (2013) 297–9.

[2] For the significance of marriage imagery in 3.20, see Racette-Campbell (2013) 303–9.

elegiac *fides*. In 3.20, the 'lyric' fascination with constancy that Propertius reclaims from Horace in 3.12 is re-embedded in elegy; a dialogue between these poems equips elegy's reader to appreciate the willing credulity that elegiac fidelity requires of lovers, and of readers. Similarly, the transparent use in 3.6 of the erotic as a metaphor for the literary – and vice versa – provides key insight into the new deal which 3.20 offers for elegy. 3.6 reveals that a poet's words are to be trusted no more than a lover's.[3] But in 3.20 recognition that the lovers (and poets) will tell lies is no longer a matter of destabilisation but instead a positive step towards a *new* contract between lovers (as between reader and poet); indeed, this contract finally brings into being the elusive *concordia* invoked plaintively at the conclusion of 3.6. Rather than positioning the reader/beloved as the helpless victim of deception, 3.20 invites its addressee – and so its readers – to demonstrate actively their understanding of how love and poetry work.

Faithful Lovers and Elegiac *Puellae*

As the poem begins, Propertius purports to instruct an unnamed female addressee whose naivety in the ways of lovers has led her to overvalue her erstwhile partner's integrity:

> Credis eum iam posse tuae meminisse figurae,
>   uidisti a lecto quem dare uela tuo?
> durus, qui lucro potuit mutare puellam!
>   tantine, ut lacrimes, Africa tota fuit?
> at tu, stulta, deos, tu fingis inania uerba:
>   fortisan ille alio pectus amore terat.
> est tibi forma potens, sunt castae Palladis artes,
>   splendidaque a docto fama refulget auo.
> fortunata domus, modo sit tibi fidus amicus!
>   fidus ero: in nostros curre, puella, toros!
>   3.20.1–10

Do you believe that he can still recall your beauty, the man whom you have seen set sail from your bed? Hard-hearted the man who is able to

---

[3] James (2003b) 13 points to the conflation of reader and beloved in the figure of the *puella*; see also Habinek (1998) 134.

Faithful Lovers and Elegiac *Puellae*

exchange a girl for money! Was all Africa worth so much that you should weep? But you, foolish girl, dream up gods and empty words: perhaps he warms his chest in another's loving embrace. You have potent beauty, and the skills of chaste Pallas, and your fame shines down brilliantly from your learned grandfather. Your house is blessed – if only you have a faithful lover! I shall be faithful: run, girl, into my bed.

Clearly Propertius' instruction is also his seduction.[4] Just as the poet's flatteries (7–8) are intended to impress the *puella*, so is the pointed juxtaposition he makes between his own constancy and the inconstancy of his rival: with the girl's affections at stake, Propertius would have her believe that the two men are as different as can be.[5] Yet, for the poem's reader, the structure and context of the poem conspire precisely to undermine the poet's claimed point of difference.[6] To begin with, Propertius' promise *fidus ero* (10) is a conventional cry – a reader familiar with Propertius' poetry will remember that he has promised to be true (to Cynthia) from the very beginning.[7] For some readers, the frequency of Propertius' insistence on his own faithfulness is enough in itself to invite suspicion.[8] In this instance, Propertius' emblematic claim to good faith is treated with overt irony: the anonymity of the girl whom Propertius addresses and the clear suggestion in the middle of the poem that he is approaching her for the first time (*nox mihi prima uenit! primae da tempora nocti! longius in primo, Luna, morare toro*, 'The first night approaches for me! Make time for the first night! Moon, linger longer on our first bedding', 3.20.13–14) implies that the poet now reiterates his promise always to be faithful precisely in a poem in which he appears to be leaving Cynthia for a new mistress.[9]

---

[4] James (2003b) 13.
[5] Williams (1968) 416, Racette-Campbell (2013) 300.
[6] The reminiscence, via the myth of Ariadne, in the poem's opening couplet of the beginning of 1.3 – in which Propertius had seemingly abandoned Cynthia for an evening with another girl – furthers the irony with which the lover now pledges his loyalty: Racette-Campbell (2013) 309–11.
[7] E.g. 1.4.1–4, 1.8.21–6, 1.12.19–20, 1.15.29–32, 2.7.19, 2.20.34, 2.26.27, 3.15.9–10. See Lilja (1965) 172–86, Lyne (1980) 65–7; cf. Lieberg (2006) 954–8.
[8] See Lilja (1965) 185.
[9] Heyworth & Morwood (2011) 299–300. Cf. Butler & Barber (1933) 312, who assumes that the emphasis on novelty must mean that 3.20 recalls the beginning

More fundamentally, while the poem's first two sections seemingly reinforce the distinction Propertius claims between himself and the girl's former lover by focusing on faithlessness and faithfulness in turn, a switch back to the theme of infidelity in the final section gives the poem a 'wry symmetry',[10] and suggests in fact an ironic resemblance between the poem's two male characters:

> ergo, qui pactas in foedera ruperit aras,
>   pollueritque nouo sacra marita toro,
> illi sint quicumque solent in amore dolores,
>   et caput argutae praebeat historiae;
> nec flenti dominae patefiant nocte fenestrae:
>   semper amet, fructu semper amoris egens.
>   3.20.25–30

Therefore, for the man who breaks the altars pledged as a contract and defiles the sanctity of a marriage by turning to a new bed, for him might there be all the sorrows that are customary in love, and might he present his head for shrill notoriety. May his mistress's windows remained barred to his weeping by night: may he love always, yet may he always lack the enjoyment of love.

No doubt this closing censure of male infidelity is intended to remind the *puella* of her abandonment, but it should remind the reader of the Propertian poet–lover instead. For a start, Propertius denounces the (other) fickle man who has sought 'a new bed' (*nouo toro*, 26), yet the one character in the poem indubitably seeking a 'new love' (*nouo amore*, 16) is Propertius himself. More strikingly, the erotic anguish Propertius invokes as punishment for the faithless man corresponds closely to the programmatic condition already afflicting the Propertian lover, whose Venus 'levies on him nights of bitterness', for whom 'fruitless Love is never absent' (*in me nostra Venus noctes exercet amaras|et nullo uacuus tempore defit Amor*, 1.1.33–4). It is Propertius himself whose access to the *puella* is usually barred

---

of Propertius' affair with Cynthia. Less likely still, others assume the resumption of the affair after a break: Baker (1968a) 338–9, Baker (1969), Barsby (1975) 37–8, Fedeli (1985) 586, Clarke (2004) 138, Cairns (2006) 355.

[10] Richardson (1977) 398.

Faithful Lovers and Elegiac *Puellae*

(29), and whose public reputation suffers from hostile gossip (28; cf. esp. 2.24.1–8).

If Propertius' character comes unwittingly to resemble the rival whom he has used a foil (and vice versa), the enigmatic character of the poem's *puella* creates an elusive association with previous *puellae* in Propertian elegy.[11] On the one hand, given the poem's position late in Book 3 most readers are surely right to regard the *puella* in 3.20 as a new mistress who plays the closural role of 'not-Cynthia'.[12] On the other hand, in Propertius' description at 3.20.7–9 of the *puella*'s literary lineage and artistic accomplishments, other readers are not mistaken in (nearly) recognising a miniature portrait of Cynthia herself.[13] We might remember that, even at this late stage, Book 3 has not yet named Propertius' mistress: in one sense, the poem's almost-evocation of Cynthia – in a narrative context where finding Cynthia makes little sense – provides a teasing acknowledgement of the way the poetry has increasingly withheld positive identification of elegy's mistress (it will be no coincidence that Cynthia is finally named in the very next poem, 3.21). In a broader sense, the poem's play with identity comments knowingly on the increasing challenge of maintaining belief in the individuality of Propertius' mistress. The use of Cynthia's name has declined markedly since Book 1:[14] in the first collection, the name Cynthia appears thirty-one times, followed by twenty-three times in the (considerably longer) second book, and only three times in Book 3, all of

---

[11] On the *puella*'s indefinite identity, see Lilja (1965) 70, Shackleton Bailey (1956) 204 and Lieberg (2006) 954 n. 1; on such uncertainty as part of a wider theme in 3.20, see Racette-Campbell (2013) 312.

[12] See e.g. Camps (1966) 146–7, Williams (1968) 413–17, Courtney (1970) 50–1, Richardson (1977) 397–8, James (2003b) 266 n. 53, Newman (2006) 348–9, Heyworth & Morwood (2011) 299–300.

[13] Hubbard (1974) 89; see also Courtney (1970) 49, Barsby (1975) 34, Fedeli (1985) 585. On this point, cf. James (2003b) 266 n. 53, Heyworth & Morwood (2011) 299. 3.20 includes a reference to the girl's *doctus auus* ('learned ancestor', 3.20.8), a detail often used as support for Apuleius' notorious claim that Cynthia's 'real' name was Hostia, since we know of an epic poet Hostius writing about a century before Propertius: see e.g. Syme (1978) 202, Coarelli (2004), esp. 110–15.

[14] On namelessness as a means of 'silencing' the elegiac *puella*, see Gold (2007) 60.

which occur after 3.20.[15] Here the question of the girl's identity in the present poem directly engages the space created by Cynthia's gradual disappearance. The poem's opening statement (3.20.1) about the lover's inability to remember the *figura* of the poem's beloved might well find metapoetic resonance in the poetry's reader, for whom it has been some considerable time since there was certainty of reading *Cynthia*.

In this bigger picture, however, the real value of 3.20's elusive *puella* lies in her essential anonymity itself. 3.20 reminds us that Cynthia herself has long since yielded to a number of generic beloveds, each of whom bears a greater or lesser resemblance to the Cynthia of Propertius' early poetry.[16] This transition is well marked at a programmatic level. Whereas Books 1 and 2 open with poems that ostensibly declare allegiance to one woman as both beloved and poetic inspiration, Book 3 opens with an invocation of poets and (love) poetry itself. Among the early programmatic gestures in the third book is reference to the poet's 'crowd of girls' (*turba puellarum*, 3.2.10),[17] building on the implication as early as 2.5 that the poet's beloved mistress is one of numerous *puellae* fit to be elegy's subject.[18] This is the Propertius imitated with knowing insight in subsequent Ovidian elegy. While Ovid (like Propertius) outwardly maintains the romantic notion of elegiac exclusivity (e.g. *Am.* 1.3.15–20, 2.17.33–4, 3.12.16; cf. esp. Prop. 1.19), Ovid also makes explicit the scale of elegy's erotic ambition: 'Whatever girls in the whole city someone might commend, my love has designs upon them all' (*noster in has omnes ambitiosus amor, Am.* 2.4.47–8).[19]

---

[15] A Propertian *puella* appears unnamed in poems 6, 8, 10, 11, 15, 16, 19, 23. 'Cynthia' is named in poems 21 and 24. See Williams (1968) 483–92, esp. 488f., for a discussion of the possible identification of Cynthia in other poems.

[16] On the gradual switch in Propertian elegy from 'realistic' mistress towards an adaptable female symbol, see Wyke (1987a) 154.

[17] On 3.20 and Propertius' *turba puellarum*, see Newman (2006) 349.

[18] Esp. 2.5.5–6: *inueniam tamen e multis fallacibus unam | quae fieri nostro carmine nota uelit* ('Out of the many deceitful women nonetheless I shall find one who would be glad to be made famous in my poetry'). See similarly Prop. 2.22.1–10, 35–6.

[19] See here Keith (1994) 35. For the theme of (plural) *puellae* in Ovidian elegy, see also *Am.* 2.1.37–8, and generally 2.7 and 2.10.

Faithful Lovers and Elegiac *Puellae*

In fact, it is Ovid in the *Ars Amatoria* who best unmasks Propertius' claim *fidus ero* as a promise the poet has made to any number of potential 'Cynthias'. Early in Book 1, Ovid echoes once again the faithful utterance of elegiac poets before him. But on this occasion the Ovidian narrator quotes specifically from Propertius himself (Prop. 2.7.19):

> dum licet, et loris passim potes ire solutis,
> elige cui dicas 'tu mihi sola places'.
> *Ars Am.* 1.41–2

> While you are free, and able to range widely with loosened rein, choose the one to whom you will say 'You alone please me'.

Within the poem's didactic paradigm, the Ovidian instructor presents the lover's oath of fidelity as an insincere 'script to be performed'.[20] To the extent that the *Ars Amatoria* is also a critique of the elegiac genre, Ovid's use of a quotation from Propertius to illustrate the lover's oath itself affirms that Propertian elegy is characterised by the very same performativity; the 'student' reader of Ovid's poem is taught not only to feign sincerity, but to feign it 'like Propertius'. From this perspective, the opening ten lines of 3.20 rehearse the Ovidian dictum that the *fidus ero* (or its equivalent) is the lie that every lover tells to his beloved. As the poem begins, Propertius chides the *puella* as being foolish for trusting the *inania uerba* of a lover, before wooing her with seductive words of his own (7–10). From Propertius' perspective, the poem's anonymous *puella* resembles the series of girls he has addressed similarly in the past. From the point of view of the *puella*, Propertius and her former lover are merely two instances of the same character: Propertius is simply the next lover, and the phrase *fidus ero* comprises the *inania uerba* themselves – that which Propertius says now, and what (it is a reasonable guess) would have been said by her lover before him.

---

[20] Kennedy (1993) 65; see too Myerowitz (1985) 26.

Renewing an Elegiac Contract: Propertius 3.20

Being Faithful in Literary Love

Recognising the Propertian lover's promise to be faithful in this poem as an element in a wider literary trope reinforces the sense that the claim is very difficult to take seriously. The lover's cry *fidus ero* is at once a personal pledge and an echo of the cries of previous lovers (among them Propertius himself, as we have seen). For an Augustan poet, this broader context is informed particularly by Catullan and Horatian erotic perspective, where not only is a lasting erotic union a naive and unattainable ideal, but where love poetry itself is often a whimsical or seductive game played by poets with their readers.[21]

In 3.20 Propertius seeks to reinforce his verbal pledge to be faithful by enshrining it in a written contract:

> foedera sunt ponenda prius signandaque iura
> et scribenda mihi lex in amore nouo.
> haec Amor ipse suo constringit pignora signo:
> testis sidereae torta corona deae.
> namque ubi non certo uincitur foedere lectus,
> non habet ultores nox uigilanda deos,
> et quibus imposuit, soluit mox uincla libido:
> contineant nobis omina prima fidem.
>
> 3.20.15–24

First treaties must be set up and statutes must be signed and a law written for my new love. Love himself seals these with his own signet ring: the twisted crown of the starry goddess is witness. For when a bed is not bound by a settled contract, the sleepless night finds no avenging gods, and lust soon releases the bonds from those on whom it has imposed them: in our case may the first omens preserve our faith.

Propertius' intent is positive but his rhetoric is pessimistic. Significantly, in anticipation of the coming rendezvous with a new mistress, Propertius prioritises the writing and signing of such erotic treaties ahead of any sex that might occur.[22] Within the poem's narrative the contract is a defensive measure. It is

---

[21] An 'erotic' relationship between poet and reader is examined in the context of Catullus by Fitzgerald (1995) 34–58.

[22] Cf. James (2003b) 43–6, where the promise of 'marriage' is one of the stratagems by which the lover woos the *puella* into bed. Yet here the sex is explicitly put on hold until the *foedus* is signed.

Being Faithful in Literary Love

an erotic talisman whose purpose is to guard against the inevitable desire to be unfaithful – a condition seemingly intrinsic to lovers (23), and here symbolised by the departure of the girl's erstwhile partner.[23] But, in this regard, even the terms of the contract reflect the poet's pessimism. The *foedus* seems unable to prevent any such infidelity, instead offering divine redress should either party be untrue (21–2).

Invoking an amatory 'treaty' is also overtly allusive. Most of all, Propertius' legal terminology invokes the precedent of Catullus, who conspicuously adopted the language of Roman public life to describe his private poetic relationship with his mistress Lesbia;[24] indeed, in his 'final' love poem, Catullus refers to the ideal of a long-lasting erotic union precisely as 'this eternal treaty of inviolable friendship' (*aeternum hoc sanctae foedus amicitiae*, Cat. 109.6).[25] When in 3.20 Propertius seeks to embed his pledge of good faith in an erotic contract, the elegist essentially restates the idealism behind Catullus' original *foedus* – but with an ironic effect suggesting the futility of believing that such an oath might ever endure. The ostensible optimism in Catullus' contract at the conclusion of 109 gains poignancy from the 'unchronological' ordering of Catullus' collection, where the poems describing the eventual breakdown of Catullus' relationship with Lesbia (esp. Cat. 8, 11) come near the beginning. By the time we reach Catullus' final love poem, we know full well that Lesbia will not live up to her faithful promise (109.1–2) which Catullus' contract seeks to make permanent.

In a more subtle way 3.20 also continues Propertius' engagement with the erotic morality of Horace's *Odes*.[26] The dramatic scenario with which Propertius opens 3.20 – an abandoned girl whose erstwhile lover has departed for foreign lands – reprises

---

[23] E.g. James (2003b) 48. For discussion of a sexual contract in Plautus' *Asinaria* as evidence of male anxiety about female promiscuity, see James (2006) 228–32.
[24] E.g. Richardson (1977) 399; see too Hallett (1973) 109–11, and Fitzgerald (1995) 117–20, Racette-Campbell (2013) 301.
[25] See also Cat. 76.3, 87.3.
[26] Even the playfulness surrounding the identity of the *puella* responds in an elegiac context to the cheerful ambivalence that attends the identities of the (named) mistresses of Horace's lyric poetry (for which see Nisbet & Rudd (2004) xxiii).

Renewing an Elegiac Contract: Propertius 3.20

the erotic setting of Propertius 3.12,[27] where Postumus had left his Galla behind in order to pursue military glory as an Augustan soldier. But in doing so 3.20 reprises the interaction that 3.12 stages with *Odes* 3.7 – and Horace's presence in the background exposes Propertius' apparent volte-face in terms of the ethics of amatory constancy. These three poems have in common a central focus on amatory fidelity in the face of distance. In *Od.* 3.7, Horace separates a pair of lovers, Gyges and Asterie, and presents each as (potentially) vulnerable to the erotic attentions of third parties (Chloe and Enipeus, respectively) during their absence from each other. The Horatian narrator sides with the separated lovers, reassuring Asterie of the constancy of Gyges, and urging her in turn to resist the (suggestively elegiac) overtures of Enipeus. In 3.12 Propertius also celebrates an enduring bond between his lovers, praising the surpassing faithfulness of Galla during the absence of Postumus – and thus seeking to outdo Horace at his own game in an intertextual contest between lyric and elegiac values.

But in 3.20 Propertius shifts perspective in a startling manner. In one sense Propertius continues to honour faithfulness, seeking to enshrine his and the *puella*'s fidelity in an erotic *foedus*. But when the narratives of 3.12 and *Od.* 3.7 are brought together, we can see with new clarity that in 3.20 Propertius in fact assumes an erotically disruptive role even as he pledges his fidelity – Propertius plays the role of Horace's deceptively seductive Enipeus, the one who (we might assume) promises constancy only so as to persuade Asterie to be *un*faithful. More broadly still, a triangulation with *Odes* 3.7 draws attention to the way that Propertius qualifies what had been a (Horatian) idealisation of constancy in 3.12. As we saw in chapter 4, faithfulness in a girl (*qua* Galla) does reflect an ideal and a surprisingly common 'reality' in Propertian elegy. But it is apparent here that the only faithfulness that matters is that which a girl displays to Propertius himself (in fact, the third-person homily of Galla and Postumus might even be the kind

---

[27] Racette-Campbell (2013) 299.

of tale one recites to a girl whose fidelity one wishes to win). Most importantly of all, the complex Horatian love triangles that lie behind both 3.12 and 3.20 provide tacit perspective to the primary relationships in these Propertian poems. By drawing Horace's own suggestive eroticism, Propertius contrives to point out that fidelity to the elegiac lover 'almost certainly means infidelity to someone else'.[28]

Closure and Renewal

Though it might generate a certain self-satisfaction to be able to see through the poet's declaration of fidelity in 3.20, we should expect there to be more to the poem than the continued unpicking of amatory verse that such a spell-breaking revelation represents, especially given a pervasive double-voicing in 3.17 and 3.18 with regard to the poet's commitment to (erotic) elegy. The poem's central narrative of 'taking a new mistress' – seen both in Propertius himself (*amore nouo*, 16) and in the poem's second male character (*alio amore*, 6) – is certainly recognisable as one of several typical strategies for overcoming an unhappy affair that gather in the final third of Book 3 (alongside wine in 3.17 and travel in 3.21, and paying blunt attention to a girl's faults in 3.24);[29] read in this way, 3.20 offers to cohere with a broader literary narrative that eventually frees the writer from writing love poetry.[30] Yet this turns out to be only half the story. One of the most striking features of the poem remains its exultant embrace of a sense of beginning: *prima nox*, *primae noctis*, *primo toro* (13–14). Rather surprisingly, as much as it might prepare us for an end to amatory writing, 3.20 also offers to take us right back to the start, ready to do it all over again. The difference is that, next time around, we enter the relationship with our eyes open.

---

[28] Sharrock (2000) 273.
[29] All these 'cures' for love will be proposed by Ovid in his *Remedia Amoris*: wine at 803–10, taking another mistress at 441–88, travel at 213–48 and exposing a girl's blemishes at 315–56.
[30] So Courtney (1970) 50–1.

Renewing an Elegiac Contract: Propertius 3.20

One of the most important ways in which 3.20 lays bare elegy's erotic conceit stems metapoetically from a narrative in which both the *puella*'s erstwhile lover and Propertius himself exchange an old mistress for a new one. Propertius employs this central commonplace of promiscuous lover(s) to explore the poet's ultimate control over his material – here, specifically, to 'change his girl' (*mutare puellam*, 3) whenever he desires.[31] In essence Propertius narrates a central truth about his poetry from the beginning: as the poet–lover's erotic subject, elegy's mistress is changeable and, indeed, exchangeable. The ironic manner in which the motif *mutare puellam* is treated within the amatory narrative also offers a parallel for a wider game the poet plays with his reader. The narrating lover rejects the idea of changing girls – but this is because the rejection forms part of the lover's seduction of the *puella*, who sits in for us as the poem's primary audience. When we place the poem in its context, however, it becomes clear that this is precisely the moment when the narrator *does* change girls. For the reader who seeks always to find 'Cynthia' in Propertius' erotic narrative,[32] the result is confrontation with a poem whose message is that one can never be sure whom the poet addresses as his mistress. In fact, 3.20 teases such a reader with the promise and yet impossibility of identifying the *puella* in the poem – with the consequent sense of disorientation emphasised by a juxtaposition with 3.21 in which the apparent 'certainty' of reading about 'Cynthia' is finally provided. Finally, by suggesting that the girl in this poem could be anyone, Propertius both suggests an inherent plurality within the identity of his poetic 'mistress' and so destabilises the reader's ability to trust in a coherent romantic narrative, let alone an exclusive poetry of 'Propertius and Cynthia'.

Yet what makes this confession of elegiac deception different from its presentation in 3.6 is that it occurs now in an essentially optimistic poem; 3.20 anticipates with excitement a new

---

[31] On Cynthia's adaptability to narrative need, see esp. Wyke (1989a) 30, Gold (1993) 87–90.
[32] E.g. Cairns (2006) 348 n. 83: 'Where a mistress who is not named appears in a Propertian elegy, I assume that she is Cynthia (if this matters).'

Closure and Renewal

beginning, whereas 3.6 articulates fear of an ending. The contract with which the lover hopes to formalise a new relationship symbolises a restart not only for Propertius' love life but for his love poetry too, in a way that (for us, especially) takes stock of the lessons learned across the breadth of Book 3. To the extent that the *foedus* in 3.20 evokes the values associated with Roman marriage,[33] it has typically been read as enacting 'the true death of elegy' for the reason that 'all the episodes, events, and emotions of elegy require the lover and the beloved *not* to be married'.[34] But such an approach overlooks a crucial lesson from the middle of the collection: 3.12 has shown us that marriage can (and does) exist as part of elegy's symbolic language; moreover, it has shown that the idealised exclusivity, consistency and certainty represented by a marriage contract are in fact the conventional values that the elegiac lover has always espoused.[35] Rather than effect elegiac closure, the *foedus* in 3.20 gives particularly elegiac expression to the formal union of Postumus and Galla celebrated in 3.12, rearticulating the enduring faithfulness symbolised by their marriage in the context of Propertius' own persuasive manner. More broadly still, the proposed contract in 3.20 offers a moment of reconciliation for the lover and beloved (and for their reader) with the duplicity in erotic discourse that the poem itself and 3.6 before it have exposed. Only by recognising the strategy in the lover's cry *fidus ero* might the emblematic phrase gain a paradoxical sincerity; now, as the end of the book approaches, all parties are given the chance to give their informed consent to beginning again.

This will matter, as we look ahead. We will all admit that some measure of knowing self-deception is vital in the beginning of a love affair (indeed, Ovid will later advise women precisely to allow themselves to be deceived by their pretending lover: *Ars Am.* 1.617–18).[36] Rather than reading the *stulta*

---

[33] E.g. James (2003b) 47.
[34] James (1998) 12.
[35] E.g. Greene (1998) 316–17.
[36] Kennedy (1993) 69.

puella in 3.20 as a naive victim of male duplicity, we might even recuperate her as a willing participant, provided she signs the lover's contract. In the end, the *foedus* of 3.20 – bound up as it is with the idea of a new beginning – offers the freedom to renew a love affair with the work precisely because the artifice of the erotic discourse has been revealed. In his discussion of the potency of romantic irony, Don Fowler offers apt summation in words that apply to both love and poetry:

> It is not normally thought a good tactic for seducers in literature or life to bring up the subject of deception. Would you believe a man who declared his love like this? Can we allow ourselves to be taken in by a poem that so blatantly tells us that it deceives? The answer of course is 'yes': that is the name of the game.[37]

At this point it is finally possible to read 3.20 *as* a love poem. In one sense, the conspicuous allusiveness of Propertius' promise *fidus ero* and of his proffered *foedus* aligns this love poem with the more overtly literary poetics of the third book; here 3.20 is a performative poem about love and literature in a tradition influenced especially by the erotic writing of Catullus and Horace. At the same time, at a personal level there is an ironic sense in which, precisely by coming clean about the nature of his patterned seduction and by emphasising the textual, fictive basis of his love, Propertius releases the poem's reader now to *believe* in a seductive sincerity within the poet's declaration of fidelity – in a way less possible before.

---

[37] Fowler (2000) 13.

CHAPTER 9

BREAKING UP (WITH) *CYNTHIA*

Propertius 3.24

There can be no doubt that Propertius 3.24 is an ambitiously closural poem: it is an elegy that utilises its position at the end of the book to engage actively with representations of 'ending up'.[1] The most overt strategy that Propertius adopts at this point is to conflate the end of the collection of poetry with a narrative in which he escapes his mistress's erotic thrall. In objective terms, this makes a fine ending for a book of verse – even an ending, as the poem itself suggests, for three books of verse.[2] The manner of ending in 3.24 offers a perspective from which the preceding body of poetry can be seen to make sense (as, perhaps, representing an errant period of 'youthful excess' from which the poet now withdraws in an authorial act of 'growing up');[3] and, in so far as a text's ending should enable one to leave the work behind and move on, Propertius adopts precisely this narrative as his closural move, and suggests to his readers that they do the same.

But the paradox that arises from Propertius' decision to perform a *renuntiatio amoris* in the collection's final poem is that the reader must synthesise symbolic closure with a generic history of refusing to end. Readers of love poetry have learned to be wary of trusting too quickly in any protestation from a lover that he is giving up love:[4] in a Roman context, this is the lesson

---

An earlier version of this chapter was published as Wallis, J. A. C. (2013): 'Reading False Closure in(to) Propertian Elegy', in: Grewing, Acosta-Hughes & Kirichenko (2013): The Door Ajar. False Closure in Greek and Roman Literature and Art, Heidelberg: **Universitätsverlag Winter**, 229–46.

[1] On the issue of the unity of '3.24–5', see Richardson (1977) 409–10, Fedeli (1985) 672–4, Heyworth (2007b) 412.
[2] On the structural unity of Propertius Books 1–3 see esp. Putnam (1980) 108–11 and Barsby (1974) 135–7.
[3] Fear (2005).
[4] E.g. Sharrock (1994) 92–3: 'The rejection of love is part of the discourse of love – it *is* love.'

201

especially of Catullus' archetypally hopeless attempts to drag himself from Lesbia; it is also a truism seemingly confirmed by an Ovidian poet–lover (perhaps the closest reader of love elegy) who will conclude with cheerful perspicacity that *uincit amor* every time. In the case of elegy itself, even Propertius' purported forsaking of Cynthia in 3.24 as his source of poetic inspiration accords, at a deep level, with an established game of elegiac brinkmanship involving 'a degree of suspense as to whether the poet will abandon or betray his calling'.[5] In the end, the inconclusive closure of 3.24 reflects the competing demands of a developing genre and a central elegiac credo that 'Cynthia' would be forever.

Propertius has been signalling for some time his increasing distance from the fictitious realism that attended *Cynthia*, and from the effete slavishness of his persona in Book 1 that sits at odds now with the potent and public capacity we have seen him claim regularly in Book 3. In this context, when Propertius 'unmasks' Cynthia as an erotic fantasy in 3.24, he dismisses his reliance on the affected autobiographical pose of his early poetry, and the central (if not exclusive) thematic focus on his mistress that came with it. Yet the poem's mannered refusal to let go of Cynthia entirely continues the performance of a fundamental elegiac game (inseparable from its signature erotic theme) predicated on an inability to close. 3.24 might shatter the illusion of Cynthia, but this does not mean that there is no place for *amor* (or, as it will turn out, for Cynthia herself) in any ensuing Propertian poetry. This, indeed, has been the message of the collection's foregoing elegies and their combined interrogation of the evolving nature of elegiac verse.

Finally, it is worth remembering that we have been in (nearly) this position before. At the heart of Book 2, a sequence of poems 2.8–13 follows 'a conventional pattern in setting out the

---

[5] Wilson (2009) 197. Nonetheless Prop. 3.24 itself is generally understood only in a firmly closural sense, an approach invariably connected to a belief in an objectively distinct poetic voice in Book 4, preceded by (and necessitating) a clean break at the end of Book 3: e.g. Camps (1966) 154, Baker (1969) 335–6, Barsby (1974) 135–7, Jacobson (1976) 171. Cf. the awkwardness in e.g. Cairns (2006) 355–6 over the reappearance of Cynthia at 4.7–8.

An Elegiac Ending

rejection which precedes poetic renewal'.[6] The precedent of such narrative in Propertius' earlier poetry itself gives cause for wondering, when the pattern of rejection begins to reappear towards the end of Book 3, whether it too should be followed – at some point, in some manner yet unexplored – by further poetic renewal. (It is even possible that Propertius deployed this pattern across a book ending: if our 'Book 2' is indeed a conflation of two books,[7] one scenario argues that the original second collection ended at 2.11, with a poem that presents a literary epitaph for a rejected Cynthia that, like 3.24, purports to indicate Propertius' lack of interest in further elegiac writing;[8] 'Book 3' then began with an inceptive sequence of poems (2.12–15) which articulates the opening of a new collection by staging the resumption of the poet's interest in love.)[9] When we arrive at 3.24 – does Propertius mean it, this time? or does the resumption of elegy in Book 4 mean that the message is one of reinforcement: that *amor* really is as omnipotent a force as Propertius has always claimed?

An Elegiac Ending

In 3.24 Propertius marshalls an array of closural devices which seek to close down the source of deviant erotic inspiration that the poet had used to begin his first collection, thereby framing Books 1–3 as a self-contained amatory unity from which the now ex-lover/poet has emerged intact and heart-whole.[10] In terms of Book 3 itself, Propertius rounds off the collection's dominant metaphor of journeying by presenting the

---

[6] Wyke (1987b) 54. Wyke argues that Book 2 should stand as a unity, containing an internal investigation of the 'poetics of renewal' (56).
[7] Goold (1990) 16–18; Fedeli (2005) 21f., Heyworth (2007a) lxii–lxiv; cf. Butrica (1996) esp. 89–98, Syndikus (2006) 273 n. 93.
[8] See generally Lyne (1998b). Lyne argues that the original Book 2 ended with a unified 2.10/11, although there is no consensus on where the ending might have been: cf. Murgia (2000) 147–91, Heyworth (2007b) x–xi.
[9] Lyne (1998b) 31. Cf. Horace's resumption of lyric writing in *Od.* 4.1, where the renewal of erotic interest figures the resumption of lyric writing, after the lyric poet had prepared the close of *Odes* 1–3 by 'retiring' from love in *Od.* 3.26.
[10] See e.g. Richardson (1977) 410, Putnam (1980) 109–10, Fedeli (1985) 682, Debrohun (2003) 131–4.

triumphant harbouring of his poetic ship, its journey safely completed:[11]

> ecce coronatae portum tetigere carinae,
> traiectae Syrtes, ancora iacta mihi est.
> 3.24.15–16

Look, my garlanded ships have reached harbour, the Syrtes have been crossed, my anchor has been cast.

This bold image combines the representation of achieving emotional tranquillity with a more general statement of attaining literary closure that draws especially on Virgilian precedent. In placing this couplet at the climax of a series of revelations (3.24.9–14) which unwrite the programmatic conditions of erotic delinquency that had attended his emergence as a love poet, Propertius positions the literary movement of Book 3 precisely as a successful progression out of a poetic madness that had begun in Book 1.[12] The poet's claim to have recovered an orthodox common sense itself reaches a climax in the poem's central couplet:

> Mens Bona, si qua dea es, tua me in sacraria dono!
> exciderant surdo tot mea uota Ioui.
> 3.24.19–20

Good Sense, if you are a goddess, I dedicate myself to your sanctuary: so many of my vows have been lost upon a deaf Jove.

In seeking association with the goddess of clear thinking Propertius strives to mark out his foregoing poetry as a foolish mistake, in both form and content; the poem's final image of an aged and haggish Cynthia (3.24.31–8) then reinforces vividly the poet's forsaking of an erotic aesthetic. In short, the rejection of Cynthia as Book 3 closes is deeply complicit with what must seem the writer's declared intention to cease writing Cynthian, amatory discourse.

---

[11] For the significance of journeys in Book 3 see Putnam (1980) 107, and esp. Clarke (2004).

[12] Wyke (1987a) 154; for a powerful reading of the end of Book 3 as a recovery of mainstream values, see Fear (2005).

An Elegiac Ending

The narration of the end of the poet's affair also serves as an emphatic marker for the end of the book(s) for the poet's reader.[13] On this level, a further significant feature of the final poem's closural effect is the way in which Propertius' escape from Cynthia's spell offers a suggestive prompt for the reader's own withdrawal from the act of reading as the collection comes to an end. Addressed ostensibly to Cynthia, the opening lines of this final poem have the doubled effect of undermining the trust that readers might have placed in Propertius' depictions of his mistress:

> Falsa est ista tuae, mulier, fiducia formae,
> olim oculis nimium facta superba meis.
> noster amor talis tribuit tibi, Cynthia, laudes:
> uersibus insignem te pudet esse meis.
> mixtam te uaria laudaui saepe figura,
> ut, quod non esses, esse putaret amor.
> 3.24.1–6

That confidence in your appearance is false, woman, you who were once made proud by my eyes. Our love has granted you such praises: it shames me that you are famous through my verses. The you I often praised was put together from the appearance of various women, such that love thought you were what you were not.

At the level of metapoetry these lines amount to an extraordinary closing declaration of what the reader may have long suspected – that the details of Cynthia's biography are fictive, that *Cynthia* has been a deceptive text.[14] To begin with, such a revelation of authorial manipulation brings closural force in itself by reminding the reader of the text's artificiality.[15] But, in the second half of the poem, the effect is furthered through the presentation of the poet–lover as a victim of such deception himself – and here Propertius adopts a position analogous to that of susceptible readers of his poetry who have shared

---

[13] Cf. the similar closural functions of Hor. *Od.* 3.26 and Tib. 1.9.
[14] See here Sharrock (2000) 264–5 on the delicate balance elegy seeks to maintain between inviting its readers to suspend their disbelief and yet appreciate the text's artificiality. One closural move in 3.24 is to upset this balance.
[15] Fowler (2000) 11. On exposing the author's manipulative tools in 3.24, see also Debrohun (2003) 131–4.

Breaking up (with) *Cynthia*: Propertius 3.24

the lover's gaze at Cynthia for the past three books.[16] This is a regular metacritical move on Propertius' part. Pertinently for 3.24, for instance, Hérica Valladares discusses the identification (in 1.3) of the Propertian lover not only as protagonist within the drama of the poetry but also as an observer – resembling the external reader – 'who has become entangled in the emotional dynamics of viewing a work of art, Cynthia'.[17] But in 3.24 Propertius only replicates his readers' vulnerability in order to offer a closural role model of self-empowerment. This is the poem where Propertius finally puts a stop to his own self-deception:

> nil moueor lacrimis: ista sum captus ab arte;
> semper ab insidiis, Cynthia, flere soles.
> flebo ego discedens, sed fletum iniuria uincit:
> tu bene conueniens non sinis ire iugum.
> 3.24.25–8

> I am not moved at all by your tears; I have been deceived by that trick of yours; always as a trap are you accustomed to weep, Cynthia. I myself shall weep as I leave, but the injury surpasses the weeping: though well-matched, you do not allow the yoke to move forward.

In lines underpinned by the earnest resolve of Catullus to free himself from Lesbia – the Roman archetype of love gone wrong – Propertius' metapoetic recognition here of his poetry's 'real' nature is linked explicitly with the end of poetic discourse. Propertius connects imagery of stoppage and departure (*non sinis ire iugum*, 28; *ego discedens*, 27) with his new-found awareness that he has been deceived (*ista sum captus ab arte*, 25) and his consequent resistance to Cynthia's tricks (*nil moueor lacrimis*, 25). And, in doing so, Propertius provides his fellow Cynthian voyeurs with the opportunity through his own example to see *Cynthia* for the artifice it is, and so to extract

---

[16] The connection of pleasure, control and vulnerability with the act of looking (foregrounded here with *oculis meis*, 3.24.2; cf. *suis ocellis*, 1.1.1) is fundamental to Propertian erotics – see e.g. 2.22a.1–12. Heyworth (2007a) emends *oculis* to *elegis*, on the grounds that Cynthia's *forma* in this poem is better regarded as written rather than seen: see Heyworth (2007b) 409. Yet a connection between 'beauty' and 'vision' is exceedingly straightforward, and there is much to be gained by retaining a poem that describes written praise of an observed appearance.
[17] Valladares (2005) 228. In Book 3, cf. esp. 3.6 (see chapter 2).

themselves at the end of the book from the illusory world of literature by recovering their own real-world sense of *mens bona*.[18]

Catullan Background

For the Roman elegists, the desperate struggle with the seeming impasse of *amor* and *odium* derives inescapably from Catullus.[19] In the present instance, the vehemence of the older poet's attempts to cease loving Lesbia certainly authenticates Propertius' apparent determination to leave love behind. At the same time, the ultimate lack of resolution to Catullus' battle with love and hatred inevitably calls into question the very possibility of achieving the sort of erotic emancipation that Propertius claims so bitterly to have attained in 3.24. Prefiguring the kind of self-awareness of one's own folly that Propertius declares at the end of Book 3, Catullus had written:

> Miser Catulle, desinas ineptire,
> et quod uides perisse perditum ducas.
> Cat. 8.1–2

> Wretched Catullus, you should stop playing the fool, and what you see is lost, count as lost.

There follows a poem in which Catullus calls on himself repeatedly to cease his obsession with Lesbia and to stand firm (*perfer, obdura*, Cat. 8.11). But, rather than establishing a precedent for erotic closure, this poem offers a now-celebrated example of a false ending: the failure of the poem to finish when seemingly it should articulate the inability of Catullus to put an end to his obsessive love for his mistress.[20] For successive Roman love poets and their readers, the significance of this poem and its brethren lies in creating a poetic programme

---

[18] See Fowler (2000) 25 for a closing text's 'recall to reality'. Cf. Sharrock (1996) 152 for a focused reflection on reading as 'delusion'.
[19] For the primacy of Catullus for the later Roman love poets, see Hinds (1998) 26–9.
[20] Fowler (1989) 98–9.

based around futile attempts to leave love behind.[21] One of Catullus' most potent contributions to Roman literary love was, in other words, to become the symbol for a type of love from which one is unable to tear oneself away.[22]

Not only does Propertius' 'successful' narrative in 3.24 sit at odds with a tradition dominated by Catullan failure, but Book 3's final elegy pivots about a false ending of its own which undermines still further the belief a reader might have in Propertius' claim to be free of love. As we have seen, in 3.24 Propertius draws (his own) attention to the creative fiction inherent in Cynthia and Cynthian poetry, and recounts the successful measure he has taken to cure himself from the madness of love; in the poem's second half he curses Cynthia herself with the onset of old age. Crucially, it is at the point between these two sections (and right at the poem's centre) that Propertius symbolically dedicates himself to the sanctuary of *Mens Bona* (19–20). If Propertius is truly possessed of his freedom from the grip of *amor* as he claims, then this 'triumphant climax'[23] would provide an excellent point to stop. *Mens Bona*, and the mainstream common sense with which she is associated, represents the antithesis of an irrational elegiac lifestyle; thus Ovid would choose to depict his *Mens Bona* symbolically as tightly bound into submission when beginning his amatory career (*Mens Bona ducetur manibus post terga retortis*, *Am.* 1.2.31); and the fine opportunity for an ending that this couplet provides has led several editors to divide the elegy in two at this point. But the fact that the text continues past this point (whether as the same poem or as one further poem) has the effect of complicating any clear sense of elegiac stoppage that *Mens Bona* provides – especially as the final lines return obsessively to, of all people, Cynthia. Of course, this move makes sense for a Propertius desperate to portray effectively the death of his desire; in this sense the image of an old and unattractive

---

[21] E.g. Cat. 11, 72, 75 and esp. 76 – a poem in which Catullus explicitly questions the possibility of carrying out even what is now cited as his only course of action (*hoc facias, siue id non pote siue pote*, Cat. 76.16).
[22] Fitzgerald (1995) 114.
[23] Richardson (1977) 410.

anus is mustered to reinforce the message of *Mens Bona*, the poet being now released to imagine and realise his mistress in this abhorrent guise. But the closing vituperation of a white-haired and wrinkly Cynthia has Propertius end the book still doing what he has stated at the poem's beginning that he used to do, and what he professes no longer to do: indulging in a neurotic manipulation of his mistress's *uaria figura* (cf. 3.24.5). Approached in this way, we recognise the dynamic of a failed amatory ending that perpetuates a core erotic aesthetic even in claiming to write it off.[24] At the very least, the bitter unveiling of a decrepit Cynthia as a symbol for the end of love and love poetry indicates, by its continuing presence, that female *forma* (3.24.1) still dominates the poet's thoughts and sense of inspiration.

Ovidian Reflection

While Catullus is figured frequently as the instigator of a Roman erotic aesthetic, Ovid presents himself explicitly as one who has inherited an amatory tradition. Thus Ovid's *Amores* are more than sophisticated love poetry in their own right: they are also a self-conscious reading of foregoing love poetry – the poetry of Catullus and Propertius in particular.[25] In the present context, one of the significant features of Ovidian erotic verse is his (mostly) upbeat acceptance of love's endlessness. In the context of Roman erotic tradition Ovid thus distinguishes himself from the repeated struggles of his predecessors with the authority of *amor*. Yet Ovid's own contented submission to *amor* ultimately reflects the eventual outcomes of those earlier struggles, and so comments on the essential fruitlessness of wrestling with a force that a lover will never defeat.

The Catullan inability to escape erotic obsession which informs Propertius 3.24 is also targeted by Ovid in his third book of *Amores*. In 3.11a Ovid calls upon the apparent strength of Catullus' resolve in Poem 8 to bolster his own courage in

---

[24] Wilson (2009) 186.
[25] E.g. Cairns (1979) 137f.

Breaking up (with) *Cynthia*: Propertius 3.24

rejecting his mistress (*perfer et obdura! dolor hic tibi proderit olim*, 'persist and endure! this pain will benefit you some day', 3.11a.7);[26] in 3.11b Ovid then plays up the generic pointlessness of this quest by having resurgent love open the ensuing poem. In doing so, Ovid has *amor* not only bringing the unwilling poet to heel but boldy resolving a famous Catullan dilemma at the same time:[27]

> luctantur pectusque leue in contraria tendunt
> hac amor hac odium, sed, puto, uincit amor.
> 3.11b.33–4

Love on this side, and hate on the other, wrestle and pull my fickle heart in opposing directions; but love, I think, is the winner.

Thus in 3.11a Ovid begins properly by acknowledging Catullus' Roman pre-eminence in the formal *topos* of erotic *renuntiatio*; but by also pinning the second (half of the) poem to Catullus, Ovid makes explicit to Catullan poetics what had only been implied in Catullus 8, and is in fact an unstated truth of Catullus' poetry more broadly – that in a lover's struggle with *amor*, *amor* will always win in the end.

Like Propertius in 3.24, Ovid creates his own false ending in 3.11a when he claims to have dismissed his mistress and triumphed over love:

> iam mea uotiua puppis redimita corona
> lenta tumescentes aequoris audit aquas.
> desine blanditias et uerba, potentia quondam,
> perdere – non ego sum stultus, ut ante fui!
> 3.11a.27–32

My vessel is already decked with a votive garland, and listens unperturbed to the swelling waters of the ocean. Stop wasting your caresses and your words that once had power – I am not the fool I was before!

As again in the Propertian poem, here Ovid's garlanded ship seems to symbolise the poet's successfully completed journey.

---

[26] See Perkins (2002) 119–20. Perkins views the allusion to Catullus as revealing a 'lack of determination' (120) on the part of the Ovidian lover, whereas I read the allusive matrix as marking a determination that inevitably fails.
[27] Cf. Cat. 85; Hinds (1998) 29.

Ovidian Reflection

Beyond this, familiar closural devices are brought into play – the call to stop (*desine*, 31; cf. *desinas ineptire*, Cat. 8.1; *non sinis ire iugum*, Prop. 3.24.28) and the claim to be aware of having been played for a fool in the past (*non ego sum stultus*, 32; cf. *desinas ineptire*, Cat. 8.1; *ista sum captus ab arte*, Prop. 3.24.25). But all these symbols signal the approach of a merely mistaken sense of escape: Ovid's poetry and his erotic desire immediately continue, so reflecting and validating an erotic tradition in which the claim to clear-headedness proves to be yet more delusion. As he too resigns himself to the ever-renewed dominion of Amor in 3.11, Ovid annotates an 'actual' moment of erotic clarity when he acknowledges that even he cannot rely upon the sentiment of his own prayers, whether they lead him to desire separation from his beloved, or indeed to return to her:

> sic ego nec sine te ne tecum uiuere possum
> et uideor uoti nescius esse mei.
> 3.11b.39–40

So it is that I can neither live without you nor with you, and I seem not to know my own wishes.

Ovid offers here an allusive Catullan commentary[28] on the preceding poem that positions his former steadfastness as a misunderstood (and misleading) determination to leave love behind. But, in line with his broader sense of elegiac poetics, Ovid appropriates and then transforms a tortured Catullan confusion into a state of productive ignorance which proves integral to the continuation of elegiac writing. In drawing out a closural context for Roman erotic poetry, it is significant that Ovid never seeks to 'close down' amatory inspiration in the way that Propertius attempts in Book 3 by claiming to see Cynthia for what she really is. The threat that such a position poses for elegy is sidestepped by Ovid in his penultimate love poem when he requests that his mistress *not* reveal her true nature to

---

[28] Ovid's psychological uncertainty in 3.11 rests on Catullus' emblematic confusion as expressed succinctly in Cat. 85 (already the target of an allusion at the beginning of 3.11b). Here the Ovidian *uideor nescius* (*Am.* 3.11b.40) in part establishes the later poet self-consciously as 'being seen' to re-enact the Catullan *nescio* (Cat. 85.2).

him – allowing instead the Ovidian lover to embrace a 'foolish credulity' (*stulta credulitate*, *Am.* 3.14.30; cf. the 'false' *non ego sum stultus*, *Am.* 3.11a.27) that permits his love to continue pain-free in perpetuity. In keeping with the lesson that love does not and cannot be stopped, Ovid finally offers a farewell to his role as a writer of love poetry more in the manner of a Horatian *sphragis* than a Propertian *renuntiatio*, claiming explicitly that his 'work' (*opus*, 3.15.20 – a suggestively erotic word) will carry on beyond the poet's own death.

Ovid's handling in a *renuntiatio* of the particular nautical imagery already used by Propertius in 3.24 is clearly significant for reading the staged 'end' of the Propertian amatory corpus.[29] Taken in thematic isolation, Ovid's choice of metaphor in validating his own claim to be immune to love's miseries must reinforce the closural value of Propertius' garlanded ship at the end of Book 3. In this context, *Amores* 3.11a is one of several poems within *Amores* 3 which allude to Ovid's intention soon to switch genres and, thus, to a coming end for love (poetry).[30] But it turns out that there is more love poetry to be written first; and the fact that Ovid follows this ostensibly 'final' poem with an elegy in which love reclaims its position of authority over the poet also positions his symbolic ship precisely at the point of what becomes false closure – that point which purports to have effected thematic shutdown, only to be shown up by the continuing erotic text not to have done so. This broader context now suggests an Ovidian reading of attempted elegiac/amatory closure in which the symbol of the poet's ship anchored safely in port is treated as being ultimately misleading for both the poet and reader.

The groundwork for such a reading has been prepared by Ovid in *Amores* 2.9, a poem which also examines the power

---

[29] The closural metaphor of a poetic ship reaching its destination is not a Propertian invention; for the Augustan poets it is associated especially with Virgil's *Georgics*: see *Geo.* 2.541–2, 4.116–17, with Harrison (2007), esp. 5–9. Prop. 3.24.15 in fact alludes to Virg. *Geo.* 1.303 (*portum tetigere carinae*, 'the ships have attained harbour'), a passage neither metaphorical nor closural. See n. 32.

[30] E.g. *Amores* 3.1, 3.9, 3.13.

of love to reclaim a resisting lover, and which is the subject of close reference in 3.11.[31] In 2.9 Ovid sends up the closural value of steering one's literary ship into port in lines which allude directly to Propertius 3.24:[32]

> ut subitus, prope iam prensa tellure, carinam
> tangentem portus uentus in alta rapit,
> sic me saepe refert incerta Cupidinis aura,
> notaque purpureus tela resumit Amor.
> <div align="right">Ovid <i>Am.</i> 2.9.31–4</div>

As suddenly, when land is almost already gained, the wind sweeps the ship out to the deep even as it reaches the harbour, so the shifting breeze of Cupid carries me away again, and bright Love takes up again its well-known weapons.

> ecce coronatae portum tetigere carinae,
> traiectae Syrtes, ancora iacta mihi est.
> Prop. 3.24.15–16

Within the didactic context of his own poem, Ovid adapts the now familiar nautical metaphor to fit a simile that has the purpose of explaining his lover's poor track record in giving up love. In a wider allusive sense Ovid makes an ironic target of Propertius at the very moment (the present participle *tangentem*, *Am.* 2.9.32) Propertius signals his climactic erotic emancipation – perhaps, then as now, the most celebrated example of elegiac *renuntiatio amoris*. In doing so, at an intertextual level Ovid does more than merely subvert the older poet's symbol: he dramatises explicitly the vulnerability that this outwardly closural metaphor has to being read as a false ending, regardless even of what its author intended. The metaphorical ship will quite easily return to sea, swept by forces beyond its captain's control.

---

[31] See generally Cairns (1979).
[32] Both these passages derive their formulation ultimately from Virg. *Geo.* 1.303. But does Ovid here allude to Virgil or Propertius? For a reader of love poetry, the context of the *renuntiatio* means that the Propertian passage must be the first port of call.

Breaking up (with) *Cynthia*: Propertius 3.24

A Romantic Ending

The aim of this chapter has been to examine ways in which a reader of love poetry might react to Propertius' claim to have finished with love at the end of Book 3. In closural terms, Propertius positions his awareness of his own erotic self-deception as a hortatory role model for his readers in pulling themselves out of a literary spell as the book comes to an end. But, at a programmatic level, Propertius' use of a *renuntiatio amoris* at the end of his book also asks his readers to accept what should amount essentially to the poet's own literary self-annihilation. In 3.24 Propertius rejects Cynthia and, in seeking the sanctuary of *Mens Bona*, rejects *amor* as well (in any case Cynthia and *amor* are inseparable, or should be). We have known since Book 1 that the end of love would be the end of poetry – and since the book also comes to an end, so it seems to be. Yet there is much at play here. The language of erotic closure is inescapably also the language of love's failed endings:[33] as Propertius claims closure by cursing Cynthia with encroaching old age, the reader – primed especially by Catullan precedent – will recognise a poet failing to abandon *amor* even as he professes (and in his professing) to do so; especially so, since teasing the reader with an apparent intent to abandon love elegy is a game the Propertian narrator has played many times before. Then again, the twinning of the rejection of love with the ending of the book adds new urgency to the game being played with the reader's credulity – indeed, if the motifs of false closure can in the end also symbolise actual closure, then, in the absence of more poetry, just possibly this time Propertius means it. The extent to which this game of 'will he or will he not' remains live at the end of Book 3 is underlined when the poetry does subsequently resume in a fourth book. In 4.1 Propertius immediately takes up what seems to be a new aetiological programme (*pace* Ovid, below) and as such appears to uphold the erotic closure stated at the end of Book

---

[33] Cf. the paradox noted well by Cairns (1979) 138, 140, that in *Am.* 3.11 Ovid starts out all the more confident of rejecting his mistress precisely because in that poem he will have accepted that he is powerless to do so.

A Romantic Ending

3; but even before this initial poem reaches its midpoint the poet's new ambition is opposed directly by the sudden intervention of the astrologer Horos, who seeks to direct Propertius back to his accustomed love elegy – a move that, inasmuch as it marks out the new programme as a conspicuous thematic departure, also must position any such departure as being still a contested issue.

With reference to Book 4 we come back to the truism that Book 3 does not in the end act out the death throes of Propertian elegy. Clearly, at the point of transition between the books, the issue of closure (or its interpretation) is significant – a reader who takes seriously the *renuntiatio amoris* of 3.24 will approach 4.1 as a new beginning, and will read for the ways in which Book 4 forms a distinctly novel collection within the poet's corpus (such a reader will perhaps be disappointed that Propertius never quite sustains the new mode in the way he has said he would); a reader who is stubborn in her belief that Propertius – whatever he might claim – would never actually abandon his subversive erotic voice will look for traces of the old poet among the new poems (this reader will struggle to account for the strongly Augustan tones of several of these elegies, and for the frequent absence of the poet's own voice entirely). But this is too simplistic. As we have seen, Ovid appropriates the symbolism of Propertian closure – which would and does form the point of transition between Books 3 and 4 – in a way that emphasises its complicity in the continuation of erotic writing. In part this is because Ovidian *amor* must always go on, even if he must therefore change mistresses (or take several) for it to do so; the Propertian *renuntiatio amoris* of 3.24 cannot mean the end – when Ovid reads it. In one sense, the upbeat focus on erotic continuity in Ovid's own poetry expresses the relative licence ceded to the free-loving Ovidian persona when compared with the tragic romanticism of his predecessor(s), who, in insisting on the absolute indivisibility of life, poetry, love and mistress, constantly face off a literary death should love ever fail them (epigrammatically: *Cynthia prima fuit, Cynthia finis erit* at Prop. 1.12.20, a poem just past halfway through Book 1; cf. 4.7 below). But Ovid's relentless connivance in ensuring that his own love/writing continues also emphasises once more the fact that, if Propertius was serious about sending Cynthia away in 3.24, then it ought to have been impossible for him to continue writing elegy. And so, as it happens, Propertius himself declares to us in the midst of his subsequent book. In 4.7 a supposedly past love (cf. Hor. *Od.* 4.1) returns to the present as a ghost, in a dream, to haunt the poet and chastise him for his neglect; and the irrepressible vitality of 4.8 – the final Cynthia poem – reinstates the mistress to her position of authority over the poet for all time, in a brilliant poetic recantation of any and all past claims to have become love-free.[34] It is true that Cynthian poetry was never quite the same again after the end of Book 3. It is equally true that, if Propertius had thought that 3.24 was the end for *Cynthia*, then he was deceiving both himself and us.

[34] Heyworth (2010) 100–1.

EPILOGUE

The Apotheosis of Amor: *Propertius 3.22*

When Propertius reached the end of the twenty-second elegy, Book 3 contained the same number of poems as Book 1. Only two short elegies remained in the third collection, each a farewell – the first wistful in tone, the second bitter – to erotic elegy as the pseudo-autobiographical lament of a Roman lover for his errant mistress. Propertius uses this moment of symmetry to signal ostentatiously that he was wrapping things up (for the time being) by addressing a poem once more to Tullus, the elegist's erstwhile patron whom he had last addressed in the twenty-second (and final) elegy in Book 1. After coming full-circle in 3.22, 3.23–4 provide a closural coda.

Propertius addressed Tullus four times in the first collection: in the opening poem (where he also introduced us to Cynthia as a vehicle for articulating his dissident lifestyle to his conformist patron), as well as in the sixth and fourteenth poems – and the second of these (1.6) is the more important for setting up 3.22 as a symbolic resolution of foundational elegiac tensions.[1] In 1.6, Tullus had left Italy on imperial business, after failing to persuade Propertius to go with him; now, in 3.22, it is Propertius who attempts to persuade Tullus to return to Rome. More importantly, in 1.6 the geographical separation of Propertius and Tullus carried vital programmatic significance for elegy, by characterising love (and love poetry) in opposition to the conventional performance of Roman duty and pursuit of public life, and even to the physical reach of Roman *imperium*: whereas Tullus travels and does his soldiering for *Roma*, Propertius stays put and battles for *amor*

---

[1] Zetzel (1982) 99, Heyworth (2007c) 96.

Epilogue

(1.6.21–2, 29–30). Now, at the end of Book 3, not only does Propertius himself embrace thoughts of travel (and to locations precluded by his love for Cynthia at 1.6.13–14; cf. 3.21.1–2), but his eagerness to be reunited with Tullus in Rome signals that the early symbolic value of their separation is no longer pressing.

What has changed, that has the potential to bring Propertius and Tullus together again? The answer, as Propertius presents it, is the transcendence of *amor* in the always competitive collision of cultural values that has coloured elegy's engagement with Roman society since its inception. Tullus' role in Propertian elegy is fundamentally embedded in this contest. One of the central narratives of Book 1 employs 'Cynthia' as a focalising tool in a competition between these two men (and several others),[2] as erotic material shared by them and as an instrument with which Propertius sought to demonstrate the superiority of his own indolent values when compared with the conventional masculinity (or literary taste) symbolised by the men to whom his poems are addressed. The language of competition is marked in these exchanges and, of course, underpins the metaphor of *militia amoris* with which Propertius distinguishes his preference for peace from Tullus' for war, and yet seeks rhetorically to coopt Tullus' own sense of duty and to turn his patron's martial orthodoxy against him. Programmatically, neither side is backing down: so Tullus is a man whose 'life has never yielded to love' (*tua non aetas umquam cessauit amori*, 1.6.21); of course, love itself does not yield – and certainly not to the material wealth that comes with Rome's imperial expansion, which therefore does not enable Tullus' opulent lifestyle to compete against Propertius' life with Cynthia (*non tamen ista meo ualeant contendere amori:|nescit Amor magnis cedere diuitiis*, 1.14.7–8).[3] The mutual intransigence of Tullus and Propertius causes their separation, and ensures that the contest will continue.

---

[2] For Propertius' poetry as participation in homosocial cooperation and competition, see esp. Keith (2008) 115–38. For the subordination of *amor* and Cynthia to *amicitia* and Propertius' male addressees, see Oliensis (1997).

[3] The unstated irony here is that Propertius' own leisured enjoyment of Cynthia's company is itself a perk of Roman imperialism: see esp. Keith (2008) 139–65.

Epilogue

When Propertius looks again to Tullus in 3.22, he reprises the competitive spirit which had framed the symbolic relationship with his patron in Book 1. Again the elegist asserts that Tullus' life choices pale when compared with Propertius' own – in this case, Propertius argues that whatever delights have pleased Tullus in the East are surpassed by those he might enjoy at home in Roman territory (where the poet has stayed put).[4] But now, as the end of Book 3 looms, Propertius foreshadows the resolution of their symbolic differences – and in the elegist's favour:

> omnia Romanae *cedent* miracula terrae:
> natura hic posuit, quidquid ubique fuit.
> 3.22.17–18

All wonders *will yield* to the Roman land: nature has placed here whatever has been anywhere.

This remarkable statement of mature patriotism[5] does more than represent the superiority of Roman Italy over the Greek East, or the choices made by Propertius over those made by Tullus: it removes any sense of meaningful distinction between such opposites by having Italy subsume within itself anything that might have been a point of difference. Augustan Rome and its territory are presented as a totalising concept – and this central logic of the poem is fundamental to the poet's climactic (re)turn to *amor*, once the signature division between Propertius' indolence and his patron's sense of duty.

Here we come back to that even more remarkable statement, the pitch-perfect rendition of Roman virtues with which the poem ends, and with which this study of Propertius Book 3 began:

> haec tibi, Tulle, parens, haec est pulcherrima sedes,
>   hic tibi pro digna gente petendus honos,
> hic tibi ad eloquium ciues, hic ampla nepotum
>   spes et uenturae coniugis aptus amor.
> 3.22.39–42

This, Tullus, is your motherland, this your most beautiful home, here the public honour for you to seek as befits your distinguished family,

---

[4] On Propertius' conflation of (Augustan) Rome and Italy itself, see Cairns (2006) 353.
[5] Johnson (2009) 112–13.

Epilogue

here the citizens to move you to eloquence, here the ample hope of offspring and the suitable love of a wife to be.

Public office, civil rhetoric, marriage and the production of children: Propertius concludes his appeal for Tullus to return by urging him to fulfil his duty as a Roman citizen, husband and father. But the extraordinary thing about this small catalogue of Roman virtues is that it now includes, rather than excludes, the elegist's signature theme of *amor* (albeit qualified as *coniugis amor* – wifely love – to which we return presently).[6] Indeed, *amor* is the poem's final word, and the very moment that Book 3 attains numerical equality with Book 1, where *amor* had been elegy's definitional motif, and where Tullus had been both the poet's dedicatee and his thematic foil. Propertius uses this flamboyant moment of circularity to emphasise just how much the resonance of elegy's signature theme has been adapted. In a very real sense, the final four lines of 3.22 represent the epitome of Propertius' programme in Book 3 to reinvent elegiac *amor* as a poetic theme with overt social capacity; beginning in 3.1–3, Propertius has increasingly inverted the reference points within the always doubled language of 'erotic' elegy by playing up the genre's latent flipside of heroism or moral orthodoxy or (in this case) sense of dutiful commitment – the very themes, in other words, with which elegy is notionally incompatible. Now, in a poem whose logic depends on Augustan *Roma* transcending geographical difference to become all-encompassing, so Propertian *amor* now embraces openly the opposed elements in the binary cultural discourse of which it forms part. In a nutshell, Propertius concludes his latest poem still urging *amor* upon Tullus, just as he had in Book 1. But, uncannily, in Book 3 to embrace *amor* is to do one's duty as a Roman, rather than to avoid it (and yet the prompted rereading of 1.6 should remind us that there is a rhetorical sense, at least, in which it always was).[7]

---

[6] On *amor* at 3.22.42 as both elegiac and unelegiac, Keith (2008) 131.
[7] E.g. Zetzel (1982) 99: in 1.6 'Propertius ... represents *both the rigors and the decadence* of staying in Rome' (my emphasis).

Epilogue

If we can find here the denouement of Propertius' introspective re-evaluation of elegiac motifs, in 3.22 we might also see a terminus for Propertius' other significant third-book arc – his engagement with the revolutionary poetry (and its values) of his Augustan contemporaries Virgil and Horace. Most obviously, in his seeming enthusiasm for married love as the poem ends, Propertius commends to Tullus his celebration of marital fidelity of Postumus and (especially) Galla at the heart of the book in 3.12, where the elegist's response to the moral challenge of Horace's lyric showed that elegy is comfortable with the ideal of Roman marriage (if not its realisation nor necessarily its politics, as we will see). But it is the *Romanitas* of Virgil's *Georgics* and imminent *Aeneid* that most influences the shape of 3.22. At 3.22.19–26 Propertius echoes in elegiac couplets Virgil's so-called *laudes Italiae* (*Geo.* 2.136–74),[8] a climactic passage of praise for the serene equilibrium of the Italian landscape that represents the culmination of the elegist's engagement with the Roman programme of *Georgics* in his own programmatic waypoints at 3.1, 3.9 and 3.17. In addition, the particular moral balance which Propertius embeds in his Italian soil directly anticipates the interplay of *ira* and *pietas* that will drive Virgil's *Aeneid* (e.g. *Aen.* 6.851–3, 12.827),[9] and which sits at the heart of Augustan ideology.[10] In fact, in his elegiac brevity Propertius portrays the balance of Roman steel and restraint more positively than will Virgil, whose epic dwells persistently on the antagonism of Augustan symbols, and on the dilemma (merely implicit in Propertius) for an individual tasked with executing 'pietistic allegiance through force of arms'.[11] In short, in 3.22's Roman landscape Propertius brings together a mainstream personal ethic provoked by Horatian lyric, and a positive spin on the national values underpinning Virgil's epic, to frame a new and remarkably centrist voice for elegy where *amor* can be the final word in a patriotic endorsement of Roman Duty.

---

[8] Tränkle (1960) 101–3, Williams (1968) 421–6, Nethercut (1970a) 403–6.
[9] Cairns (2006) 353.
[10] Cairns (2006) 353, Keith (2008) 159–60, Johnson (2009) 112–13.
[11] Putnam (1977) 245.

Epilogue

Yet if this seems a surprise – well, it certainly should. For all that Propertius' 'astonishing change of heart and mind'[12] can be explained (perhaps, explained *away*) as the belated embrace of a repressed orthodoxy lying at the heart of the genre, we should not understate the sense of cultural whiplash that stems from the seeming ease with which an elegist now aligns the pursuit of love with the performance of other Roman responsibilities – not least of which is producing children for the good of the nation (cf., of course, 2.7.13–14). It is only a small step from here to Ovid's openly parodic advertisement of love as an honest *labor* requiring the kind of reputable hard work and dedication expected of a soldier or a sailor in his *Ars Amatoria* (Ovid's wit lies in the sustained juxtaposition of antithetical symbols, but this is also his satirical insight into the paradoxical poetics of an amatory tradition).

Reading 3.22 itself as parody has provided one way out of the poem's awkward politics;[13] reading the elegy's mainstream stance as confirmation of Propertius' Augustan conversion provides another.[14] Yet a stronger approach than either would surely be to regard 3.22 as calling upon the kind of multi-voicing we have seen in a number of third-book poems, and most recently in Propertius' lament for Marcellus in 3.18. Defending 3.22 against criticism (also levelled at 3.18) that it fails to meet the standard of its Virgilian model, Nethercut presents poem's differing sentiment positively as 'an *elegist*'s tribute to Rome',[15] and there is value in the sympathetic aspects of his reading; Johnson, notwithstanding his treatment of the poem as an argument designed to fail, nonetheless sees Propertius' homage to Virgil's *Georgics* as being 'as concise as it is lovely'.[16] At the same time, Propertius' simple (and perhaps simplistic) enthusiasm for an Augustan counterpoint of *ira* and *pietas* begs comparison with the *Aeneid*'s deeper treatment of these as 'a moral paradox';[17] Propertius' praise for Roman clemency

---

[12] Johnson (2009) 115.
[13] E.g. Stahl (1985) 205–12, Johnson (2009) 109–17, Heyworth & Morwood (2011) 316.
[14] Cairns (2006) 352–4.
[15] Nethercut (1970a) 405.
[16] Johnson (2009) 113.
[17] Putnam (1977) 243.

Epilogue

(*uictrices temperat ira manus*, 'anger moderates our hands in victory, 3.22.22) comes in a poem addressed to Tullus – whose last poem from Propertius (1.22) identified the elegist with the losing faction at the infamous Perusine siege in 41 BCE at which Octavian's brutal lack of clemency was now infamous.

Finally – to return once more to the poem's closing pair of couplets with which we began – the most potent opportunity for a multivalent reading comes in Propertius' gesture to 'the ample hope of offspring' (*ampla nepotum spes*, 3.22.41–2). In a positive sense, Propertius reunites with Tullus at last in a shared desire to escape the limitations of mortality in their respective spheres. In Tullus' case, Propertius asserts, the continuation of his *nomen* will come about through a succession of descendents, much as Aeneas will see his son's name extend into the Roman future (and Augustan present) in *Aeneid* 6.[18] For Propertius himself, we are reminded in closing of the poet's obsession with his posthumous reputation in the collection's opening poem, and of the solace he takes in the praise he will receive from Rome's own future generations (*meque inter seros laudabit Roma nepotes*, 3.1.35).

But for the Augustan project – whose most prominent values Propertius appears in 3.22 to coopt – the message can read very differently. While Propertius' optimism in the promise of offspring closes out a poem informed by the Roman idealism of *Aeneid* 6, the phrase *ampla nepotum spes* itself offers allusion to the epic's second book, to the words *spes tanta nepotum* ('such great hope of descendents', *Aen.* 2.503) with which Aeneas laments the very moment of Troy's fall, and refers with laconic nihilism to a fecund potential in Priam's palace that will never be realised. When we read this poem within such an Augustan frame, suddenly Propertius' closing endorsement of Roman values rings hollow. The poem's double allusion to Virgil juxtaposes the proud procession of Roman *gentes* with the thwarted promise of barren bedrooms; indeed, by bringing *Aeneid* 2 and 6 together, Propertius' (now ironic) reference to

---

[18] For resonances here of Anchises' speech in Virgil's underworld (especially of the link between *nomen* and *nepotes*), see Putnam (1977) 248.

Epilogue

nepotes recalls most of all the final appearance of the word in Anchises' speech,[19] as he mourns the future death of his descendant Marcellus (*Aen.* 6.884) and, implicitly, the lack of children to ensure a future for Augustus' own family (cf., of course, 3.18 and chapter 7).

Just possibly, harnessing the competitiveness in Horace's lyric monument that would last 'longer' than the bronzed memorials of kings (*exegi monumentum aere perennius, Od.* 3.30.1), so Propertius' doubled voice in 3.22 contrasts a belief in Italy's fecundity – and so the prosperity of Tullus' family and the poet's own literary longevity – with what might have seemed in 23 BCE a foreshortened Augustan dynasty. All of a sudden, the poem's cultural landscape seems an uncannily familiar place in which to find an elegist.

[19] Putnam (1977) 248.

BIBLIOGRAPHY

Adams, J. N. (1982) *The Latin Sexual Vocabulary*. Baltimore.
Alfonsi, L. (1961) 'L'Antiope di Pacuvio e Properzio III 15,' *Dioniso* 35/2: 5–10.
Austin, R. G. (1977) *P. Vergili Maronis Aeneidos Liber Sextus*. Oxford.
Baker, R. J. (1968a) 'Miles annosus: The Military Motif in Propertius,' *Latomus* 27: 322–49.
——— (1968b) 'Propertius III 1, 1–6 Again: Intimations of Immortality?,' *Mnemosyne* 21: 35–9.
——— (1969) 'Propertius' Lost *Bona*,' *AJPh* 95: 333–7.
Balot, R. K. (1998) 'Pindar, Virgil, and the Proem to "Georgic" 3,' *Phoenix* 52: 83–94.
Barchiesi, A. (2005) 'Learned Eyes: Poets, Viewers, Image Makers,' in K. Galinksy (ed.) *The Cambridge Companion to the Age of Augustus*, 281–305. Cambridge.
——— (2007) '*Carmina*: *Odes* and *Carmen Saeculare*,' in S. J. Harrison (ed.) *The Cambridge Companion to Horace*, 144–61. Cambridge.
Barsby, J. A. (1974) 'The Composition and Publication of the First Three Books of Propertius,' *G&R* 21: 128–37.
——— (1975) 'Propertius III.20,' *Mnemosyne* 28: 30–9.
Bartsch, S. (2006) *The Mirror of the Self: Sexuality, Self-Knowledge, and the Gaze in the Early Roman Empire*. Chicago.
Batinski, E. E. (1991) 'Horace's Rehabilitation of Bacchus,' *CW* 84: 361–78.
Becker, C. (1971) 'Die späten Elegien des Properz,' *Hermes* 99: 449–80.
Bennett, A. W. (1968) 'The Patron and Political Inspiration,' *Hermes* 96: 318–40.
——— (1972) 'The Elegiac Lie: Propertius 1.15,' *Phoenix* 26: 28–39.
Biddau, F. (2005) '"*Redeamus in orbem*": Nota a Properzio 3, 2, 1–2,' *MD* 55: 185–91.
Boucher, J.-P. (1965) *Études sur Properce: Problèmes d'inspiration et d'art*. Paris.
Boyle, A. J. (1986) *The Chaonian Dove: Studies in the Eclogues, Georgics and Aeneid of Virgil*. Leiden.
Bradley, K. R. (1987) *Slaves and Masters in the Roman Empire: A Study in Social Control*. Oxford.
——— (1994) *Slavery and Society at Rome*. Cambridge.

Bibliography

Bradshaw, A. (1978) 'Horace and the Therapeutic Myth: *Odes* 3,7; 3,11; and 3,27,' *Hermes* 106: 156–76.
Bramble, J. C. (1973) 'Critical Appreciations 1: Propertius iii.10,' *G&R* 20: 155–61.
Breed, B. (2010) 'Propertius on Not Writing about Civil Wars,' in B. Breed, C. Damon & A. Rossi (eds.) *Citizens of Discord: Rome and Its Civil Wars*, 233–48. Oxford.
Brouwers, J. H. (2006) 'On the Summary of the Adventures of Odysseus in Propertius 3.12,' in A. P. M. H. Lardinois, M. G. M. van der Poel & V. Hunink (eds) *Land of Dreams: Greek and Latin Studies in Honour of A. H. M. Kessels*, 215–28. Leiden.
Buchheit, V. (1972) *Der Anspruch des Dichters in Vergils Georgika: Dichtertum und Heilsweg*. Darmstadt.
Burck, E. (1959) 'Abschied von der Liebesdichtung (Properz 3, 24 und 3, 25),' *Hermes* 87: 191–211.
Burke, P. F. (1979) 'Roman Rites for the Dead and "Aeneid 6",' *CJ* 74: 220–8.
Butler, H. E. & Barber, E. A. (1933) *The Elegies of Propertius*. Oxford.
Butrica, J. L. (1983) 'Propertius 3.6,' *EMC* 27: 17–37.
 (1994) 'Myth and Meaning in Propertius 3.15,' *Phoenix* 48/2: 135–51.
 (1996) 'The *Amores* of Propertius: Unity and Structure in Books 2–4,' *ICS* 21: 87–158.
Cairns, F. (1971) 'Propertius 3,10 and Roman Birthdays,' *Hermes* 99: 149–55.
 (1972) *Generic Composition in Greek and Roman Poetry*. Edinburgh.
 (1979) *Tibullus: A Hellenistic Poet at Rome*. Cambridge.
 (1995) 'Horace, *Odes* 3.7: Elegy, Lyric, Myth, Learning, and Interpretation,' in S. J. Harrison (ed.) *Homage to Horace: A Bimillenary Celebration*, 65–99. Oxford.
 (2006) *Sextus Propertius: The Augustan Elegist*. Cambridge.
 (2010) 'The Mistress's Midnight Summons: Propertius 3.16,' *Hermes* 138: 70–91.
Camps, W. A. (1966) *Propertius, Elegies Book III*. Cambridge.
 (1967) *Propertius, Elegies Book II*. Cambridge.
Castriota, D. (1995) *The Ara Pacis Augustae and the Imagery of Abundance in Later Greek and Early Roman Imperial Art*. Princeton.
Clarke, J. (2004) '"Goodbye to All That": Propertius' *magnum iter* between Elegies 3.16 and 3.21,' *Mouseion* 4: 127–43.
Coarelli, F. (2004) 'Assisi, Roma, Tivoli: I luoghi di Properzio,' in C. Santini & F. Santucci (eds) *Properzio tra storia arte mito: Atti del convegno internazionale. Assisi, 24–26 maggio 2002*, 99–115. Assisi.
Comber, M. (1998) 'A Book Made New: Reading Propertius Reading Pound. A Study in Reception,' *JRS* 88: 37–55.
Commager, S. (1962) *The Odes of Horace: A Critical Study*. New Haven.
Connolly, J. (2000) 'Asymptotes of Pleasure: Thoughts on the Nature of Roman Erotic Elegy,' *Arethusa* 33: 71–98.

Bibliography

Connor, P. J. (1971) 'Enthusiasm, Poetry, and Politics: A Consideration of Horace, Odes, III.25,' *AJPh* 92/2: 266–74.

Conte, G.B. (1992) 'Proems in the Middle,' *YClS* 29: 147–59.

(1994a) *Genres and Readers*. Baltimore.

(1994b) *Latin Literature: A History*. Baltimore.

Courtney, E. (1968) 'The Structure of Propertius Book 1 and Some Textual Consequences,' *Phoenix* 22: 250–8.

(1970) 'The Structure of Propertius Book 3,' *Phoenix* 24: 48–53.

Crowther, N. B. (1979) 'Water and Wine as Symbols of Inspiration,' *Mnemosyne* 32: 1–11.

Davis, G. (1975) 'The Persona of Licymnia: A Revaluation of Horace, *Carm.* 2.12,' *Philologus* 119: 70–83.

(1991) *Polyhymnia: The Rhetoric of Horatian Lyric Discourse*. Berkeley.

(2005) 'From Lyric to Elegy: The Inscription of the Elegiac Subject in Heroides 15 (Sappho to Phaon),' in W. W. Batstone & G. Tissol (eds) *Defining Genre and Gender in Latin Literature: Essays Presented to William S. Anderson on His Seventy-Fifth Birthday*, 175–91. New York.

DeBrohun, J. B. (2003) *Roman Propertius and the Reinvention of Elegy*. Ann Arbor.

Eder, W. (2005) 'Augustus and the Power of Tradition,' in K. Galinsky (ed.) *The Cambridge Companion to the Age of Augustus*, 13–32. Cambridge.

Falkner, T. M. (1977) 'Myth, Setting, and Immortality in Propertius 3.18,' *CJ* 73: 11–18.

Fantham, E. (2000) 'Roman Elegy: Problems of Self-Definition, and Redirection,' *L'Histoire Littéraire Immanente dans la Poésie Latine*, Tome 47, 183–211.

(2006) 'The Image of Women in Propertius' Poetry,' in H.-C. Günther (ed.) *Brill's Companion to Propertius*, 183–98. Leiden.

Fantuzzi, M. & Hunter, R. (2004) *Tradition and Innovation in Hellenistic Poetry*. Cambridge.

Farrell, J. (2003) 'Classical Genre in Theory and Practice,' *New Literary History* 34: 383–408.

Fear, T. (2005) 'Propertian Closure: The Elegiac Inscription of the Liminal Male and Ideological Contestation in Augustan Rome,' in R. Ancona & E. Greene (eds) *Gendered Dynamics in Latin Love Poetry*, 13–40. Baltimore.

Fedeli, P. (1984) *Propertius*. Stuttgart.

(1985) *Sesto Properzio, Il Libro Terzo delle Elegie*. Bari.

(2005) *Properzio, Elegie Libro II*. Cambridge.

Feeney, D. (1986) 'History and Revelation in Vergil's Underworld,' *PCPhS* 32: 1–24.

Fitzgerald, W. (1995) *Catullan Provocations: Lyric Poetry and the Drama of Position*. Berkeley.

(2000) *Slavery and the Roman Literary Imagination*. Cambridge.

Bibliography

Fowler, D. (1989) 'First Thoughts on Closure: Problems and Prospects,' *MD* 22: 75–122.
— (1995) 'Horace and the Aesthetics of Politics,' in S. J. Harrison (ed.) *Homage to Horace: A Bimillenary Celebration*, 248–66. Oxford.
— (2000) *Roman Constructions: Readings in Postmodern Latin*. Oxford.
— (2002) 'Masculinity under Threat? The Poetics and Politics of Inspiration in Latin Poetry,' in E. Spentzou & D. P. Fowler (eds) *Cultivating the Muse: Struggles for Power and Inspiration in Classical Literature*, 141–60. Oxford.
Fraenkel, E. (1957) *Horace*. Oxford.
Gale, M. (2000) *Virgil on the Nature of Things: The Georgics, Lucretius and the Didactic Tradition*. Cambridge.
Galinsky, K. (1969) 'The Triumph Theme in the Augustan Elegy,' *WS* 82: 75–107.
Gibson, R. K. (2006) 'Politics of Moderation in *Ars Amatoria* 3,' in R. K. Gibson, S. Green & A. R. Sharrock (eds) *The Art of Love: Bimillennial Essays on Ovid's Ars Amatoria and Remedia Amoris*, 121–42. Oxford.
— (2007) *Excess and Restraint: Propertius, Horace, and Ovid's Ars Amatoria*. London.
Gold, B. K. (1982) 'Propertius 3.9: Maecenas as *eques, dux, fautor*,' in B. K. Gold (ed.) *Literary and Artistic Patronage in Ancient Rome*, 103–17. Austin.
— (1993) '"But Ariadne Was Never There in the First Place": Finding the Female in Roman Poetry,' in N. S. Rabinowitz & A. Richlin (eds) *Feminist Theory and the Classics*, 75–101. London.
— (2007) 'The Silence of Women in Propertius,' *Antichthon* 41: 54–72.
Goold, G. P. (1990) *The Elegies of Propertius*. Cambridge, MA.
Greene, E. (1995) 'Elegiac Woman: Fantasy, *materia* and Male Desire in Propertius 1.3 and 1.11,' *AJPh* 116/2: 303–18.
— (1998) *The Erotics of Domination: Male Desire and the Mistress in Latin Love Poetry*. Baltimore.
— (2000) 'Gender Identity and the Elegiac Hero in Propertius 2.1,' *Arethusa* 33: 241–61.
— (2005) 'Gender and Genre in Propertius 2.8 and 2.9,' in W. W. Batstone & G. Tissol (eds) *Defining Genre and Gender in Latin Literature: Essays Presented to William S. Anderson on His Seventy-Fifth Birthday*, 211–38. New York.
Griffin, J. (1977) 'Propertius and Antony,' *JRS* 67: 17–26.
— (1985) *Latin Poets and Roman Life*. Duckworth.
Gruen, E. S. (2005) 'Augustus and the Making of the Principate,' in K. Galinsky (ed.) *The Cambridge Companion to the Age of Augustus*, 33–51. Cambridge.
Günther, H.-C. (2006) 'The Fourth Book,' in H.-C. Günther (ed.) *Brill's Companion to Propertius*, 353–95. Leiden.

Bibliography

Gurval, R. A. (1995) *Actium and Augustus: The Politics and Emotions of Civil War*. Ann Arbor.
Habinek, T. (1998) *The Politics of Latin Literature*. Princeton.
Hallett, J. P. (1973) 'The Role of Women in Roman Elegy: Counter-Cultural Feminism,' *Arethusa* 6: 103–24.
Harrison, S. J. (1988) 'Horace, *Odes* 3.7: An Erotic Odyssey?' *CQ* 38: 186–92.
  (2004) 'Lyric Middles: The Turn at Centre in Horace's *Odes*,' in S. Kyriakidis & F. De Martino (eds) *Middles in Latin Poetry*, 81–102. Bari.
  (2006) *Generic Enrichment in Vergil and Horace*. Oxford.
  (2007) 'The Primal Voyage and the Ocean of Epos: Two Aspects of Metapoetic Imagery in Catullus, Virgil and Horace,' *Dictynna* 4: 1–17.
Henderson, J. (1998) *Fighting for Rome*. Cambridge.
Heyworth, S. J. (1994) 'Some Allusions to Callimachus in Latin Poetry,' *MD* 33: 51–79.
  (1995) 'Propertius: Division, Transmission, and the Editor's Task,' *Papers of the Leeds International Latin Seminar* 8: 165–85.
  (2007a) *Sexti Properti Elegos*. Oxford.
  (2007b) *Cynthia: A Companion to the Text of Propertius*. Oxford.
  (2007c) 'Propertius, Patronage and Politics,' *BICS* 50: 93–128.
  (2010) 'An Elegist's Career: From Cynthia to Cornelia,' in P. R. Hardie & H. Moore (eds) *Classical Literary Careers and their Literary Reception*, 89–104. Cambridge.
Heyworth, S. & Morwood, J. H. W. (2011) *A Commentary on Propertius: Book 3*. Oxford.
Hinds, S. (1985) 'Booking the Return Trip: Ovid and *Tristia* 1,' *PCPhS* 31: 13–32.
  (1987) *The Metamorphosis of Persephone: Ovid and the Self-Conscious Muse*. Cambridge.
  (1998) *Allusion and Intertext: Dynamics of Appropriation in Roman Poetry*. Cambridge.
  (2000) 'Essential Epic: Genre and Gender from Macer to Statius,' in M. Depew & D. Obbink (eds) *Matrices of Genre: Authors, Canons and Society*, 221–44. Cambridge, MA.
Horsfall, N. M. (1982) 'The Structure and Purpose of Vergil's Parade of Heroes,' *AncSoc* 12: 12–18.
  (1991) 'Virgil and the Poetry of Explanations,' *G&R* 38: 203–11.
  (2001) 'Virgil Reads; Octavia Faints: Grounds for Doubt,' *Proceedings of the Virgil Society* 24: 135–37.
Houghton, L. B. T. (2007) 'The Drowned and the Saved: Shipwrecks and the *cursus* of Latin Love Elegy,' *CCJ (PCPS)* 53: 161–79.
Hubbard, M. (1974) *Propertius*. Bristol.
Hunter, R. (2006) *The Shadow of Callimachus: Studies in the Reception of Hellenistic Poetry at Rome*. Cambridge.
Hutchinson, G. O. (1984) 'Propertius and the Unity of the Book,' *JRS* 74: 99–106.

Bibliography

(2002) 'The Publication and Individuality of Horace's *Odes* Books 1-3,' *CQ* 52: 517-37.
Jacobson, H. (1976) 'Structure and Meaning in Propertius Book 3,' *ICS* 1: 160-73.
James, S. L. (1998) 'Introduction: Constructions of Gender and Genre in Roman Comedy and Elegy,' *Helios* 25: 1-16.
— (2003a) 'Her Turn to Cry: The Politics of Weeping in Roman Love Elegy,' *TAPhA* 133: 99-122.
— (2003b) *Learned Girls and Male Persuasion: Gender and Reading in Roman Love Elegy*. Berkeley.
— (2006) 'A Courtesan's Choreography: Female Liberty and Male Anxiety at the Roman Dinner Party,' in C. A. Faraone & L. K. McClure (eds) *Prostitutes and Courtesans in the Ancient World*, 224-51. Madison.
Janan, M. (2001) *The Politics of Desire: Propertius IV*. Berkeley.
Johnson, W. R. (1976) *Darkness Visible: A Study of Virgil's Aeneid*. Berkeley.
— (2009) *A Latin Lover in Ancient Rome: Readings in Propertius and His Genre*. Columbus.
Karamalengou, H. (2003) 'Poétique ou poétiques chez les poètes augustéens?,' *REL* 81: 133-56.
Keith, A. M. (1994) '*Corpus Eroticum*: Elegiac Poetics and Elegiac *Puellae* in Ovid's Amores,' *CW* 88: 27-40.
— (2008) *Propertius: Poet of Love and Leisure*. London.
Kennedy, D. F. (1992) ' "Augustan" and "Anti-Augustan": Reflections of Terms of Reference,' in A. Powell (ed.) *Roman Poetry and Propaganda in the Age of Augustus*, 26-58. Bristol.
— (1993) *The Arts of Love: Five Studies in the Discourse of Roman Love Elegy*. Cambridge.
Kirichenko, A. (2013) 'Virgil's Augustan Temples: Image and Intertext in the Aeneid,' *JRS* 103: 1-23.
Knox, P. E. (1985) 'Wine, Water, and Callimachean Polemics,' *HSPh* 99: 107-19.
Koniaris, G. L. (1971) 'On Propertius 3.24: A Reply,' *CP* 66: 253-8.
Kraggerud, E. (1998) 'Vergil Announcing the *Aeneid*: On *Georgics* 3.1-48,' in H. P. Stahl (ed.) *Vergil's Aeneid: Augustan Epic and Political Context*, 1-20. London.
Kyriakidis, S. & De Martino, F. (eds) (2004) *Middles in Latin Poetry*. Bari.
Lardinois, A. P. M. H., van der Poel, M. G. M. & Hunink, V. (eds) (2006) *Land of Dreams: Greek and Latin Studies in Honour of A. H. M. Kessels*. Leiden.
Lee, G. (1996) *Propertius: The Poems*. Oxford.
Lefèvre, E. (1991) 'Propertius Pindaricus: Der Sinn der Elegie 3,17 und ihr Verhältnis zu 3,18,' *Studi di filologia classica in onore di Giusto Monaco* (Palermo), II: 1001-5.
Lieberg, G. (1999) 'Formale und inhaltliche Analyse von Properz III,12,' *Latomus* 58: 785-98.

Bibliography

(2006) 'Properz' Elegie III, 20 als Offene Form,' *Latomus* 65: 954–60.
Lilja, S. (1965) *The Roman Elegists' Attitude toward Women*. Helsinki.
Littlewood, R. J. (1975) 'Two Elegiac Hymns: Propertius, 3.17 and Ovid, *Fasti*, 5.663–692,' *Latomus* 34: 662–74.
Lowrie, M. (1997) *Horace's Narrative Odes*. Oxford.
Luck, G. (1957) 'The Cave and the Source,' *CQ* 51: 175–9.
  (1969) *The Latin Love Elegy*. London.
Lyne, R. O. A. M. (1980) *The Latin Love Poets: From Catullus to Horace*. Oxford.
  (1995) *Horace: Behind the Public Poetry*. New Haven.
  (1998a) 'Propertius and Tibullus: Early Exchanges,' *CQ* 48/2: 519–44.
  (1998b) 'Propertius 2.10 and 11 and the Structure of Books "2A" and "2B",' *JRS* 88: 21–36.
Lyne, R. O. A. M. & Morwood, J. H. W. (1973) 'Critical Appreciations 1: Propertius iii.10,' *G&R* 20: 38–48.
Mader, G. (1993) 'Architecture, Aemulatio and Elegiac Self-Definition in Propertius 3.2,' *CJ* 88/4: 321–40.
  (1994) 'Propertius' Hymn to Bacchus (3, 17) and the Poetic Design of the Third Book,' *Studies in Latin Literature and Roman History* 7: 369–85.
Maltby, R. (1981) 'Love and Marriage in Propertius 4,3,' in F. Cairns (ed.) *Papers of the Liverpool Latin Seminar: 3rd Volume*, 243–7. Liverpool.
Marr, J. L. (1978) 'Structure and Sense in Propertius III,' *Mnemosyne* 31: 265–73.
McKeown, J. C. (1998) *Ovid: Amores III: A Commentary on Book Two*. Leeds.
Meban, D. (2008) 'Temple Building, *Primus* Language, and the Proem to Virgil's Third *Georgic*,' *CP* 103/2: 150–74.
Miller, J. F. (1983a) 'Propertius 3.2 and Horace,' *TAPhS* 113: 289–99.
  (1983b) 'Ennius and the Elegists,' *ICS* 8: 277–95.
  (1991) 'Propertius' Hymn to Bacchus and Contemporary Poetry,' *AJPh* 11: 77–86.
  (2009) *Apollo, Augustus, and the Poets*. Cambridge.
Miller, P. A. (2001) 'Why Propertius Is a Woman: French Feminism and Augustan Elegy,' *CP* 96: 127–46.
  (2004) *Subjecting Verses: Latin Love Elegy and the Emergence of the Real*. Princeton.
Moritz, L. A. (1968) 'Some "Central" Thoughts on Horace's *Odes*,' *CQ* 18: 116–31.
Murgia, C. E. (2000) 'The Division of Propertius 2,' *MD* 44: 147–242.
Myerowitz, M. (1985) *Ovid's Games of Love*. Detroit.
Mynors, R. A. B. (1990) *Virgil, Georgics*. Oxford.
Nappa, C. (2005) *Reading after Actium: Vergil's Georgics, Octavian, and Rome*. Ann Arbor.
Nethercut, W. R. (1968) 'Notes on the Structure of Propertius, Book IV,' *AJPh* 89: 449–64.

Bibliography

(1970a) 'The Ironic Priest. Propertius' 'Roman Elegies', III, 1–5: Imitations of Horace and Vergil,' *AJPh* 91: 382–407.
(1970b) 'Propertius 3.12–14,' *CP* 65: 99–102.
(1971) 'Propertius 3.11,' *TAPhS* 102: 411–43.
(1975) 'Propertius III 1, 1–6 again,' *Mnemosyne* 28: 73–5.
Neumeister, K. (1983) *Die Überwindung der elegischen Liebe bei Properz (Buch I–III)*. Studien zur klassischen Philologie 7. Frankfurt.
Newman, J. K. (1985) 'Pindar and Callimachus,' *ICS* 10: 169–89.
(1997) *Augustan Propertius: Recapitulation of a Genre*. Zürich.
(2006) 'The Third Book: Defining a Poetic Self,' in H.-C. Günther (ed.) *Brill's Companion to Propertius*, 319–52. Leiden.
Nisbet, R. G. M. & Hubbard, M. (1970) *A Commentary on Horace, Odes, Book I*. Oxford.
(1978) *A Commentary on Horace, Odes, Book II*. Oxford.
Nisbet, R. G. M. & Rudd, N. (2004) *A Commentary on Horace, Odes, Book III*. Oxford.
Oliensis, E. (1997) 'The Erotics of *Amicitia*: Readings in Tibullus, Propertius and Horace,' in J. P. Hallett & M. B. Skinner (eds) *Roman Sexualities*, 151–71. Princeton.
(1998) *Horace and the Rhetoric of Authority*. Cambridge.
O'Neill, K. N. (2000) 'Propertius 4.2: Slumming with Vertumnus?,' *AJPh* 121: 259–77.
(2005) 'The Lover's Gaze and Cynthia's Glance,' in R. Ancona & E. Greene (eds) *Gendered Dynamics in Latin Love Poetry*, 243–68. Baltimore.
O'Rourke, D. (2011) 'The Representation and Misrepresentation of Virgilian Poetry in Propertius 2.34,' *AJPh* 132: 457–97.
Otis, B. (1963) *Virgil: A Study in Civilized Poetry*. Oxford.
(1965) 'Propertius' Single Book,' *HSPh* 70: 1–44.
Owens, W. M. (1992) '*Nuntius Vafer et Fallax*: An Alternative Reading of Horace, *C* 3.7,' *CW* 85: 161–71.
Pasquali, G. (1920) *Orazio lirico*. Florence.
Pelling, C. B. R. (2002) '*Duplices Tabellae*: A Reading – and Rereading – of Propertius 3.23,' *SIFC* 20: 171–81.
Perkins, C. (2002) 'Protest and Paradox in Ovid, *Amores* 3.11,' *CW* 94: 117–25.
Phillips, T. (2011) 'Propertius and the Poetics of the Book': 1.18 and 3.15–17,' *CCJ* 57: 105–35.
Putnam, M. C. J. (1973) 'Horace c3.30: The Lyricist as Hero,' *Ramus* 2: 1–17.
(1977) 'Propertius 22: Tullus' Return,' *ICS* 2: 240–54.
(1980) 'Propertius' Third Book: Patterns of Cohesion,' *Arethusa* 13: 97–113.
(1998) *Virgil's Epic Designs: Ekphrasis in the Aeneid*. New Haven.
Racette-Campbell, M. (2013) 'Marriage Contracts, *Fides* and Gender Roles in Propertius 3.20,' *CJ* 108: 297–317.
Reed, J. (2001) 'Anchises Reading Aeneas Reading Marcellus,' *SyllClass* 12: 146–68.

Bibliography

Reitzenstein, E. (1931) 'Zur Stiltheorie des Kallimachos,' *Festschrift Richard Reitzenstein*: 49–51.

Richardson, L. (1977) *Propertius, Elegies I–IV*. Norman.

Rosati, G. (2006) 'The Art of the *Remedia Amoris*: Unlearning to Love?,' in R. K. Gibson, S. Green & A. R. Sharrock (eds) *The Art of Love: Bimillennial Essays on Ovid's Ars Amatoria and Remedia Amoris*, 143–65. Oxford.

Ross, D. O. (1975) *Backgrounds to Augustan Poetry: Gallus, Elegy, and Rome*. Cambridge.

Rudd, N. (ed.) (1993) *Horace 2000: A Celebration. Essays for the Bimillenium*. London.

Rutherford, R. (2007) 'Poetics and Literary Criticism,' in S. J. Harrison (ed.) *The Cambridge Companion to Horace*, 248–61. Cambridge.

Santirocco, M. S. (1980a) 'Horace's Odes and the Ancient Poetry Book,' *Arethusa* 13: 43–57.

— (1980b) 'Strategy and Structure in Horace *C.* 2.12,' in C. Deroux (ed.) *Studies in Latin Literature and Roman History 2*, Collection Latomus 168, 223–36. Brussels.

— (1984) 'The Maecenas Odes,' *TAPhA* 114: 241–53.

— (1986) *Unity and Design in Horace's Odes*. Chapel Hill.

— (1995) 'Horace and Augustan Ideology,' *Arethusa* 28: 225–43.

Schauer, M. (2007) *Aeneas Dux: Eine literarische Fiktion in augusteischer Zeit*. Munich.

Schmidt, P. L. (1984) 'Structure and Sources of Horace, Ode 2,12,' in H. Evjen (ed.) *Mnemai: Classical Studies in Memory of Karl K. Hulley*, 139–49. Chico.

Shackleton Bailey, D. R. (1956) *Propertiana*. Cambridge.

Sharrock, A. R. (1994) *Seduction and Repetition in Ovid's Ars Amatoria 2*. Oxford.

— (1995) 'The Drooping Rose: Elegiac Failure in *Amores* 3.7,' *Ramus* 24: 152–80.

— (1996) 'The Art of Deceit: Pseudolus and the Nature of Reading,' *CQ* 46/1: 152–74.

— (2000) 'Constructing Characters in Propertius,' *Arethusa* 33: 263–84.

Skard, E. (1965) 'Die Heldenschau in Vergils *Aeneis*,' *Symbolae Osloenses* 40: 53–65.

Stahl, H.-P. (1985) *Propertius: 'Love' and 'War': Individual and State under Augustus*. Berkeley.

Sullivan, J. P. (1976) *Propertius: A Critical Introduction*. Cambridge.

Syme, R. (1978) *History in Ovid*. Oxford.

Syndikus, H. P. (1972–3) *Die Lyrik des Horaz*. 2 vols. Darmstadt.

— (2006) 'The Second Book,' in H.-C. Günther (ed.) *Brill's Companion to Propertius*, 245–318. Leiden.

Tatum, J. W. (2000) 'Aspirations and Divagations: The Poetics of Place in Propertius 2.10,' *TAPhA* 130: 393–410.

Bibliography

Tarrant, R. J. (2016) *Texts, Editors, and Readers: Methods and Problems in Latin Textual Criticism*. Cambridge.
Thomas, R. F. (1983) 'Callimachus, the *Victoria Berenices*, and Roman Poetry,' *CQ* 33: 92–113.
 (1988) *Virgil, Georgics*. 2 vols. Cambridge.
 (1998) 'Virgil's Pindar?,' in P. E. Knox & C. Foss (eds) *Style and Tradition: Studies in Honor of Wendell Clausen*, 99–120. Stuttgart.
 (1999) *Reading Virgil and His Texts: Studies in Intertextuality*. Ann Arbor.
 (2001) *Virgil and the Augustan Reception*. Cambridge.
Tissol, G. (2005) 'Maimed Books and Maimed Authors,' in W. W. Batstone & G. Tissol (eds) *Defining Genre and Gender in Latin Literature: Essays Presented to William S. Anderson on His Seventy-Fifth Birthday*, 97–112. New York.
Tränkle, H. (1960) *Die Sprachkunst des Properz und die Tradition der lateinischen Dichtersprache*. Wiesbaden.
Treggiari, S. (2005) 'Women in the Time of Augustus,' in K. Galinsky (ed.) *The Cambridge Companion to the Age of Augustus*, 130–47. Cambridge.
Tronson, A. (1998) 'Vergil, the Augustans, and the Invention of Cleopatra's Suicide: One Asp or Two?,' *Vergilius* 44: 31–50.
 (1999) 'What the Poet Saw: Octavian's Triple Triumph, 29 B.C. Jeremiah Markland's Conjectures at Propertius 3.11.52–53,' *AClass* 42: 171–86.
Troxler-Keller, I. (1964) *Die Dichterlandschaft des Horaz*. Heidelberg.
Valeri-Tomaszuk, P. (1976) 'A Reconsideration of Propertius, III 10,' *Latomus* 35: 827–33.
Valladares, H. (2005) 'The Lover as a Model Viewer,' in R. Ancona & E. Greene (eds) *Gendered Dynamics in Latin Love Poetry*, 206–42. Baltimore.
Veyne, P. (1988) *Roman Erotic Elegy: Love, Poetry, and the West*. Chicago.
Warden, J. (1980) *Fallax Opus: Poet and Reader in the Elegies of Propertius*. Toronto.
Weinlich, B. P. (2003) 'Re-Constructing Relationships: The Significance of Name and Place in Propertius 3.22,' *Ramus* 32: 102–21.
 (2005) 'Properz III, 11: Eine Neubetrachtung im Kontext des "Liebesromans",' *GB* 24: 135–50.
Welch, T. S. (2005) *The Elegiac Cityscape: Propertius and the Meaning of Roman Monuments*. Columbus.
 (2012) 'Whose Reading of What Propertius'?, in E. Greene & T. S. Welch (eds) *Propertius*, 1–27. Oxford.
West, D. (2002) *Horace Odes III: Dulce Periculum*. Oxford.
White, P. (1995) 'Postumus, Curtius Postumus, and Rabirius Postumus,' *CP* 90: 151–61.
 (2007) 'Friendship, Patronage, and Horatian Sociopoetics,' in S. J. Harrison (ed.) *The Cambridge Companion to Horace*, 195–206. Cambridge.
Wiggers, N. (1977) 'Reconsideration of Propertius II. 1,' *CJ* 72: 334–41.

Bibliography

Wilkinson, L. P. (1966) 'The Continuity of Propertius II.13,' *CR* 16: 141–4.
  (1969) *The Georgics of Virgil: A Critical Survey*. Cambridge.
  (1970) 'Pindar and the Proem to the Third *Georgic*,' in W. Wimmel (ed.) *Forschungen zur römischen Literatur: Festschrift zum 60. Geburtstag von Karl Büchner*, 286–90. Wiesbaden.
Williams, G. (1968) *Tradition and Originality in Roman Poetry*. Oxford.
  (1974) 'Horace *Odes* i.12 and the Succession to Augustus,' *Hermathena* 118: 147–55.
Williams, M. F. (1996) 'Poetic Seacoasts: Mortale's *i Morti* and Propertius 3.18, 1.11, 3.5,' *Classical and Modern Literature* 17: 149–69.
Williams, R. D. (1964) 'The Sixth Book of the "Aeneid",' *G&R* 11: 48–63.
Wilson, M. (2009) 'The Politics of Elegy: Propertius and Tibullus,' in W. S. Dominik, J. Garthwaite & P. A. Roche (eds) *Writing Politics in Imperial Rome*, 173–202. Leiden.
Wimmel, W. (1960) *Kallimachos in Rom: Die Nachfolge seines apologetischen Dichtens in der Augusteerzeit*. Wiesbaden.
Woolley, A. (1967) 'The Structure of Propertius Book iii,' *BICS* 14: 80–3.
Wyke, M. (1987a) 'The Elegiac Woman at Rome,' *PCPhS* 33: 153–78.
  (1987b) 'Written Women: Propertius' *scripta puella*,' *JRS* 77: 47–61.
  (1989a) 'Mistress and Metaphor in Augustan Elegy,' *Helios* 16: 25–47.
  (1989b) 'Reading Female Flesh: *Amores* 3.1,' in A. Cameron (ed.) *History as Text: The Writing of Ancient History*, 111–43. Chapel Hill.
  (1994) 'Taking the Woman's Part: Engendering Roman Love Elegy,' *Ramus* 23: 110–28.
  (2002) *The Roman Mistress*. Oxford.
Yardley, J. C. (1972) 'Comic Influences in Propertius,' *Phoenix* 26: 134–9.
Zanker, P. (1988) *The Power of Images in the Age of Augustus*. Ann Arbor.
Zetzel, J. E. G. (1982) 'The Poetics of Patronage in Late First Century B.C.,' in B. K. Gold (ed.) *Literary and Artistic Patronage in Ancient Rome*, 87–102. Austin.
  (1989) 'Romane Memento: Justice and Judgment in Aeneid 6,' *TAPhA* 119: 263–84.

GENERAL INDEX

Aeneas, 2, 175, 177–79
afterlife, 181
amor, see love
Amphion, 36, 151
Anchises, 176–78
Antony, Mark, 63, 83, 132, 140–41, 141n. 21, 147
Apollo, 37, 43–44, 132, 137, 140, 142–43, 148–49, 155, 158
Ariadne, 134
Asterie, 100–3, 105, 116, 196
Augustus, 10, 12–14, 17, 19, 30–31, 71, 83, 87–89, 111, 132, 140, 142, 145–47, 153, 160, 165, 177, 224
Avernus, Lake, 168–69

Bacchus, 126, 131–63, 170
Baiae, 167–74, 180
birthday, 64, 74, 76, 82

Caesar, see Augustus
Callimachus, 2, 24, 26–27, 29, 40, 42, 125, 132, 134, 137, 160
    Callimachean landscape, 24, 125, 149
    Callimachean restraint, 70–71, 150
Calliope, 37, 42–45, 67, 146, 149
Catullus, 195, 200, 207–8, 209, 210
    Propertian engagement with, 195
centrality, 119–22, 124–25, 128
Chloe, 102, 112–13
civil war, 10, 88, 141
Cleopatra, 17, 63, 83–89
closure, 17, 172, 187, 201–7
    false, 202, 208, 212–5
comedy, 47–49
contract, 187–88, 194–96, 199–200
culture, Augustan, 10–11, 13–14, 112, 140–42
Cynthia, 4, 16–17, 37–41, 43–44, 46, 74, 76–83, 95, 99, 107, 116–17, 125, 134, 139, 170–75, 191–92, 198, 202, 204–5, 208–9, 214, 218

death, 122, 125, 174n. 28
deception, 50, 57, 60, 188, 193, 198–200, 205–6
delay, 129, 167
Delia, 161
Dionysus, see Bacchus
duty, 1, 217–19, 220–21

elegy, 3–4, 7, 13–14, 17, 19, 22–23, 29–30, 35, 39, 43–45, 59, 63, 101, 103, 109, 111–12, 114–17, 131, 133, 154–55, 166, 172, 193, 202, 217
    Propertian innovation, 24–25, 35, 37, 40–41, 133, 167, 172, 175, 183–86, 220–21
Enipeus, 103, 115, 196
Ennius, 42, 149
epic, 15, 28–30, 43, 45, 66, 70, 91, 110, 149, see also Virgil: *Aeneid*
epigram, 47

fame, 27, 31
fidelity, 16, 17–18, 46, 51–56, 60, 94–95, 97–98, 100–3, 113, 116, 187–88, 190, 193–97, 221
fides, see fidelity
foedus, see contract

Galatea, 36, 151
Galla, Aelia, 3, 18, 63, 93, 95–97, 100, 104–9, 111, 114, 117, 196
gender, 85, 87, 89, 218
    female audience, 36–37
    female power, 85–87
    female sorrow, see tears, elegiac
    male authority, 86, 89

236

General Index

genre, *see* elegy, epic, lyric
grotto, 146, 149
Gyges, 100–1, 103, 113, 116, 196

Helicon, Mount, 11, 15, 45
Hercules, 147
Homer, 28–29, 30, 32, 106, 149
Horace
   Odes, 4, 10, 12–15, 22, 27, 31,
     65, 72, 86, 94, 100–3, 103, 111–15,
     123, 131, 139, 142–48, 164
   Propertian engagement with, 25, 27,
     32, 34–35, 37, 113–14, 142, 154,
     195–97, 221
   Satires, 126
Horos, 215

imagery
   nautical, 69–70, 204, 210, 212–13
   slavery, 61, 90, 139
   travel, 110, 123, 203
intertextuality, 25, 32, 69, 114, 138, 156,
   162, 182, 186, 196, 213
intratextuality, 16, 42–44, 171–73, 217
irony, romantic, 200

journey, 6, 78, 118–27, 218, *see also*
   imagery: travel
Jove, 87

lament, 19, 139, 161, 166, 172, 175, 184,
   186, 217
landscape, 24, 169, 217, 219, 221
Lesbia, 195, 206–7
literature, Augustan, 22, 86, 91, 131
love, 4, 13, 33, 41, 77, 80, 112, 135,
   207–11, 214, 217–21
Lucretius
   De Rerum Natura, 67–68
Lucrine, Lake, 168–69
Lygdamus, 46–51, 53–61
lyric, 12–13, 31–32, 111–12, 136, 143,
   152–53, 221, *see also* Horace:
   Odes

Maecenas, 11, 15, 63–73, 84, 88,
   91, 157
magic, 53, 57
Marcellus, 19, 164–86

marriage, 94, 109, 187, 199, 221
Medea, 85
mens bona, 207–8
metapoetics, 17, 46–49, 57, 64, 79,
   88–89, 99, 109, 126–128, 173, 192,
   198, 205–6
middles, *see* centrality
midnight, 120, 122
militia amoris, 218
mime, 47
mora, *see* delay
morality, Augustan, 13, 133
Muses, 11–12, 74–75, 159
myth, 36, 85, 150–52, 184

Octavian, *see* Augustus
Odysseus, 106, 110, 114
Omphale, 85
Orpheus, 36, 151
Ovid
   Amores, 192, 209–13
   Ars Amatoria, 52, 193, 222
   Tristia, 128

Paetus, 2–3, 62, 97, 105, 118
Penelope, 55, 106–7, 115
Penthesilea, 85
Philitas, 24, 27, 40, 42, 134
Pindar, 136, 137, 160–61
Plautus
   Pseudolus, 48
politics, Augustan, 10, 83, 132, 152, 165,
   182
Pollux, 147
Polyphemus, 36, 151
Pompey, Sextus, 168
Postumus, 95–97, 100–1, 104, 106,
   109–11, 196
priest, 12, 15, 25–26, 29, 32, 148
puella, 3, 6, 35, 37–40, 53, 55–58,
   68, 83, 93, 99, 107, 116,
   188–93, 198

readers, 37–39, 47, 50, 56, 59,
   127–28, 188, 194, 198,
   201, 205–6, 214
reception, 4–10
recusatio, 64, 72–73, 91, 149
renuntiatio amoris, 3, 201, 213, 214–15

237

General Index

Roma, see Rome
Rome, 1, 4, 17, 26, 29, 33, 41, 87, 145, 177, 217, 219–20

sacerdos, see priest
satire, 47
Semiramis, 86
Seneca
  de consolatione ad Marciam, 164
seruitium, see slavery
slavery, 84, 91, 126, 130, 136, 150
slaves, 46–49, 52–53, 59
Styx, River, 169
succession, 176, 179, 184

tears, elegiac, 55–56, 59–61, 111n. 25
temple
  Bacchic, 158–59, 160–61, 186
  Caesarian, 11–12, 16, 159–60, 186

Terence
  Heauton Timorumenos, 47
Tibullus, 131, 138, 161
Tibur, 118, 120, 129
tomb, 118, 124–5
  of Marcellus, 181
tragedy, 63, 136, 155n. 60
triumph
  poetic, 11, 15, 25–26, 153
triumphator, 26–27, 29, 142, 153
Tullus, 1, 217–19, 223

Virgil
  Aeneid, 4–5, 10–12, 14, 19, 22, 162, 175–79, 182, 184–85, 221, 223
  Georgics, 11–12, 15, 25, 69–71, 131, 156–59, 162, 221
  Propertian engagement with, 15–16, 25, 28–30, 69–72, 161, 186, 221, 223

INDEX LOCORUM

Catullus
  8.1–2, 207

Horace
  Epistles 1.20, 127
  Odes 1.12, 164
  Odes 1.22, 13, 123
  Odes 2.12, 72
  Odes 2.19, 132, 142–43
  Odes 2.19.1–8, 144
  Odes 3.3.9–15, 146
  Odes 3.4.37–42, 146
  Odes 3.7, 13, 100, 112, 196
  Odes 3.7.1–5, 101
  Odes 3.7.9–12, 102
  Odes 3.7.17–22, 112
  Odes 3.7.21–22, 114
  Odes 3.7.21–32, 102
  Odes 3.17.39–40, 152
  Odes 3.25, 132, 142, 152–53
  Odes 3.25.17–18, 152
  Odes 3.30.1–5, 31

Lucretius
  De Rerum Natura 6.92–95, 67

Ovid
  Amores 2.9, 212
  Amores 2.9.31–34, 213
  Amores 3.11a, 209, 212
  Amores 3.11a.27–32, 210
  Amores 3.11b, 210
  Amores 3.11b.33–34, 210
  Amores 3.11b.39–40, 211
  Ars Amatoria 1.41–42, 193
  Ars Amatoria 1.611–12, 52

Plautus
  Pseudolus 401–5, 48

Propertius
  1.1, 16, 87
  1.1.5, 93
  1.1.33–34, 190
  1.2, 80–81
  1.3, 155
  1.6, 217
  1.6.1–6, 110
  1.7.21–24, 40–41
  1.11, 98–99, 169–73, 185
  1.11.1–6, 27–30, 169
  1.11.7–8, 171
  1.11.7–18, 99
  1.11.9–12, 173
  1.11–12, 16
  1.12, 172
  1.16, 154
  1.21–22, 30
  2.1.1–4, 68
  2.6.41–42, 109
  2.7.7–10, 109
  2.9.3–8, 107
  2.9.29–30, 107
  2.10, 29
  2.15.41–44, 140
  2.29.23–24, 98, 116–17
  2.34.61–66, 22n. 2, 30
  2.34.65–66, 10
  3.1, 15–16, 24–32, 42, 132, 137, 153
  3.1.1–18, 25
  3.1.3–4, 148
  3.1.5–6, 27
  3.1.21–25, 28
  3.1.33–36, 32
  3.2, 15, 33–41, 42, 150
  3.2.1–2, 33
  3.2.3–8, 36
  3.2.3–10, 150
  3.2.9–10, 37–38

Index Locorum

Propertius (*cont.*)
- 3.2.17–26, 34
- 3.3, 15, 41–45
- 3.3.19–20, 98
- 3.3.22, 175
- 3.3.27–30, 149
- 3.3.35–36, 149
- 3.3.47–50, 44
- 3.6, 17, 46–62, 188
- 3.6.1–8, 49
- 3.6.9–18, 54
- 3.6.19–30, 57
- 3.6.31–34, 57
- 3.6.35–38, 60
- 3.6.41–42, 58
- 3.7, 2
- 3.8.23–24, 56
- 3.9, 15–16, 63, 64–74, 75, 90–91, 132
- 3.9.1–4, 65
- 3.9.5–6, 90
- 3.9.21–22, 85
- 3.9.47–52, 67
- 3.9.59–60, 73
- 3.10, 17, 74–83
- 3.10.1–4, 75
- 3.10.11–18, 81
- 3.10.15–18, 77
- 3.10.29–32, 78
- 3.11, 17, 63, 83–92
- 3.11.1–4, 84
- 3.11.3–4, 90
- 3.11.7–8, 85
- 3.11.27–32, 86
- 3.12, 3, 18, 63, 93–117, 196, 221
- 3.12.1–4, 109
- 3.12.1–14, 96
- 3.12.15–16, 104
- 3.12.17–20, 105
- 3.12.33–34, 114
- 3.12.37, 115
- 3.12.37–38, 106
- 3.13.3, 138
- 3.15, 63
- 3.16, 17, 118–30
- 3.16.1–2, 120, 129
- 3.16.5–6, 127
- 3.16.5–8, 120
- 3.16.11–20, 122
- 3.16.21–30, 124
- 3.17, 15, 126, 131–63, 186
- 3.17.1–2, 157
- 3.17.1–10, 134
- 3.17.13–21, 135
- 3.17.37–38, 158
- 3.17.39–42, 135
- 3.17.42, 138
- 3.18, 3, 18, 164–86
- 3.18.1–2, 180
- 3.18.1–10, 168
- 3.18.11–14, 179
- 3.18.15–16, 173
- 3.18.24, 174
- 3.18.31–34, 181
- 3.20, 17, 187–200
- 3.20.1–10, 188
- 3.20.7–9, 191
- 3.20.15–24, 194
- 3.20.25–30, 190
- 3.22, 1–2, 217–22
- 3.22.17–18, 219
- 3.22.19–26, 221
- 3.22.39–42, 1, 219
- 3.23.3–6, 52
- 3.24, 16, 201–16
- 3.24.1–6, 205
- 3.24.15–16, 204, 213
- 3.24.19–20, 204
- 3.24.25–26, 59
- 3.24.25–28, 206
- 4.1, 214
- 4.7, 216
- 4.8, 216

Tibullus
- 1.2, 161
- 1.2.1–2, 138

Virgil
- *Aeneid* 2.503, 223
- *Aeneid* 6.788–90, 177
- *Aeneid* 6.860–86, 175
- *Aeneid* 6.884, 224
- *Georgics* 2.2, 41, 157
- *Georgics* 2.39–46, 11, 69, 157
- *Georgics* 2.136–74, 221

Index Locorum

Georgics 2.136–75, 157
Georgics 2.541–41, 212n. 29
Georgics 3.10–13, 159
Georgics 3.13, 16, 11
Georgics 3.13–15, 71
Georgics 3.16, 162, 186
Georgics 3.26–39, 162
Georgics 3.40–42, 70
Georgics 3.46–48, 71
Georgics 4.116–17, 212n. 29